Mainstreaming Exceptional Learners in Music

Mainstreaming Exceptional Learners in Music

Betty W. Atterbury
University of Southern Maine

PRENTICE HALL, Englewood Cliffs, New Jersey 07632

Library of Congress Cataloging-in-Publication Data

Atterbury, Betty Wilson.
    Mainstreaming exceptional learners in music
                    Betty W. Atterbury.
        p.   cm.
    Includes bibliographical references.
    ISBN 0-13-545351-8
    1. Special education--Music. 2. Handicapped children--Education-
-Music. 3. School music--Instruction and study.   I. Title.
MT17.A87 1990
371.9'04487--dc20   89-38967
                                                            CIP
                                                            MN

Editorial/production supervision and
  interior design: Carole R. Crouse
Cover design: 20/20 Services Inc.
Manufacturing buyer: Michael Woerner

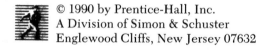 © 1990 by Prentice-Hall, Inc.
A Division of Simon & Schuster
Englewood Cliffs, New Jersey 07632

Printed in the United States of America

10 9 8 7 6 5 4 3 2 1

ISBN 0-13-545351-8

PRENTICE-HALL INTERNATIONAL (UK) LIMITED, *London*
PRENTICE-HALL OF AUSTRALIA PTY. LIMITED, *Sydney*
PRENTICE-HALL CANADA INC., *Toronto*
PRENTICE-HALL HISPANOAMERICANA, S.A., *Mexico*
PRENTICE-HALL OF INDIA PRIVATE LIMITED, *New Delhi*
PRENTICE-HALL OF JAPAN, INC., *Tokyo*
SIMON & SCHUSTER ASIA PTE. LTD., *Singapore*
EDITORA PRENTICE-HALL DO BRASIL, LTDA., *Rio de Janeiro*

This book is dedicated
to my husband, Bob

Contents

Preface, xiii

CHAPTER ONE

An Introduction to Mainstreaming, 1

Contrasts in Mainstreaming Realities, 1
Early Education for the Handicapped, 4
Federal Legislation, 5
What Is the Least Restrictive Environment? 7
Mainstreaming: Pro and Con, 8
The Impact of Mainstreaming in Music Education, 10
Conclusion, 15
Questions, 16
Activities, 16

CHAPTER TWO

Educable Mentally Retarded Students, 17

One Mainstreaming Reality, 17
Definition, 19
Learning and Instruction, 21
Effects of Mainstreaming, 27

Research in Music Education, 30
Conclusion, 35
Questions, 36
Activities, 36
Bibliography, 36

CHAPTER THREE

Learning Disabilities, 37

What Happened When Joey Came to Music? 37
Definition, 39
A Model of Learning Disabilities, 40
Behavior of Learning Disabled Students, 44
Learning and Instruction, 49
Research in Music Education, 52
Conclusion, 55
Questions, 56
Activities, 56
Bibliography, 57

CHAPTER FOUR

Gifted and Talented Students, 58

One Mainstreaming Reality, 58
Definition, 60
Learning and Instruction, 64
Research in Music Education, 70
Conclusion, 75
Questions, 76
Activities, 76
Bibliography, 77

CHAPTER FIVE

Putting It All Together, 78

Introduction, 78
Main Street School, 80
Conclusion, 101
Questions, 102
Activities, 102

CHAPTER SIX

Hearing Impaired Students, 103

One Mainstreaming Reality, 103
Definitions, 104
Hearing, 104
Language, 109
Hearing Impaired Students in Music, 112
Research in Music Education, 115
Conclusion, 119
Questions, 120
Activities, 120
Bibliography, 121

CHAPTER SEVEN

Visually Impaired Students, 122

One Mainstreaming Reality, 122
Definitions, 123
Seeing, 124
Visually Impaired Students in Music, 126
Research in Music Education, 135
Conclusion, 137
Questions, 138
Activities, 139
Bibliography, 139
Sources, 139

CHAPTER EIGHT

Physically Handicapped Students, 140

One Mainstreaming Reality, 140
Definitions, 142
Learning and Instruction, 148
Research, 153
Conclusion, 155
Questions, 156
Activities, 156
Bibliography, 156

CHAPTER NINE

Emotionally Disturbed Students, 158

One Mainstreaming Reality, 158
Definitions, 160
Models, 161
Behaviors, 162
Learning and Instruction, 166
Research, 169
Conclusion, 172
Questions, 173
Activities, 173
Bibliography, 173

CHAPTER TEN

Putting It All Together, 175

Introduction, 175
Main Street School, 177
Conclusion, 196
Questions, 197
Activities, 197

CHAPTER ELEVEN

Self-Contained Classes
for Multiply Handicapped Students, 198

One Mainstreaming Reality, 198
Definitions, 200
Music Teaching, 205
Integration of Multihandicapped Students, 211
Additional Research, 214
Conclusion, 216
Questions, 217
Activities, 218
Bibliography, 218

CHAPTER TWELVE

Success for Mainstreamed Learners, 219

Introduction, 219
Musical Success, 223
Advocacy, 230
Questions, 234
Activities, 234

References, 235

Index, 247

Preface

The passage of one federal law has had an immense effect in many music classrooms in the United States. The legislators who passed this law, "The Education for All Handicapped Children Act" (1975), would be quite amazed at the many ways in which their language has been interpreted. The intent of the law was to ensure that all handicapped children would be provided with a free and appropriate public education in the least restrictive environment. In many settings, this intent has often been interpreted to mean that only some environments (music, art, physical education) are considered "least restrictive."

Mainstreaming is the term commonly used to refer to placing exceptional students in nonhandicapped classes for one period, for part of a day, or for their entire schooling. It is a reality in American education today, and it is here to stay. Its presence adds another variable that must be adequately addressed during the preparation of music teachers. Undergraduate courses for music educators already appear overwhelming in number. They include instruction in performance, theory and history, orchestration and conducting, and nonmusic areas such as learning theory, psychology, and educational history. But to provide adequate instruction for all the students in a class, present and future music educators also need to be able to understand the individual differences of a variety of students designated exceptional and must adapt their instruction in appropriate ways. These students are categorized by single labels, such as hearing impaired or learning disabled or gifted and talented. Within each of these general descriptors, there are students of all ages who have a wide range of abilities and disabilities. Understanding these possible differences is a prerequisite for adequate preparation of music educators in the 1990s.

The purpose of this text is to make that understanding a reality. Although it is primarily oriented toward music educators, the contents are also applicable to the preparation of music therapists. Only one exceptionality that therapists meet daily—speech impairment—is not specifically addressed in an individual chapter. However, this exceptionality is referred to in several chapters, including Chapter 11, where children with severe communication disorders are described.

Chapter 1 focuses on the specific language and impact of the federal law, Public Law 94-142. Chapters 2–4 provide a detailed profile of three exceptionalities whose learning abilities vary considerably: educable mentally retarded, learning disabled, and gifted and talented. Within each chapter, readers will find an introductory scenario based on real music teaching experiences, general information about the exceptionality, music teaching suggestions, and summaries of relevant research in music education.

Chapter 5 serves as a summary of the preceding three chapters. Here, readers will find a detailed fictional description of a music teacher who is trying to accommodate all three categories of exceptional learners in music classes. The teacher's planning approaches and instructional adaptations are related to how a teacher copes with the reality of more than one mainstreamed student in each music class.

In the next four chapters, other exceptionalities are again described singly. Chapters 6–8 focus on handicaps that are caused by physical deficits: hearing impairment, visual disability, and physical handicaps. The focus of Chapter 9 is students who are emotionally disturbed. Inasmuch as these students are so designated because of their outward and visible "behaviors," this chapter follows the descriptions of other discernible handicaps. Each chapter is organized similarly, with an emphasis initially on teaching, followed by definitions, general information, learning differences, and music teaching adaptations, and concluding with relevant research from music education and music therapy.

These chapters are followed by a summary in Chapter 10, which describes the inclusion of several handicapped children in music classes at three different grade levels. This account continues the fictional narrative begun in Chapter 5, in which a single teacher's planning for a variety of exceptional mainstreamed learners is described. Both chapters contain musical material from current texts and describe how musical learning can be made possible for handicapped students.

Chapter 11 contains a description of multihandicapped students. These learners are not generally mainstreamed, but an awareness of their abilities and disabilities is also part of adequate preparation of music teachers in the 1990s. Readers will find that there are attempts, however, to mainstream some of these learners, which may present a future challenge to many music educators.

The title of the final chapter, "Success for Mainstreamed Students," implies the premise of the entire text. The myriad of details about single handicapping conditions, the numerous teaching suggestions, and the summarized research provide only a background for music teachers. With this information, readers must approach the daily and weekly task of providing an appropriate musical education to all students, including those who have learning or physical or emotional differences.

No text is written without the help of others, and the author wishes to acknowledge first the important effect and cumulative impact that teaching exceptional learners in many parts of the coutnry had on the writing of this book. From Anna, with cerebral palsy and moderate retardation who could memorize multiple verses of songs and sing in tune, and from Davey, who could not walk or talk or play an instrument without help, and from Marty, who loved to "go walking" with the drum beat, and from many others—as much was learned as was taught.

In addition, the assistance of Monica Dobson and Cassandra Fitzherbert, both of the University Library at the University of Southern Maine, is highly appreciated. I am most grateful for the careful reading of three chapters by colleagues in the field of special education: Chapter 6 benefited greatly from the suggestions of Toni Rees at the University of Southern Maine; Chapter 7 was improved thanks to Lorraine Spenciner of the University of Maine at Farmington; and Charles Lyons of the University of Southern Maine provided help on Chapter 9. The former Acting Dean of the College of Arts and Sciences at the University of Southern Maine, Stephen Reno, provided time for the author to write during the academic year. A summer Faculty Scholarship Award granted by Provost Helen Greenwood of the University of Southern Maine assisted the completion of this text. To both of these supportive administrators the author expresses deep appreciation.

Betty W. Atterbury

An Introduction
to Mainstreaming

CHAPTER ONE

CONTRASTS IN MAINSTREAMING REALITIES

River Street School

It is Wednesday morning at 11:15. The music room door is open, and Mrs. Peters is waiting for her next class of fifth graders to arrive. This year, the fifth-grade classes have been grouped by their reading ability, and this class contains all the best readers. After the class has burst enthusiastically into the room and settled into their assigned places, eight other children slowly walk in and sit at the back of the class. These children, the entire "special needs" class, also have music at 11:15 on Wednesday because this is the scheduled preparation period for their classroom teacher.

Mrs. Peters has spent the last two music periods teaching the class one form: theme and variations. She begins to review the topic: "Who can arrange five class members so their clothing will illustrate a theme and variations?" The fast readers quickly look around and begin to wave their hands; the members of the special needs class look puzzled. After one blue jeans and one sweater illustration of variations, Mrs. Peters asks the class to open their books to "When Johnny Comes Marching Home" on page 116. She patiently waits until all the special needs class members have the page. During this wait, many of the children in the "regular" fifth grade look at each other and roll their eyes. After reviewing the song and illustrating the phrase structure, Mrs. Peters directs the class to listen to the beginning of "American Salute" and raise their hands when they recognize the theme. Within seconds, hands are waving—but only in the front of the class.

1

The activity for listening to the entire piece is a call sheet that Mrs. Peters has used often in fifth grades. It contains numbers and a description of the musical events in each variation. The students are directed to read the description while they are listening. The members of the special needs class hold their sheets, and Mrs. Peters moves quietly to the back of the room and points to the numbers as the music is playing. None of the children reads beyond a second-grade level.

The final planned activity for this period involves composition. The children are directed to divide themselves into groups of four; each group member is labeled either A, B, C, or D. Mrs. Peters removes a poster covering the directions on the blackboard:

>   A—Bring one xylophone to the group.
>   B—Get paper and pencil from the shelf.
>   C—Choose one rhythm instrument.
>   D—Get either a second- or a third-grade music book.

Then: Choose a familiar song and brainstorm on ways to create a composition that will illustrate theme and three musical variations.

The advanced readers are in five groups and appear to be busy deciding their song choice. Mrs. Peters looks at the back row of children. They have divided themselves into two groups but have not followed the rest of the directions on the chart. Mrs. Peters quickly realizes that the chart means reading again and heads for those two groups. On her way, however, she must first separate two groups who are sitting too close together. Children in another group are waving their hands and are calling out their questions while one student is experimenting with the dynamic extremes of a bongo drum. It is 11:45. The eight children in the special needs class see their teacher at the door and line up. Mrs. Peters waves to them and continues to move from group to group.

Roosevelt School

It is Wednesday morning at 11:15. The music room door is open, and Miss Roberts is waiting for her next class, a second grade, to arrive. Just as the class is walking down the hall, Tommy, who is in a wheelchair, is brought to class by this week's assigned helper, Jason. As the books are being passed out, Jason realizes that he has forgotten the lapboard. He raises his hand and asks permission to return to Tommy's class and get it so that Tommy will be able to hold his book. Tommy has cerebral palsy and needs this special part of his wheelchair in music class.

Miss Roberts is also teaching form this week. She wants this class to understand the similarities between several two-part songs. The class learned the first song, "Old Dan Tucker," in first grade, and as the children sing, they pat the beat on their knees during the verse and move the beat to another body part during the refrain. Miss Roberts leans over to Tommy and tells him to use his lapboard instead of his knees. During the refrain, she helps Tommy put the beat on his shoulders. When she asks the class to open their books to page 83, Jason helps Tommy turn the pages and find "All Night, All Day." After the class has learned the song, Miss Roberts adds a resonator bell accompaniment to the refrain. When it is Tommy's turn to play, he proudly holds his special mallet with the thick taped handle—Jason got it for him off the shelf.

Miss Roberts has the class stand and make a circle. Jason carefully pushes Tommy into the circle, and the class decides which two contrasting movements they will use during the verse and refrain of "Old Joe Clark." When the class moves, first to the left and then to the center, Jason pushes Tommy's chair. The second graders do not bump into Tommy, and they act as though nothing extraordinary is happening in this music class.

Are These Classrooms the Same?

Certainly, there are wide contrasts between the two music classes. There are contrasts of grade, of content, and of activities. Central to this text, however, are the implied and obvious contrasts between the classes in the placement and the musical education of exceptional children. In the first scenario, the placement of an entire self-contained special needs class with a class of advanced readers occurred because of scheduling convenience. In the second scenario, the decision to place one exceptional child as described had been made at a meeting that included the "special teachers" (music, art, and so on). Miss Roberts had made the final decision regarding whether Tommy could cope with the demands of a second-grade music class and which class would be the best social and educational setting for him to learn music.

The two scenarios present wide disparities in the types of social and educational experiences exceptional children meet when they are mainstreamed into general music classes. The social possibilities range from acceptance to bare tolerance to rejection. Exposure and active involvement are the contrasting ways of defining the musical education of mainstreamed exceptional children.

From the Colonial era to the present, one can find accounts of schooling differences in various localities. These variations are due to the traditional role of the states in the control over education and to the differing abilities and desires of individual communities to financially support schools. But the mainstreaming differences in our two examples can occur in the same community and are the result of the interpretation of one phrase, "least restrictive environment," found in the regulations of a federal law, The Education for All Handicapped Children Act (Public Law 94-142).

This law, passed in 1975, has been compared to the civil rights legislation of the 1960s because it finally provided all handicapped children with "equal protection." All exceptional learners were now guaranteed the right to a free public education. Until the passage of this legislation, the education of some exceptional children was not deemed an appropriate task of the public schools but, rather, a matter for separate institutions. These institutions, both public and private, were the descendants of schools initially established by concerned and compassionate Europeans.

EARLY EDUCATION FOR THE HANDICAPPED

Three early schools for handicapped individuals were established in Paris. One of the first educational institutions for handicapped persons was the result of a priest's encounter with two deaf children in his parish. The Abbé de l'Épée (1712–1789) devised a method of teaching the two children to talk, and very soon a school that used his methods was established for the hearing impaired. Shortly thereafter, another Frenchman, Victor Hauy, discovered that he could teach the blind to read tactually using large embossed type.

Certainly, the most famous pioneer in the education of the handicapped is Jean Marc Gaspard Itard, who documented his work with a wild boy. The 11- or 12-year-old boy had been found in the woods and resembled an animal more than a human being. Itard worked with the boy, whom he named Victor, for five years and wrote a complete report of this work, titled "The Wild Boy of Aveyron." His sensory training methods are considered the first attempt to teach a retarded child (Gearheart, 1972).

One of Itard's students, Edouard Seguin, developed his own sequential system of education and established schools for the retarded in France. By 1850, Seguin had moved to the United States, and he eventually initiated schools for the retarded in four states (Gearheart, 1972). Other early separate schools for the handicapped in the United States included the American Asylum for the Deaf, opened in 1817 by Thomas Hopkins Gallaudet, and the school that became the Perkins School for the Blind (Massachusetts), which began in 1829.

The expansion of education for the visually handicapped was largely the result of the development of a system of reading and writing by Louis Braille. Once educators had demonstrated that blind children could indeed be educated, a lessening of reliance on residential schools occurred, and day classes began to be offered in public schools in the United States. The first day class for blind children in a public school began in 1900 in Chicago (Napier, 1972). Although the children were educated in a public school, they were completely segregated from their peers.

Children defined as educable mentally retarded were also among the first to be included in public school settings. The first special class for retarded children in a public school was held in Providence, Rhode Island, in 1896 (Kanner, 1964). About the same time that American cities were including retarded classes in public schools, Alfred Binet was developing the first intelligence test in France. French schools did not include classes for retarded children, and Binet was given the task of developing a measure that would determine which children would benefit from special instruction.

The translation and adaptation of Binet's test by American psychologists and educators made it possible to separate the retarded into mental age-groups. One result of using this test, the Stanford-Binet, was that public schools did enroll children who tested with an IQ above 50, but a second result was a simultaneously established precedent that those children with an IQ below 50 did not belong in public schools. This tradition remained in effect from the development, publication, and widespread use of the intelligence test in 1916 until about 1950.

FEDERAL LEGISLATION

The legislative trail that led to Public Law 94-142 began with the passage of the Elementary and Secondary Education Act in 1965, which focused upon the improvement of educational opportunity for poor children. That federal law did not specifically mention handicapped children, but a subsequent amendment, Public Law 89-313, made available some funding for states to provide education in schools and residential centers for the handicapped. Supporters of public education for the handicapped recognized that unity was necessary to effect change at the federal level, and thanks to the support of many groups representing different types of handicaps, a Bureau of Education for the Handicapped was established in 1966 and was included in the Office of Education. At the same time, Congress created a National Advisory Committee on the Education and Training of the Handicapped. Both of these newly created agencies became strong national advocates for additional legislation and funding (Ravitch, 1983).

In addition, these advocates realized that the legislative model provided by supporters of civil rights legislation was an efficacious one.

One source of support for civil rights laws had been prior court rulings. The supporters of a federal law for exceptional children then moved to the judicial arena. The first decision on behalf of the right to a free public education for severely retarded children was handed down in 1971 in Pennsylvania by a three-judge panel in the federal district court. This decision was quickly followed by a decision in the District of Columbia (1972) that cited the due-process-of-law clause of the Fifth Amendment and stated that every school-age child in the District should be provided with "a free and suitable publicly-supported education regardless of the degree of a child's mental, physical or emotional disability or impairment" (Levine and Wexler, 1981, p. 41).

The passage in 1975 of a federal law mandating a "free appropriate public education" for all handicapped children was the result of both the precedent set in these court rulings and extensive lobbying by parents, special educators, the many organizations representing exceptional children, and the federal agencies mentioned in this chapter. This law, The Education for All Handicapped Children Act, Public Law 94-142, was the most detailed education law that Congress had ever passed. It required states and localities to fund new programs for the handicapped, and it established the educational guidelines for children's inclusion in public schools. Because this law affects most music educators today, a thorough knowledge and understanding of its wording is essential.

Public Law 94-142

There are three sections of the law that have direct bearing on the daily teaching of many music educators. They are as follows:

> It is the purpose of the Act to assure that all handicapped children have available to them, within the time periods specified in section 612(2)(B), a free appropriate public education which emphasizes special education and related services designed to meet their unique needs, to assure that the rights of handicapped children and their parents or guardians are protected, to assist States and localities to provide for the education of all handicapped children, and to assess and assure the effectiveness of efforts to educate handicapped children. . . .
> The term "free public education" means special education and related services which (A) have been provided at public expense, under public supervision and direction, and without charge, (B) meet the standards of the State educational agency, (C) include an appropriate preschool, elementary, or secondary school education in the State involved, and (D) are provided in conformity with the individualized education program required under section 614(a)(5). (20 U.S. Code 1401)

Although music is not specifically mentioned in those sections, the intent of the legislation was to ensure that all educational experiences provided to normal children would also be provided to handicapped children as a part of their free appropriate public education.

> . . . that, to the maximum extent appropriate, handicapped children . . . are educated with children who are not handicapped . . . and that special classes, separate schooling, or other removal of handicapped children from the regular school environment occurs only when the nature of severity of the handicap is such that education in regular classes with the use of supplementary aids and services cannot be achieved satisfactorily. (20 U.S. Code 1412)

The foregoing section is also known as the least restrictive environment provision (from the heading in the 1976 regulations) and has been the basis for the integration of handicapped students into music classes. The term *mainstreaming* is actually not mentioned at all in the law.

Because of the impact of mainstreaming in many music classrooms, the specific wording of these paragraphs is important for music educators to understand and remember. Many administrators truly believe that P.L. 94-142 mandates the automatic inclusion of all handicapped children in regular classrooms, but, as you can see in the preceding extract, the law actually reads, "to the maximum extent appropriate." What has occurred in many schools since the passage of P.L. 94-142 is an odd interpretation of those words. Many self-contained classes of exceptional children are placed in nonhandicapped music classes under the guise of obeying the "language of the law." The scheduling that results is often undertaken without consulting the music teacher or without an adequate consideration of the impact of mainstreaming on the handicapped child or on the normal class.

Music educators must not continue to be passive onlookers in this process. Present and future music teachers must become informed advocates for the best educational and social placement of handicapped children. An important basis of this advocacy is a thorough understanding that (1) the "least restrictive environment" may not be a normal class for some handicapped children, (2) the law does not say that every handicapped child must be mainstreamed into music, and (3) the law certainly does not say that entire groups of handicapped students are to be mainstreamed into music.

WHAT IS THE LEAST RESTRICTIVE ENVIRONMENT?

How the wording of the federal law is interpreted at the local level, therefore, is the important issue for music educators. Because state laws are, for the most part, modeled on the federal legislation, the same wording—"least restrictive environment"—is used in most state regulations. The result is that there is no uniform understanding or definition of what constitutes mainstreaming. Some schools have "special" or "composite" classes, which contain a variety of exceptional children who are mainstreamed into different self-contained classes for academic subjects but who receive music instruction in their "special" class. Other schools group their exceptional children by specific handicaps, and those children receive all their instruction, including music, in mainstreamed settings. In still other schools, groups of exceptional children in one class receive music instruction both as a class and as mainstreamed members of nonexceptional classes. Following are some actual examples of how mainstreaming in music is realized.

In Wichita, Kansas (student population 47,000), all children in grades one through eight receive one hundred minutes of music each week, during a daily music period. Some classes of exceptional children (behaviorally disordered, educable mentally handicapped, visually impaired, hearing impaired, physically handicapped) are mainstreamed, while classes of children with more severe handicaps (trainable mentally handicapped, multiply handicapped, developmentally disabled kindergarten) receive music instruction as a class from specially certified special music teachers. The placement is a cooperative decision made by the principal, the music specialist, and the special education teacher. In this city, whenever possible, entire classes of exceptional children are mainstreamed into existing music classes, since the music period provides the classroom teacher with preparation time (J. Kimpton, pers. com., 1987).

In South Portland, Maine (student population 3,300), children in grades one through four receive weekly music instruction, and the length of the period ranges from thirty to forty minutes. Fifth graders receive sixty minutes of biweekly instruction. Most exceptional children receive music instruction in their self-contained special class grouping. Some children are mainstreamed into general music classes on an individual basis, and this decision is made by the special education teacher without consulting the music teacher (R. Salamone, pers. com., 1987).

From these two examples of actual mainstreaming practice, it is clear that although each school district is reading the same language in the same law, P.L. 94-142 can have very different meanings for the readers. The interpretation of the law, therefore, can vary a great deal within each state and often within each school district. In some schools, music educators are consulted prior to the placement of handicapped students, while in others they may be told that the inclusion of an entire class of special needs students with the advanced fifth-grade readers is "the law."

MAINSTREAMING: PRO AND CON

During the period when P.L. 94-142 was being formulated, the initiative for mainstreaming came primarily from parents of retarded children and the organization of special education professionals, The Council for Exceptional Children. These proponents of integrated education based their arguments on the "right" to a public education. Additional benefits of the law have included an increase and an improvement in cooperation between parents, schools, and other agencies that serve handicapped children. Certainly, the most important benefit has been the inclusion of previously uneducated children in public schools and the development of effective teaching techniques to use with those students. Indeed, as a result of the law's passage in 1975, special education is now considered a legitimate part of the school program.

It is also argued that the practice of mainstreaming exceptional students has benefits for nonhandicapped as well as handicapped learners. Proponents believe that children who have close contact with exceptional students will learn of human similarities and differences at an early age. Supporters of the concept of modeling argue that exceptional children, when mainstreamed, are provided opportunities to imitate behaviors that are socially and educationally appropriate.

It is more than ten years since P.L. 94-142 was passed and since the specific regulations were published in the Federal Register. Many music educators who must teach classes that contain mainstreamed exceptional learners have become disenchanted with the interpretation of the law. Why has that happened? Some educators fault the wording of the law, because there is too much focus on the student's physical environment.

> The definition of "the least restrictive environment" was often taken as a physical place rather than as a set of the psychological features or conditions that promote normal social interactions among pupils of widely different ability. It was taken as an arrangement of classroom furniture and seating proximity rather than as a social system that required genuine commerce between pupils, made equitable demands on instructional time, and gave equitable opportunities for achievement and progress. (Murray, 1986, p. 43).

This assessment of mainstreaming practices is certainly applicable to some music classrooms.

Academic improvement and social integration were two expected outcomes of P.L. 94-142. Authorities in both learning disabilities (Chandler, 1986) and retardation (Gottlieb, 1981) have concluded that academic achievement has not been improved by mainstreaming. A review of research in the social behavior of mainstreamed children indicates that these students are poorly accepted, interact less often and more negatively, and are more often isolated and rejected by their classmates (Gresham, 1982).

Only one research report in music education has focused on differences in social interaction and acceptance of handicapped children in music classes (Jellison, Brooks, and Huck, 1984). In this experiment, severely retarded children were mainstreamed into three different classes. The instructional strategies included (1) large group with no changes in teaching conditions; (2) small groups with instructions to work cooperatively; (3) small groups with instructions to work cooperatively and with a reward. The observation and acceptance data indicate that the small cooperative group with reward had the highest degree of positive interactions with the exceptional students. Mere physical proximity of handicapped children (group 1) did not result in changes in acceptance or increased social interactions. These research results suggest that changes in instruction must occur if students are to socially interact in mainstreamed music teaching situations.

It is also vitally important for music educators to understand that the funding of P.L. 94-142 has had an impact on educational budgets throughout the nation and an indirect effect on music budgets as well. The original intent of the law was to apportion to each state a percentage of the cost of educating handicapped children, to begin at 5 percent and move to 40 percent. However, that percentage does not begin to cover the costs of educating handicapped children (which are almost double those of educating normal children), and since 1977, the changes in the financial condition of the federal government have reduced the amount of funding considerably. As of 1988, the maximum amount ever provided by the federal government was 12 percent.

The lack of adequate federal financial support, combined with federal regulations requiring the public education of all handicapped children, has placed an immense burden on local school districts. The resulting rise in local property taxes has certainly been a partial explanation for the success of Proposition 13 in California and Proposition 2 ½ in Massachusetts. In addition, the funneling of increased amounts of money to special education has meant less money for programs (including music) for nonhandicapped children.

THE IMPACT OF MAINSTREAMING IN MUSIC EDUCATION

Several researchers have attempted to discover the extent and the impact of mainstreaming in music education. The earliest report on teachers' reactions to mainstreaming was published in 1981 (Gilbert and Asmus). This national survey of more than seven hundred music teachers indicated that the respondents who had the most contact with mainstreamed children were the elementary and general music educators, the teachers who teach classroom groups aged 5–13. These teachers responded that a significant gap existed between their experiences with exceptional children and their knowledge of the appropriate methods for teaching music to integrated groups.

Regional surveys of music teachers have been reported by White (1984), Atterbury (1987), and Gfeller and Hedden (1987). White had previously surveyed music teachers' attitudes toward mainstreamed children (Damer, 1979), and her second survey was conducted with the same respondents ($n = 36$). One finding was that there was an increase in the numbers of handicapped students mainstreamed into music classes. The second finding was that the general music teachers, those music educators who had the most contact with exceptional students, exhibited the largest percentage of attitude change toward mainstreamed children. Specifically, 50 percent of the teachers who reported in 1979 that they felt qualified to handle educable mentally retarded students reported five years later that they did not feel qualified. In fact, in total amounts of change, the general music teachers had three times as many changes to the negative in 1984 as to the positive. White's research also included a conclusion that many teachers felt inadequately prepared to teach classes containing mainstreamed children.

Contrasting teacher populations were surveyed by Atterbury (1987) in eleven southern states and by Gfeller and Hedden (1987) in one state, Iowa. Atterbury queried only general music teachers in a survey that probed three areas: administrative support, instructional adaptations, and the effect of mainstreaming on exceptional children. Seventy-six percent of the respondents ($n = 133$) felt they received no administrative support; 57 percent reported that they made instructional adaptations for mainstreamed children; 86 percent reported that mainstreamed children were coping with the behavioral expectations of music class.

The survey by Gfeller and Hedden of both elementary and secondary teachers investigated five areas: the extent of mainstreaming, the level of teacher preparation for working with exceptional children, the level of administrative support, the extent to which music educators perceive mainstreaming as successful, and the possible correlation between administrative support and teachers' perceptions of whether mainstreaming is successful. Less than half the respondents ($n = 114$) worked with mainstreamed students, and most of the music educators responding had little or no training in ways to teach handicapped children. The teachers reported limited administrative assistance and little involvement in the placement of exceptional children in music classes. These music educators also reported lack of preparation time to individualize lessons or materials for handicapped students. Respondents indicated a moderate amount of support for mainstreaming but did feel that handicapped children should receive music instruction in a special resource room. The researchers found a slight positive correlation between the perceived success in mainstreaming and administrative support.

One additional survey was reported in a doctoral dissertation. This smaller survey ($n = 19$) was conducted in one school district by Gavin (1983). Fifty-three percent of the music teachers were familiar with P.L. 94-142, were satisfied with current mainstreaming practices, and felt that handicapped children were appropriately placed for music instruction.

It would appear from these surveys that the impact of mainstreaming in music education is quite mixed. The greatest impact is felt by general music teachers. Although the law was passed in 1975, these teachers are still not being adequately prepared to teach classes that contain integrated exceptional learners. Many of these teachers also perceive a lack of administrative support for this endeavor. These two factors often contribute to a belief by some music educators that exceptional children would probably be best served in nonmainstreamed settings.

Individualized Education Program

Another facet of The Education for All Handicapped Children Act is the mandated development of goals and objectives for each handicapped student. This document, "The Individualized Education Program" (IEP), is to be written yearly according to the law and is a vehicle for music educators to become actively involved in the placement of exceptional students. The law states that the IEP is to be determined by a committee containing a representative of the local education agency who is qualified to supervise the provision of specially designed instruction for handicapped children (usually the director of special education), the child's teacher, the child's parents, and whenever appropriate, the child. The written statement is to include the following: the present level of educational performance; a statement of annual goals, including short-term instructional objectives; the specific educational services to be provided and the extent to which the child will participate in the regular educational program; and the beginning date, the anticipated duration, and the evaluation procedures to be used.

Three of the researchers cited earlier (Atterbury, Gavin, and Gilbert and Asmus) queried respondents regarding their participation in the development of an Individualized Education Program (IEP). The percentages of music teachers who had never participated in this required yearly planning ranged from 76 percent (Gilbert and Asmus) to 89 percent (Gavin); yet, the development of an IEP for every exceptional child is a required activity in every school as a result of P.L. 94-142. This is an important process to be aware of and become involved in. Music teacher involvement in a child's IEP will assist in advocating correct placement and will help in preparing adequate instructional materials or extra needed assistance. Examples of IEPs that include music objectives found in Graham and Beer (1980) are shown in Figures 1-1 and 1-2.

Individualized Education Program

STUDENT'S NAME (FIRST, LAST) Johnny Smith		DATE OF BIRTH September 24, 1972	PUPIL ID 8-11-01
SCHOOL George Washington Elem. School	DISTRICT IV	IEP REVIEW DATE Sept. 2, 1979	TODAY'S DATE Sept. 2, 1978
TEACHER(S) Ms. R. Jones; Ms. E. Kimbrough (Music)			GRADE/PROGRAM

PRIMARY ASSIGNMENT(S)	STARTING DATE	EXPECTED DURATION OF SERVICE
Regular Class, First Grade		
Special Education, (Reading, Arithmetic)		
Music (Special Education)		
SERVICES		
Wheelchair, Transportation		

REASON FOR ASSIGNMENT(S):
Assessment revealed poor reading and inability to handle basic number

concepts. Music assessment shows minimal ability to sustain a singing

voice and very poor rhythmic abilities.

ADMINISTRATOR/SUPERVISOR RESPONSIBLE FOR PROGRAM (NAME AND TITLE) Mr. V. Smith, Principal	
ADDRESS George Washington Elementary School. 2nd and Cherry	PHONE 765-4321

THE FOLLOWING PERSONS HAVE PARTICIPATED IN THE EDUCATIONAL PROGRAM PLANNING CONFERENCE:

SCHOOL DISTRICT REPRESENTATIVE (NAME AND TITLE)
Mr. V. Smith, Principal'

TEACHER(S)
Mrs. R. Jones, 1st grade; Ms. E. Kimbrough, Music Consultant.

OTHERS
Mr. A. Wright, Educational Psychometrist

STUDENT Johnny Smith	PARENT Ms. Elizabeth Smith

PARENT RESPONSE: I DO / DO NOT APPROVE OF THE INDIVIDUALIZED EDUCATION PROGRAM WHICH IS RECOMMENDED.

_____ Signature of Parent   _____ Date

Once you indicate approval, the program will be implemented.

If you disapprove of the educational placement or program recommended for the student, you may request a hearing to resolve any differences by checking the space provided for disapproval and signing your name. To request a hearing, you must send your request within 20 days of the date of the program planning conference. You must send in your request within 10 days if you received it by mail.

If you indicate disapproval, the program will not be implemented. No change in assignment will occur until the decision of the hearing officer is received. Please review the notice which was previously sent to you. It contains an outline of hearing procedures.

If you do not respond within 20 days of the program planning conference, it will indicate that you approve of the educational placement and program that was discussed at the conference and any revisions which are attached. No response also indicates that you waive the right to a hearing at this time.

FIGURE 1-1   Individualized Education Program. Source: Richard M. Graham and Alice S. Beer, *Teaching Music to the Exceptional Child* (Englewood Cliffs, N.J.: Prentice-Hall, 1980). Used by permission.

MENC and Mainstreaming

Further support for inclusion of the teacher in the correct placement of exceptional children in music classes can be found in the 1986 edition of *The School Music Program: Description and Standards,* published by Music Educators National Conference. This slim volume is often used as a resource by administrators and developers of curricula and should also be used by music educators to demand quality standards in their schools. The applicable statements are found on pages 25 and 26.

When handicapped students are mainstreamed into regular music classes:

a. music educators are involved in placement decisions;
b. placement is determined primarily on the basis of musical achievement;

EDUCATIONAL LEVELS & OBJECTIVES

SCHOOL	STUDENT'S NAME
George Washington Elem	Johnny Smith

ASSESSMENT PROCEDURES	CURRICULAR AREA	DESCRIPTION OF PRESENT EDUCATIONAL LEVELS	DATE	PROGRAM PLANNER
Music assessment instrument	Music	Strength: Imitates short vocal sounds, shows an interest in music. Needs: To develop better rhythmic response: unable to tap feet to music. To sing phrases.	9/10	Ms. E. Kimbrough
Reading: Peabody Individual Assessment Test	Reading	Strengths: Recognizes letters, has good visual memory Needs: To work on letter sounds, blending		Ms. R. Jones
PT/OT/functional evaluation and Denver PT test	Gross Motor Skills	Leg turns inward, awkward ambulation, poor balance, arm strength is weak		Mr. T. Walls

INSTRUCTIONAL AREA	ANNUAL GOALS	PROGRAM PLANNER
Music	Will respond to music by tapping the feet/ and imitate short phrases	Ms. E. Kimbrough
Reading	Will improve letter sounds and blending to a criterion of at least 55%	Ms. R. Jones
Physical Education	Will show substantial growth in arm strength	Mr. T. Walls

SHORT TERM OBJECTIVES	ASSESSMENT PROCEDURES	PRE - TEST		POST - TEST	
		DATE	SCORE	DATE	SCORE
Will tap feet at the sound of a drum. Will imitate short vocal sounds in a song. Will sound 5 letters correctly. Will increase strength in arms.	Will tap feet with the drum beat as teacher plays 16 measures of four four meter with 80% accuracy. Will imitate short vocal sounds in two of three consecutive sessions.				

FIGURE 1-2   Individualized Education Program. Source: Richard M. Graham and Alice S. Beer, *Teaching Music to the Exceptional Child* (Englewood Cliffs, N.J.: Prentice-Hall, 1980). Used by permission.

c. placement does not result in classes exceeding standard class size; and

d. placement does not result in a disproportionate number of handicapped students in any class.

Music instruction is provided in special education classes for those handicapped students not mainstreamed for music. . . .

Special education music classes are no larger than other special education classes, and teacher aides are provided for special education music classes if aides are provided for other special education classes.

No one who teaches general music classes should be without a copy of this important publication from MENC. The use of this professional document should complement a teacher's clear understanding of all of the language of P.L. 94-142. All this information will then assist music educators in demanding the best in educational placement for all exceptional children. The present reality of mainstreaming in music is that in many settings, the word can really be equated with "dumping." The first classroom illustration in this chapter is not a freak occurrence—

it is based on a short paragraph written by a teacher on a survey form! Present and future music educators must recognize that only through active involvement in student placement can such poor mainstreaming placements be prevented.

CONCLUSION

The focus of this chapter has been on acquainting the reader with the impact of a single law on music education. Both the brief historical overview of how mainstreaming came into existence and the specific language of P.L. 94-142 most applicable to music educators have been provided as a resource for future use by the reader. Despite the criticisms and varying interpretations of this law, the reality of American education is that the law exists and the intent of the law must be met daily in almost every classroom. A single forty-minute music class may include exceptional children with very disparate handicaps and learning styles. How can music educators be better prepared to teach twenty-five normal-achieving, three learning disabled, one physically handicapped, and one hearing impaired child simultaneously?

The remainder of this book will address that question. One purpose of this text is to provide a background in the learning styles of the many types of commonly mainstreamed handicapped children. Chapters 2–4 focus on three categories of exceptionalities that are descriptive of variations in mental abilities. Chapters 6–8 focus on disabilities that are primarily physical handicaps. Music educators who understand and can describe the learning differences between an educable mentally handicapped and a learning disabled child and who can cite specific music education research to support their requests for changed placements will be listened to with respect. The information in this text will provide such a background. Correct placements will then enable teachers to provide the best music education experiences possible for all children.

A second purpose of the succeeding chapters is to provide specific application of methods and materials to music teaching situations. Teaching groups of integrated learners, many of whom have radically different learning styles and abilities, requires a command of a variety of techniques. These chapters will acquaint the reader with alternative methods and suggested adaptations of present materials that will assist them in providing the best possible music education for mainstreamed students. Two chapters, 5 and 10, are designed to serve as summary points for the preceding descriptions of single exceptionalities. These chapters contain a fictional narrative of one music teacher's planning process for classes that included mainstreamed students. These summary narratives describe general music planning because of the findings, cited in this chapter, that these are the teachers who are most affected by mainstreaming in public schools.

In many communities, general music specialists attempt to educate between seven hundred and one thousand children each week. Those numbers are the true conclusion of this chapter. In order to be a competent music educator and do the heroic job often demanded, one must be able to argue effectively and forcefully for the correct educational setting for mainstreamed students. Only then can a music teacher proceed to the task at hand—structuring instruction that will enable *all* students to experience the love and joy of music.

QUESTIONS

1. Why were parents of severely retarded children among the strongest backers of P.L. 94-142?
2. Discuss the advocacy process that led to the passage of P.L. 94-142.
3. Define the phrase "least restrictive environment."
4. What specific language in the law serves notice that it is not necessary to mainstream every handicapped child?
5. Discuss the positive and negative results of the passage of P.L. 94-142.

ACTIVITIES

1. Write a letter to the building principal at River Street School (see p. 1). Describe the educational problems encountered by the mainstreamed class in music. Include specific references to P.L. 94-142 in your argument, and advocate a change in the present placement of the mainstreamed class.
2. Prepare a historical time line that traces the history of education for one or more of these handicapping conditions: hearing impairment, visual impairment, mental retardation.
3. Interview a director of special education. Include questions that determine (1) how mainstreaming decisions are made, (2) which professionals are included in the IEP development, and (3) the numbers of handicapped children mainstreamed into each music class.

Educable Mentally Retarded Students

CHAPTER TWO

ONE MAINSTREAMING REALITY

Roosevelt School

It is Monday afternoon at 1:20, and Miss Roberts has just finished setting the stage for today's music lesson in second grade. Children have shared the pictures they brought from home that illustrate moving up or down and have sung the song "Brother Noah" while moving their arms with the descending final phrase. Now Miss Roberts asks the class to sing the song again while tiptoeing. She tells them to include a movement that will show how the melody moves at the end of the song. All the children except Sam are able to tiptoe, and all except Sam move their arms and bodies down and finish the song either sitting or squatting on the rug. After the song is finished, Sam looks around and falls down in such a way that he hits another child.

Miss Roberts ignores Sam's fall and introduces the new song "Mary Had a Baby" by singing it and showing the upward and downward melodic direction of the first three phrases with a large red arrow. After the class has learned the song and moved their hands to indicate the contrasting direction in each phrase, Miss Roberts hands each child a red arrow. She asks the children to move their arrows and show the direction of the melody while they listen to the recording of the song. Sam folds his arrow many times and puts it in his pocket. Once the record begins, Miss Roberts realizes that Sam has no arrow and she gives him another. Sam looks around and follows the movements of the child behind him.

The class listened to the "Gavotte" (*Holt MUSIC*, p. 10) earlier in the year during a unit on steady beat. Now Miss Roberts tells the class that they are to listen to the recording and watch as she moves her arrow on the flannel board. She illustrates the contour of the phrases that alternate ascending and descending patterns. While the music is playing, Sam slides along the rug and gets very close to the shelf that holds the drums. Miss Roberts has to stop the lesson and move Sam back to his original space. When the class listens the second and third times, Miss Roberts will have them move their bodies to the upward and downward sounds and then move their own arrows. She moves to be near Sam so that she can model the correct movements for him during the second listening. When the children move their arrows, she brings Sam to the flannel board and helps him point an arrow in the correct direction.

Why Is Sam in This Class?

Sam is mainstreamed into this second-grade music class because he is the same age as the other children in the class. He joins this class only for music, art, and physical education. Sam's mental age is between 4 and 5 years. That means that even though he is 7 years old like the other second graders, his ability to learn is that of a younger child.

The teaching of a sequential and conceptual music curriculum to young children is based on both prior experiences and cognitive developmental levels. Second graders need an accumulation of concrete or "readiness" experiences (singing, moving, playing, listening) with high and low sounds before they are ready to understand the concept of musical direction. This abstraction cannot be taught to a child whose thinking is that of a 4- or 5-year-old. Lacking the developmental cognitive ability of his classmates, Sam participates in "follow your neighbor" music activities.

There are additional factors that contribute to Sam's inability to participate the way his classmates do. The tempo of the recording of "Mary Had a Baby" was faster than when Miss Roberts sang, and the accompaniment on the record was also very different. Sam could not hear the similarity between the song he had tried to sing and what he heard on the recording, but he saw that everyone was moving an arrow, so he did too. Sam's motor development is also delayed, and he is as yet unable to tiptoe. Therefore, in response to the movement direction, Sam could only concentrate on his feet—he could not listen to the music.

Sam is spending time each week in a music class. He is not receiving a music education. During the rest of his school day, he is a member of a class for educable mentally retarded (EMR) children.

DEFINITION

The definition of mental retardation found in Public Law 94-142 is as follows:

"Mentally retarded" means significantly subaverage general intellectual functioning existing concurrently with deficits in adaptive behavior and manifested during the developmental period, which adversely affects a child's educational performance. (Federal Register)

There are three key phrases in this definition: "significantly subaverage general intellectual functioning," "deficits in adaptive behavior," and "manifested during the developmental period." These phrases will be discussed in the following sections. An understanding of the definition of each phrase is a prerequisite of an informed discussion of mainstreaming placement.

Intellectual Functioning

Intellectual ability is usually described by a numerical quotient that is the score from an individual intelligence test. This measure is administered by a trained professional, often the school psychologist. When music educators read a child's folder, they will find a number indicating the results of either the Stanford-Binet or the Wechsler (Revised) test. The score indicated refers to a position within the normal curve of distribution as shown in Figure 2-1 (standard deviation is 15 points). This illustration is an abstract way of showing the intelligence scores of the entire population.

When one's IQ is normal, chronological age and mental age (ability to learn) agree. A child of 10 who scores as well as the average 12-year-old has an IQ of 120. A child of 10 who scores as well as an 8-year-old has an IQ of 80. A simple formula, IQ = Mental Age ÷ Chronological Age × 100, is used to determine this descriptive statistic.

In our opening scenario, Sam, age 7, whose test scores indicate an IQ of 70, had a mental age of 4.9 years. In the second-grade music class, Sam had difficulty understanding an abstract concept because he was

FIGURE 2-1 Normal Curve of Distribution

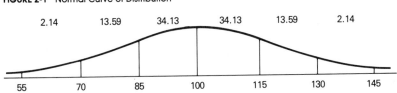

| 2.14 | 13.59 | 34.13 | 34.13 | 13.59 | 2.14 |

| 55 | 70 | 85 | 100 | 115 | 130 | 145 |

still at a stage of musical development where he should be involved in concrete musical experiences.

Children with scores between 50 and 70 (the higher number may vary in different localities) are labeled educable mentally retarded. These students are often mainstreamed into music either individually or by class. Children with scores between 40 and 55 are labeled trainable mentally retarded and are rarely mainstreamed, receiving music instruction in the self-contained classroom setting (see Chapter 11). As Figure 2-1 shows, approximately 2 percent of the total population statistically falls within the numerical scores from 40 to 70.

Adaptive Behaviors

The evaluation of adaptive behavior is often less specific than that of intelligence. Such evaluation may be quite subjective, and most often it is based on the reports of others. Some schools use a standardized test published by the American Association on Mental Deficiency (Nihira, 1974); others use the Vineland Social Maturity Scale (Doll, 1965) or rely on an interview with parents or teachers. The types of behaviors that are defined as adaptive include language, sensorimotor skills, self-help skills, and socialization. Adaptive behavior in older children also includes the ability to use academic knowledge in situations outside of school.

There are clear patterns and stages of language and motor skill development, and many young retarded infants fall behind those developmental milestones. The inability to roll over at 4 months or to sit up at 6 months may be the parents' first clue that their infant is mentally handicapped. Children with mild retardation, however, are often not identified until they are in school and are unable to perform academically at the same rate as their peers. In our opening example, Sam was mainstreamed into music on the basis of his chronological age (7), but his attention, memory, and ability to follow directions, all signs of adequate adaptive behavior in second grade, were not the equivalent of his age-mates.

Developmental Period

The time from conception until age 18 is defined as the developmental period by all authorities in mental retardation. The possible causes of mental retardation span a wide time and social spectrum from prenatal brain damage to abnormal chromosomes to familial-cultural. An exploration of the differences in the etiology of mental retardation is outside the scope of this text (see Apgar and Beck). However, one particular label, Down's syndrome, does deserve brief mention, since the term is quite common and the physical characteristics of these children are usually quite recognizable.

Down's syndrome is named for Dr. Langdon Down, who initially described the characteristics of this one group in 1854. Individuals who have this type of retardation have been found to have an extra chromosome (chromosome 21 or trisomy 21) and have somewhat similar physical characteristics. These features include smaller ears and a smaller nose, which contribute to the impression of a broad flat face; small stubby hands; shorter physique; and a smaller head. While all children with Down's syndrome are also retarded, there is a wide range of mental and motor development within this classification.

LEARNING AND INSTRUCTION

Children who are educable mentally retarded (EMR) are commonly mainstreamed, either singly or in groups, into general music classes in public schools. In most settings, the students are matched for chronological, not mental, age. Therefore, their learning will differ from that of their classmates. Retarded children have been found to perform more poorly in the three major correlates of learning: attention, memory, and organizational ability. In the following sections, each of these topics will be discussed in conjunction with illustrations of how to adapt music instruction for mainstreamed retarded students.

General Music

Attention.   Attention to relevant details and the ability to discriminate appropriate and important items are salient aspects of effective learning. When EMR children are mainstreamed into a music class, they need assistance in distinguishing the important from the unimportant. Music teachers should therefore try to highlight the most significant aspects of the lesson, but instead of using a yellow marking pen, general music teachers need to incorporate visual and aural cues that will help EMR children focus their attention. A word on the blackboard, a new bulletin board that illustrates a musical concept, and a clear teacher statement of "what we are going to learn" are helpful lesson introductions.

Many music teachers assume that all children are able to determine the lesson objective(s) because they are experiencing the same musical concepts in different activities. Incidental or associative learning cannot be assumed for retarded learners. Classes with mainstreamed EMR children should always include continual references to the important musical goals, and the lesson structure should include time for a pointed summary that, again, focuses on the importance of *what* was learned while singing, dancing, playing, listening, or moving.

In addition to a highlighted lesson structure, the use of textbooks and charts should be carefully considered when EMR children are integrated in a music class. Important details are often difficult to discriminate in the colorful and visually attractive music textbooks. Teachers need to incorporate strategies that unobtrusively assist retarded students in coping with complex visual or aural information. For example, a mainstreamed fifth-grade EMR student may experience difficulty finding the third measure of the second staff while listening for syncopated rhythms. The preparation of an overhead transparency of the page and the use of a marking pen to circle the measure direct the class's attention to the specific measure(s) and help the EMR student focus on the important rhythm.

Music notation is a difficult symbol system for normal-achieving learners to master. Details that really matter may have to be very carefully emphasized for mainstreamed retarded students. Two examples are black versus white noteheads and single versus joined stems in stick notation. Music educators must remember that retarded children may not see details that are obvious to their classmates. Such an understanding will enable teachers to foresee which contrasts and differences will need to be stressed.

Unfortunately for retarded students, how a song text is printed is based primarily on economic factors. Most teachers are familiar with the general inconsistency in the way song verses are printed, and the many formats are also confusing to retarded learners. Teachers must remember to always clearly and carefully illustrate where the verses are printed and where the refrain is found.

SUMMARY OF TEACHING SUGGESTIONS TO AID ATTENTION

Clarify important aspects of the lesson.
Refer often to the goal of the lesson.
Include a clear summary of the lesson.
Direct attention to important parts of printed pages.
Emphasize differences in notation detail.
Illustrate differences in verse/refrain format.

Memory.   The ability to process and remember information is an essential component in learning, and in this area, also, retarded children have a deficit, particularly in short-term memory. When EMR children are mainstreamed into music classes, attention to the two Rs—rate and repetition—will assist these memory deficits.

There are several teaching strategies, effective for classes with mainstreamed children, that provide a way to adjust the rate at which material is presented. Many general music teachers introduce new songs by playing the prepared series recordings, but the tempo and the accompaniment of the recordings are often frustrating for EMR learners. A more effective alternative is to sing the song without accompaniment and at a tempo that allows clear enunciation of the words.

Memory limitations must also be considered when teaching structured dances, since multiple directions combined with movement expectations can be frustrating for EMR learners. These activities require a careful presentation of the movement sequences by the teacher. A useful way to provide rehearsal time for mainstreamed children is to include a hand practice before trying the dance and practice each part using hand movements to the left, right, forward, back, and so on before asking the class to move. In some classes, having a small group illustrate the movements will provide an additional opportunity to memorize the expected movements. Of course, teachers must always be a model for all movements.

The sequence of prepared practice used by teachers who are familiar with Orff-*Schulwerk* is also recommended for retarded children. Practicing mallet movements by using *patschen* and then in the air is an effective preplaying rehearsal technique. This type of preplaying practice can easily be adapted for other instrumental accompaniments as well.

A real instructional challenge is to provide adequate repetition for mainstreamed EMR children without boring normal-achieving learners. Teaching a song by having the students join in on a repeated word, phrase, or rhythm pattern is one way to provide needed repetition of text and melody for EMR learners. The use of visual cues can be a simple strategy that provides more interest when repeating a song or a listening example.

Visual cues will also assist the short-term memory deficits of retarded children. For example, a set of pictures of a rabbit, a garden, peas, a cabbage, a tomato, and a sweet potato (use a seed catalog) is helpful in teaching "John the Rabbit" (*Silver Burdett MUSIC*, Centennial Edition, Grade 2, p. 2) to primary children. The pictures help the mainstreamed children remember the order of the words. This particular song is especially suitable for classes with mainstreamed children, since it includes a simple, repeated two-note response that enables them to participate even if they do forget the words for a phrase or two.

Mainstreamed retarded children may also exhibit memory deficits from week to week if lessons are not carefully structured. When two of five activities emphasize changing tempos but the lesson parts are separated by songs or playing experiences that emphasize beat or duration, a retarded child will not remember that last week's topic was tempo. If the two activities are taught in succession, with an emphasis on the musical concept common to both, the retarded student will be helped to associate and remember musical learnings.

Repetition in music classes is needed not only within a lesson but also between lessons. General music teachers may teach a third-grade lesson to four or six classes in one week. By the end of the week, the teacher is tired of the material and therefore plans new songs and activities for the following week. But the children only participated in the musical experiences once! A choice of songs and music that do not bore the teacher and that can be used to teach multiple musical elements is helpful in providing repetition for mainstreamed students.

Another way to reinforce musical learnings is to enlist the assistance of the classroom teacher. It may be possible to place the tape of a new song in a classroom that has "listening corners." When older EMR children are mainstreamed, music teachers should ask classroom teachers to use song texts in reading or writing assignments. Cooperative planning can prepare EMR learners for success rather than failure when reading is required in music.

SUMMARY OF TEACHING SUGGESTIONS TO AID MEMORY

Introduce new songs without recordings.
Provide adequate rehearsal for structured movements.
Include prepractice for instrumental accompaniments.
Provide adequate repetition of song texts.
Use visual cues for text order.
Order lesson activities to emphasize musical goals.
Choose good musical material so *you* won't be bored.
Enlist the assistance of classroom teachers.

Organization.   Efficient learning relies on the ability to organize and apply information both in an initial situation and in new settings. Again, this aspect of how one learns has been found to be less effectively used by mentally retarded individuals. Music teachers can help retarded children organize and use previous learnings about musical concepts by planning one or more unchanging bulletin boards that provide a visual reminder of important musical ideas: An illustration of meter or register or steady beat can be provided with pictures from magazines or coloring books.

One successful organizational strategy, called chunking, requires that the learner combine relevant information as a memory aid. General music teachers need to include concrete visual, verbal, and aural cues that will help retarded children "chunk" musical learning. One source of visual cues is the Holt, Rinehart & Winston Music Series, *Holt MUSIC*, which includes illustrations of sound in the form of ikons. These graphic illustrations of musical ideas are the step between experience and symbolization described by Jerome Bruner (1966). The inclusion of repeated iconic representations of musical ideas in addition to notation and words may provide retarded children with cues to chunk and organize abstract musical data.

Students need to be carefully directed to relate new learnings to previous musical experiences. Each lesson should focus on single or multiple concepts, with continual references to similar previous learning. In this way, students will be helped to understand that every song has melodic direction, a steady beat, a distinctive tempo, and so on.

SUMMARY OF TEACHING SUGGESTIONS
TO AID ORGANIZATION

Provide bulletin boards that are references.
Include iconic representations.
Relate previous and present learning.

Instrumental Music

All the teaching situations and suggestions discussed thus far have focused on general music classes because of the overwhelming preponderance of mainstreamed students in those classes. However, there is evidence (Williams, 1985) that retarded children can successfully learn to play instruments and participate in instrumental organizations. Instrumental settings offer an ideal setting for adaptations in instruction because of the small size of most group lessons. However, music educators should note that one successful instructor of instrumental music for EMR children (Rosene, 1976) advocates individual lessons prior to participation in group lessons.

The correlates of successful learning discussed previously also apply to how one learns to play an instrument. Attention, memory, and organization need to be carefully considered in the small-group setting. Fortunately, instrumental teachers usually have the freedom to group students according to grade or instrument and can carefully structure the lesson group that will include a retarded learner.

Attention. Teachers of instrumental music must incorporate ways of focusing the attention of retarded learners on relevant details and must help them distinguish the important from the unimportant. Fortunately, when learners have their own books, it is much easier to truly "highlight" the page with the ubiquitous yellow marker. Indeed, teachers might consider using different-colored markers for symbols of expression. Lesson structure for these learners must be carefully organized also. Careful attention to a lesson introduction, continual references to the lesson goals, and a clear summary are as important for instrumentalists as for students in general music.

Memory. Two instructional factors, rate and repetition, were described earlier in relation to general music instruction, and instrumental teachers will need to pay careful attention to each of these also. Retarded students will not be able to develop technical proficiency at a rate similar to that of their age-mates. These students must be evaluated and praised for their individual mastery, not compared with other instrumentalists.

Additional practice material can be provided from published or teacher-prepared materials. The use of two or three lesson books is one way to provide interesting but repetitive practice materials. Instrumental teachers should also consider incorporating familiar melodies that the student has previously sung in general music. Many of the songs taught in the primary grades are of limited range and contain repeated melodic and rhythm patterns. They can be transposed by the teacher into an appropriate key, and rhythms can be rewritten in augmentation or diminution to correspond to what is in the method book.

Organization. Instrumental method books are organized in terms of simple to complex fingerings and rhythms. Retarded learners will need specific instruction that will assist them to chunk the many discrete details found on successive pages. Many of the techniques that are useful in classes with mainstreamed retarded students can be adapted to instrumental teaching. These include the use of ikons, bulletin boards, and highlighting of notational or fingering differences.

In an article in *Music Educators Journal*, Paul E. Rosene described the important facets of successful instrumental teaching of EMR children: "Patience, concern, unhurried approaches, rote techniques prior to note instruction, strict adherence to rules of discipline, and sequenced procedures" (p. 37). Certainly, music educators should not ignore EMR children when recruitment time occurs in intermediate grades. Careful grouping and detailed instruction in addition to the suggested instructional adaptations may enable retarded students to achieve success in instrumental music.

SUMMARY OF TEACHING SUGGESTIONS FOR INSTRUMENTAL MUSIC

Highlight details in musical notation.
Continually focus on lesson objectives.
Adopt an appropriate rate of instruction.

Provide repetition by using several lesson books.

Aid students in chunking new and old material with ikons, bulletin boards, and highlighting.

Other Strategies

In his text on mental retardation, David L. Westling (1986, p. 123) includes the following instructional suggestions:

1. Teach retarded students to focus on single distinct dimensions when initially teaching discriminations.
2. Show retarded learners how to use rehearsal strategies to improve memory and have them practice doing so when attempting to memorize.
3. Present information in relevant clusters; do not assume common associations will be obvious.
4. Seek and use appropriate reinforcement techniques, realizing that each individual may require a different reinforcer.
5. Realize that observational and incidental learning tends to decrease with decreased IQs and structure the environment accordingly for effective learning.

Each of these general suggestions is easier to adapt to an individual when you know the capabilities of that student, and it is much more effective (and efficient) to seek a source of information regarding successful teaching strategies than to go through weekly trial-and-error situations. Each of the foregoing topics (attention, memory, organization) can be the focus of professional discussions with resource and classroom teachers. In these discussions, you can discover which rehearsal, reinforcement, and focusing strategies are effective for the student in other settings.

While the preceding section contains many generalizations about how educable mentally retarded children learn, music teachers must remember that all children with a common diagnostic label will not learn in an identical manner. Successful mainstreaming of EMR children depends upon careful teacher preparation and a clear diagnosis and understanding of each individual's learning problems. Some students may have attention problems, others may have memory deficits, and still others may be unable to organize related information in a meaningful manner. Many EMR learners may have deficits in all areas. Music teachers need to become sensitive to each child's learning style and adapt instruction in a way that will help each retarded child achieve musical success.

EFFECTS OF MAINSTREAMING

As illustrated in the opening scenario of this chapter, mainstreaming placement often results in a less than ideal educational experience for

the retarded child. While music education research that includes retarded children in mainstreamed settings is sparse (see Curtis and
Nocera, discussed on pp. 32 and 33), the literature in general and
special education contains many studies that investigate academic
achievement and the social integration of retarded children. The findings and conclusions in this research will provide music educators with
information that will contribute to effective advocacy for correct mainstreaming placement.

One thorough review of research in both the academic and the
social outcomes of mainstreaming is by Madden and Slavin (1983).
These authors were especially impressed with one study (Calhoun and
Elliot, 1977) in which EMR students were placed in regular or special
classes and tested for a period of three years. The achievement of the
mainstreamed students at the end of the three years was much higher
than that of the matched special-class sample. The two groups received
the same types of instruction, materials, and equipment, while the
teachers (all trained in special education) alternated between classes
each semester. In addition, much of the instruction was individualized.
The authors of this review of research find this study to be without
methodological flaws, since the assignment of students was done on a
random basis and the treatment was identical. However, to replicate
these conditions in everyday music classrooms would necessitate the
inclusion of continual opportunities for individualized instruction combined with an adequate training in special education, two factors that are
presently lacking in most settings.

In regard to academic achievement, Madden and Slavin conclude
the following: "When the regular class is unaltered, the students closest
in achievement level to the regular students benefit most from assignment to the regular class, whereas students with much more serious
learning problems gain most in special classes" (p. 530). This review and
its conclusion should certainly be cited by music educators in discussions about the educational environment and expectations for mainstreamed retarded learners.

This same review of research also describes the studies that have
probed the social acceptance of mainstreamed students. This research is
certainly of interest, since music class is one setting that many educators
feel is a nondemanding (that is, social) setting in which successful
mainstreaming can occur. Numerous studies are cited that all contain
similar conclusions; namely, EMR students are rejected more often and
are less socially accepted than their classmates in mainstreamed settings. The authors conclude, "It is clear that the social acceptance of
[these] students is a major problem of the mainstreamed classroom . . .
mainstreaming may exacerbate the problem to some degree" (p. 537).

In the final section of this review, the authors suggest that in order for students to develop positive social relationships, it is essential that the mainstreamed students not be identified as belonging to a special group. This conclusion should also be especially noted by music educators who may be asked to teach integrated groups that include entire classes of retarded learners.

Another review of interest to music educators (Gottlieb, Alter, and Gottlieb, 1983) also analyzes the body of research in academic achievement and social adjustment of retarded children. These authors are particularly interested in why there is no difference in academic achievement when EMR students are randomly placed in either special or mainstreamed settings. They cite an observational study that focused on types of teacher behaviors (questioning, directing, interacting) and conclude that there really was little difference in types of instruction in the two settings. Clearly, there must be instructional changes if successful educational mainstreaming is to be a reality for retarded children in music or any class.

Finally, it has been noted by Jay Gottlieb (1981) that EMR children are not successful in learning how to read: ". . . not a single study on mainstreaming . . . has reported a mean grade-equivalent reading score higher than 3.8 for EMR children, regardless of class placement" (p. 118). This finding is of special note to teachers of general music in middle and junior high schools where the reading and cognitive demands are much higher than in primary grades.

Research tells us that some

Teachers of mainstreamed students need training in special education.
Individualized instruction benefits EMR students.
EMR students are often socially rejected.
Mainstreamed students should not be identified as being "special" by their peers.
EMR students may have severe reading deficits.

Within any EMR population, there is a wide disparity of abilities and aptitudes that must be considered when mainstreaming placements occur. Indeed, within the definition, children with an IQ from 50 to 70 are quite diverse. Those students nearest the cutoff score may be most successful in a mainstreamed music class, especially during the primary grades. When the reading demands in music are above the fourth-grade level, mainstreamed retarded children may encounter frustration. Researchers have concluded that the use of individualized instruction is most efficacious with mainstreamed learners, a type of teaching that is rarely feasible in general music classes but that is possible in instrumental instruction (see Rosene, discussed on p. 34). Many administrators support a rationale that mainstreaming in music is an opportunity for socialization. Music educators who are cognizant of the research conclusions cited earlier must counter this common but erroneous assumption and advocate that only when children are not identified as special is there any possibility of social acceptance by their peers.

RESEARCH IN MUSIC EDUCATION

Retardation has been the subject of more music education research than any other exceptionality. The research that has been conducted with EMR children contains findings regarding tonal and rhythm discrimination, singing range, aptitude, achievement, rhythmic training, and instrumental training. Each of the extant studies is described in detail. These summaries are provided so that music educators will be able to incorporate relevant information into written and oral presentations when advocating appropriate mainstreaming placements.

Pitch

A report by Zenatti (1975) described the testing of 876 children in France who ranged in age from 5 years 6 months to 16 years 5 months. The subjects were normal ($n = 480$) and educable mentally retarded ($n = 396$). The test content was melodic groups of three and four notes, and children were asked to discriminate sets of same or different patterns.

The researcher reports that the tonal discrimination of the exceptional sample was appreciably inferior to that of children matched for chronological age. However, the tonal ability of the retarded children was similar to the sample matched for mental age. Of interest in this study are the content—three- and four-note patterns (shorter than what is commonly used in most music classes)—and the finding of similarities in tonal discrimination in subjects matched only for mental age.

Rhythm

Two studies focus on rhythmic ability of retarded and normal-achieving students. Similar to the tonal research, each of these studies employed author-constructed tasks. However, the ages of the sample populations in these reports were dissimilar.

The rhythmic ability of primary-age children was the subject of a dissertation by Kaplan (1977). The researcher constructed and administered a *Test of Rhythmic Responsiveness* to seventy-two children matched for *mental* age (6, 7, 8). The chronological age of the retarded sample ranged from 7 years 11 months to 12 years 9 months.

The findings of this study indicate that the two groups of children performed a steady beat, gradual changes in tempo, and metric accent in a similar manner. In only the subtest that required the subjects to echo a rhythm were there significant differences between the two groups of subjects.

Children in three groups—Down's syndrome, mentally retarded, and normal—were tested in rhythm and time by Stratford and Ching (1983). The subjects (n = 30) were also matched for mental age. The mean chronological age of the three groups was quite varied: normal—4.2 years; Down's syndrome—13 years; retarded—12.3 years. The researchers used three rhythm patterns, and the subjects were required to tap a metal plate in time with the rhythms. The mean scores for the normal and Down's syndrome groups were not significantly different, but there was a significant difference between the third group of retarded subjects and both other groups.

Both of these studies in rhythm focus on short patterns, and in both studies, subjects were similar in their mental age. The findings reinforce the conclusion that indiscriminate mainstreaming by chronological age will not lead to musical success for retarded students.

Singing Range

A report by Larson (1977) describes the individual vocal testing of a small sample of EMR (n = 11) and normal (n = 18) children, ages 7 and 8. The mean vocal range and the mean midpoint for the two samples are shown in Figure 2-2.

The statistical analysis revealed that the EMR mean midpoint was significantly lower than that of the normal sample and also lower than the midpoint of ten songs randomly selected from textbooks used by the subjects in music. Unfortunately, the small size of the sample must be noted. While these results cannot be generalized to larger groups, the findings are certainly of interest to music educators who are attempting

FIGURE 2-2 Singing Range and Mean Range of Mentally Retarded and Normal Children. Source: Larson, 1977.

COMBINED NORMAL VOICES

Mean range: 18 half steps
Mean midpoint: G

EMR VOICES

Mean range: 8 half steps
Mean midpoint: D-sharp

to develop the singing voices of children in integrated groups of learners.

Standardized Tests

Aptitude.   In a study by McLeish and Higgs (1982), two measures, the *Seashore Measures of Musical Talent* and the Bentley *Measures of Musical Abilities*, were administered to retarded subjects ($n = 121$) from special schools in England. Subjects ranged in age from 8 to 16, with mental ages from 5 to 12. The tests were administered in small groups, and the procedures were modified for the special subjects. The researchers report that the retarded subjects attained scores that were about 20 percent below the norms for each test. In addition, they found that the scores of the retarded subjects did not improve with increased age (either mental or chronological).

Another project using standardized tests was conducted by Curtis (1981), who administered the *Seashore Measures of Musical Talent* and the Gordon *Musical Aptitude Profile* (MAP) to eighty-three students in grade five who were mainstreamed into music. The sample included slow learners ($n = 26$), learning disabled ($n = 5$), and educable mentally retarded ($n = 8$). While the researcher did combine the three categories for a statistical analysis, she also reports the aptitude scores for the samples by separate categories. On the Gordon MAP test, the normal sample had a composite mean score of 47.8, and the EMR sample's mean score was 37.8. The Seashore scores are reported only by subtests, and the EMR subjects' mean scores were lower on all the subtests, with a significant difference only on the Time subtest. Again, readers are cautioned that the size of the EMR sample is not sufficient to generalize these findings. Readers are also directed to a thorough review of this dissertation (and Nocera, discussed on p. 33) by Thompson (1985).

Music aptitude in an EMR population was the subject of a dissertation by Ianacone (1976), who also used the MAP with normal and EMR populations. However, the exceptional subjects were not mainstreamed into music as in Curtis's study. The subjects ($n = 135$) were divided into groups of fifteen (normal, EMR matched for chronological age, EMR matched for mental age), and the test was administered to these three sets of groups under three different conditions: no preparation, auditory test preparation, and auditory and visual test preparation. The researcher describes these conditions as an attempt to lessen the nonmusical aspects of testing. The mean age of the normal sample was 10, of the EMR sample matched for chronological age, 10.2, and of the EMR sample matched for mental age, 16.10. The test results indicated that the retarded subjects responded better to the MAP with some form of intervention (auditory or auditory and visual), but the interventions did not differentiate the scores of the normal populations. As in all the research cited in this section, the scores of the EMR subjects matched for chronological age were significantly lower than the scores of the matched normal groups—despite the different test conditions.

Achievement. Music achievement was the topic of study in a dissertation by Ellis (1982), who administered the *Music Achievement Tests One and Two* (Colwell, 1970) to intact classes of gifted (n = 107), educable mentally handicapped (n = 64), and average (n = 116) fifth and sixth graders. The results of testing indicated significant differences in total score between the educable mentally handicapped and average samples. In addition, the researcher administered the Gaston *Test of Musicality* as an aptitude measure and reports mean scores of 28.1 for the average sample and 22.8 for the retarded sample. He also administered the tonal memory subtest of the Seashore Measures as a way of measuring memory differences and reports a mean score of 16.8 for the average and 8.9 for the EMH sample. These later sets of scores were not submitted to a statistical analysis.

A study by Nocera (1981) also focused on music achievement. The researcher used a different measure, the *Silver Burdett Competency Test*, with mainstreamed retarded and normal-achieving students in grade two (n = 40) and grade five (n = 48). The statistical analysis of test results indicated a significant difference in the two sample populations at both grade levels.

Of particular interest was the researcher's structured interviews with the teachers of these children. The teachers were asked to judge the level of musical performance (singing, playing, moving) of the tested EMR subjects. The teachers generally considered the second-grade exceptional subjects able to perform as well as their peers but judged far fewer fifth graders comparable to their age-mates in these musical tasks. In addition, the teachers were asked to assess the music learnings of the tested subjects. A comparison of their assessments with the children's actual scores indicated that the teachers were "generally unable to make accurate judgments regarding the ability of mainstreamed EMR learners to successfully master . . . music learning, and [they] make more negative evaluations than are supported by the scores achieved by EMR subjects" (p. 122).

Training. Rhythmic training of EMR children aged 9–12 was the subject of a dissertation by Buker (1966). Students in self-contained classes (n = 78) were individually pretested with author-constructed tests of rhythm matching, song recognition, and rhythm reading. Following the experimental period of seven weeks, the students were retested. The researcher concluded that EMR children could learn to read rhythms successfully.

Another study of rhythmic training (Ross, Ross, and Kuchenbecker, 1973) describes a four-week program in which the EMR experimental group (n = 14) and the control group (n = 14) received daily music instruction in small groups. The subjects ranged in chronological age from 7.3 to 10 years. An author-constructed measure was individually administered as a pretest and a posttest, and the results indicated a significant difference between the two groups following training.

A text by Dickinson (1976) describes a project conducted in England with ESN (educationally subnormal) children. The term ESN includes students with an IQ of 50–70, but sometimes the IQ cutoff is higher (80). The researcher provided a music program to be taught by classroom teachers in a special school for ESN children aged 8–13. The experimental sample (n = 59) and a control group (n = 60) were tested with a version of the Bentley *Measures of Musical Abilities* that was modified for length and administration. The two groups were administered a pretest and a posttest, and the scores of the experimental group were significantly better following the year of special instruction.

Instrumental training for EMR children aged 9–12 was the topic of a dissertation by Rosene (1976). The researcher taught thirteen subjects individual lessons (flute, clarinet, cornet, trombone) twice a week for nine weeks and group lessons three times a week for five weeks. The instruction began with imitation and rote techniques and progressed to music reading. The subjects were administered the *Music Achievement Test* (Colwell, 1970) and the *Music Aptitude Profile* (Gordon, 1965) as pre- and posttest measures, and a significant gain on both measures is reported. At the end of the research period, seven public school music teachers listened to each subject's playing and rank-ordered the thirteen subjects. The discriminating factor in this ranking was mental age: The student with the highest mental age ranked first in actual playing achievement. Of particular interest was the researcher's report that at the end of the semester, eight of the subjects qualified for intermediate band membership by passing the same audition given to other beginning instrumentalists.

Research tells us that for the students in these studies,

Tonal discrimination was similar in groups matched by mental age.
Rhythm abilities (beat, tempo, accent) were similar in groups matched by mental age.
The ability to echo a rhythm pattern was *not* similar in groups matched by mental age.
The ability to perform a simultaneous rhythm pattern was *not* similar in groups matched by mental age.
The EMR students had a lower singing range.
Music aptitude was approximately 20 percent lower for EMR students than for normal-achieving students.

Music achievement was lower in EMR students.

EMR students were trained to read rhythms and to play instruments.

Summary

The body of research summarized in the preceding sections is of particular interest to general music teachers. Although a few studies were conducted with fairly small samples, most of this research is quite adequate in sample size, test instruments, and design. Every researcher who has tested retarded and normal-achieving children has reported lower scores for the retarded subjects matched for chronological age; therefore, it is clear that in both aptitude and achievement, EMR children who are mainstreamed into music by chronological age will not be similar to their age-mates. The research findings of Ross, Buker, Dickinson, and Rosene emphasize the efficacy of additional individualized or small-group music instruction for retarded children. These conclusions should be incorporated into requests for additional or completely separate music instruction for EMR students.

CONCLUSION

Unfortunately, when a child is labeled retarded, teacher expectations are often altered. In light of the research reviewed in this chapter, a lowered expectation for EMR students in some aspects of music instruction is wise. However, Nocera's findings that teachers were not able to clearly evaluate the music learnings of mainstreamed children must also be remembered.

Cognitive competence and classroom behavior are two important factors in how children are perceived by their peers. Music class offers a setting in which retarded children may participate in structured events that allow them to be perceived as successful by their peers. Clearly, the ability to provide such opportunities is a challenge for music educators.

It is difficult for teachers to consider students' futures in their daily, weekly, or yearly planning. They certainly should remember that EMR children do not live their adult lives labeled as special. Mildly handicapped students eventually leave school, and most become undifferentiated and often productive members of society. The long-term music education goal for these students, therefore, must be the same as for all students. The understanding of long-term goals is intertwined with the articulation of a philosophy. Music educators need to have a clear vision of the value of music in the lives of all people. A philosophical outlook that focuses on providing opportunities for aesthetic perception and response in all facets of music making will assist educators in providing an adequate musical education for the educable mentally retarded. These students, like all students, need to be able to experience the beauty and joy of music for the rest of their lives.

QUESTIONS

1. Define the three components of the EMR definition and tell how each is measured in educational settings.
2. Describe five ways that music instruction of integrated classes can be adapted for EMR children.
3. How do EMR children differ from their age-mates in memory, attention, and organizational ability?
4. Why does mainstreaming placement in music based on chronological age often result in frustration for EMR students?
5. Explain how instrumental instruction can be a viable musical setting for some EMR students.
6. Discuss the implications to middle school and junior high general music educators of Gottlieb's finding that EMR children do not read above a 3.8 level.
7. How can music educators provide individualized instruction for EMR children?
8. Explain why music education research findings indicate that chronological age placement of EMR students is inappropriate.

ACTIVITIES

1. Write a lesson based on the introductory scenario, and include main-streaming adaptations based on the chapter content.
2. Compare and contrast the two adaptive behavior scales described in the chapter.
3. Observe a music class that contains EMR students. Write a chronological observation report and add suggested instructional adaptations based on your understanding of this chapter.
4. Interview a director of music or a school administrator to determine how mainstreaming decisions are made for EMR students in that school district.

BIBLIOGRAPHY

Apgar, V., and J. Beck. 1972. *Is My Baby All Right?* New York: Pocket Books.

Matson, J. L., and J. A. Mulick, eds. 1983. *Handbook of Mental Retardation.* Elmsford, N.Y.: Pergamon Press.

Nocera, S. 1979. *Reaching the Special Learner through Music.* Morristown, N.J.: Silver Burdett Company.

Westling, D. L. 1986. *Introduction to Mental Retardation.* Englewood Cliffs, N.J.: Prentice-Hall.

Learning Disabilities
CHAPTER THREE

MEMO

From: T. J. Ronald, Director of Special Education

To: Mrs. Johns, Townline Middle School

Re: Joseph Barnes

As a result of this week's meeting of the Committee on the Handicapped, beginning November 14, Joey will be mainstreamed in three areas at Townline Middle School—lunch, recess, and music class. He will participate in your sixth-grade class on Wednesdays at 1:15. He is in Mr. Adams's L.D. class.

WHAT HAPPENED WHEN JOEY CAME TO MUSIC?

Townline Middle School

It is Wednesday, November 14, and Mrs. Johns is standing at her door waiting for her sixth-grade class to arrive. As the class walks down the hall, Joey Barnes is nowhere to be seen. After the children are seated and Mrs. Johns has begun her lesson, he arrives at the door of the music room. Mrs. Johns stops and introduces him to the sixth graders.

The class begins by finding page 158 in their text so that they can review the song they learned last week, "Till That Day Blues." Joey does not find the page until the class is singing the second verse, and then he sits and looks intently at the book. After a review of the blues form, Mrs. Johns gives the class instructions for small groups.

Each group will have an Autoharp, and each member is to have a turn playing the 12-bar blues chord progression. At the end of each phrase, group members are to take turns improvising a rhythmic pattern, and each group is also to make up one or more new verses for the song. The groups are already listed on the board and the instruments are placed in different sections of the room, so the children move quickly to their assigned places. Joey gets up when the rest of the class moves, and Mrs. Johns shows him his name on the board and points to the corner where his group is meeting.

When it is Joey's turn to play the Autoharp, he cannot strum the chords rhythmically and has difficulty changing the chords in the correct measures; it is the first time he has played an Autoharp, and he loses his place in the song each time he looks at the chord buttons. When it is his turn to improvise a rhythm pattern on the claves, he plays far beyond the two-and-a-half-beat rest, and the other group members begin to yell at him to stop. Mrs. Johns walks over to the group, and the children ask her to take Joey out of their group because he is "messing them up."

Mrs. Johns takes Joey to her desk and gives him a book, which is open to page 158, and an Autoharp and tells him to read the page and practice the chords. Mrs. Johns has not been told that Joey is reading at the second-grade level! She moves to help other groups in the room, and Joey spends the next part of the period watching each of the other groups practice but doesn't touch his instrument.

During the final part of the period, the groups are taped while they perform their original verses and improvised rhythms. Mrs. Jones asks the entire class to sing so that Joey can have a turn playing the Autoharp, but he still cannot find his place or move to the new chords in a rhythmic fashion. The children begin to look at each other and laugh while he is trying to find the second chord. Mrs. Johns stops the song, picks up the Autoharp, and plays while the class sings the two verses for a concluding activity.

Was Joey Successfully Mainstreamed?

Joey is 12 years old, so he was placed in a class with his chronological peers. However, the placement committee did not know that independent and grade-level reading demands would be made upon Joey in a music class. Joey has also been in an adaptive physical education class for three years, where he receives special instruction to improve his motor coordination. The placement committee did not know that there were activities in music class that required motor coordination.

Joey's parents demanded at the meeting that he be *mainstreamed,* and the committee *solved* this problem by putting Joey in three social settings in which they thought he would not have to read. The result of that decision was really a placement where the child was expected to be able to cope with the cognitive and motor demands of his age-level peers. The result for Joey was an initial unpleasant and frustrating experience in music.

DEFINITION

The description of this exceptionality in Public Law 94-142 is as follows:

> "Specific learning disabilities" means a disorder in one or more of the basic psychological processes involved in understanding or using language, spoken or written, which may manifest itself in an imperfect ability to listen, think, speak, read, write, spell, or to do mathematical calculations. The term includes such conditions as perceptual handicaps, brain injury, minimal brain dysfunction, dyslexia, and developmental aphasia. The term does not include children who have learning problems which are primarily the result of visual, hearing, or motor handicaps, of mental retardation, or of environmental, cultural, or economic disadvantage. (Federal Register)

This definition has three key ideas that merit further discussion. The first is that a learning disability is a disorder in a psychological process. This phrase implies that a dysfunction exists in the *way* a child learns but that the basic capacity to learn is intact. Although not specifically stated in the definition, there is an assumption of tested normal intelligence as the initial delineator of a learning disability.

The definition also includes the words "imperfect ability to listen, think, speak, read, write, spell, or to do mathematical calculations." This section is often referred to as the discrepancy clause. Children who are learning disabled demonstrate a gap between their tested potential to learn as indicated by an intelligence test and their actual achievement in one or more school subjects. Because of the many academic areas listed in the definition, *learning disability* is really an umbrella term and covers a wide variety of learning problems.

The final sentence of the definition is often called the exclusion clause. This section confines the term *learning disability* to a very specific section of the population. This category, therefore, does not include students with physical and mental handicaps or disabilities that are the result of environmental, cultural, or economic disadvantage.

Music educators must be aware, however, that another group of students exists for whom there is often no label. These students test between the cutoff for educable mental retardation (70) and the beginning of "normal" intelligence (85). In some states, the term *slow learners* is applied to members of this group. Since that term does not exist in P.L. 94-142, support services for such students are not federally funded. Often, therefore, districts will label these slow learners as learning disabled.

Researchers have reported this misuse of the learning disability label in educational practice. Whorton and Daniel (1987) reported that of 290 children labeled learning disabled in their study, 181 had IQs of 85 or lower. The same authors stated that between 1976/77 and 1983/84, there was an increase in students labeled learning disabled—a 127 percent increase.

A MODEL OF LEARNING DISABILITIES

The term *learning disabilities* has a very short history. The words were first used in 1963 in a speech by Samuel Kirk to describe children who had deficits in several areas—language, speech, and reading. The concept, however, was based on the work of medical researchers such as Broca, Wernicke, and Goldstein in the nineteenth and twentieth centuries who investigated adults with different types of aphasia, the loss of speech caused by brain injury. Educators of exceptional children in the 1940s and 1950s (Orton, Strauss, Fernald) adapted the observable behaviors of aphasic adults such as hyperactivity and distractibility and used them to partially describe and diagnose children with learning problems.

One model of learning disabilities, used at Northwestern University in Evanston, Illinois, is based on the work of Johnson and Myklebust (1967). This model offers music educators a clear and concise framework for determining how to adapt music instruction for each learning disabled child. The three processes employed in learning—receiving information, or input; processing information, or integration; and expressing a response, or output—are illustrated in the three columns of the model shown in Figure 3-1.

This model provides the clinician, the learning disability resource teacher, and the music teacher with a framework that is useful in determining an individual child's learning strengths and weaknesses. To use this model, however, teachers need a clear understanding of each category and how it can be applied to learning in music. The use of this model, then, allows teachers to interpret children's learning and adapt their instructional techniques accordingly.

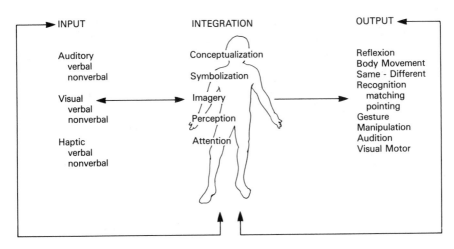

FIGURE 3-1 Learning Disability Model of Johnson and Myklebust

While the model appears quite complicated, a closer look at each column reveals the use of fairly simple ideas. The three categories on the left—auditory, visual, and haptic—refer, of course, to the senses of hearing, seeing, and feeling. Verbal inputs and responses imply the use of language. Nonverbal input can include gesture, sound, and symbols, while nonverbal responses in music include movement, playing an instrument, and pointing to the correct symbol or picture. In the following sections, each of the columns of the model is discussed in relation to music instruction and learning.

Input

Auditory. In music class, of course, heavy demands are made upon children's auditory abilities. Auditory verbal input ranges from spoken directions to recorded song lyrics. Auditory nonverbal input includes rhythm patterns, melodic ostinatos, and harmonic progressions. When a learning disabled student has difficulty with a single input, the teacher's task is to find an alternative way of presenting the material. For example, rewording a complex direction to put it in simple parts or preparing pictorial representations of a song text may assist a student with verbal input deficits.

Often, of course, auditory verbal and nonverbal inputs are used simultaneously—for example, a song and a rhythm pattern ostinato. When a learning disabled child experiences difficulty in an activity that uses more than one type of input, the teacher's task is to determine the specific problem. Is it reading the words of the song, finding the refrain or the third verse, or performing the abstract sounds of the rhythm pattern? After finding the answer, the teacher can then plan adequate instructional adaptations.

Visual. Visual verbal input implies reading. Many learning disabled children have reading deficits, but the underlying reasons can vary from child to child. Possibilities range from an inability to perceive individual sounds to an inability to remember or combine sounds and associate them with individual letters. A term that describes some reading disorders is *dyslexia.* A common belief is that dyslexic children see *d* as *b* or *dab* as *bad,* while the actual definition of dyslexia is "failure to learn to read." The difficulty can indeed include such reversals, but it most often includes more complex factors.

Reading and learning disability specialists investigate how children hear and process sounds and individual words, in addition to how children read in context. This information is invaluable to a music teacher who wants to provide meaningful music instruction for a dyslexic child. No learner should be expected to read (especially aloud) when he or she cannot. Certainly, teachers will want to explore the possibility that a child who has deficits in sounding letters may also have difficulty perceiving musical sounds.

The combination of visual verbal and nonverbal inputs implies looking at information that is not language and being able to understand and respond to the symbol system. While this category is often applied to mathematics, it is also obviously applicable to our notational system. If the information is presented in isolation, a student's difficulty can be fairly easily diagnosed. Complex combinations of words, melodic and rhythmic notation, and chord symbols may present problems to different learners for different reasons. The teacher's task then is to determine which type of input is confusing to the learner.

Haptic. Haptic input implies the use of the sense of touch and is often used in primary grades as a means of reinforcing verbal or nonverbal information. For example, many primary teachers use sets of objects when teaching basic number facts, and the students manipulate the rods, sticks, and so on to discover the properties of addition and subtraction. Similarly, many primary music educators use Popsicle sticks for stick notation or sets of shapes to illustrate form. This category, although used much less frequently in all areas of instruction, must also be considered when trying to determine the most effective means of instruction for learning disabled children.

Integration

The middle column in the model refers to what takes place within the learner before an observable response occurs. The terms are arranged in a hierarchical fashion from the simplest—attention—to the most complex—conceptualization. During the learning process, the learner may have to attend to only visual verbal material (read), or he or she may have to integrate the entire left column to find meaning.

An illustration of how children must integrate several different inputs in music class is the activity described in the opening scenario. Joey was expected to read and sing a song while playing a harmonic accompaniment that illustrated the 12-bar blues. A teacher can determine if a learning disabled child is integrating or acquiring meaning from inputs by observing carefully. Is the child attending, able to remember complex directions, and reading similarly to the rest of the class? Can the student coordinate the visual verbal (reading) with a motor act (playing)?

The term *diagnostic teaching* refers explicitly to this process. The teacher considers all the factors involved in a musical activity and observes how the child performs. When the child has difficulty, the next crucial step involves checking to see if each individual part of the process is clear to the learner. In Joey's case, this would have included a determination of his ability in each of the following: singing a song, reading the words of a song, reading the accompaniment of a song, playing the accompaniment, understanding what a rhythm pattern is, improvising patterns, and comprehending the concept of blues form in music.

Output

The right column in the learning model lists responses from simple to complex. As you can see, the use of movement as a response is simpler than matching or manipulation. However, the listing of movement as a "simpler" response is confined to unstructured, nonlocomotor movements. Locomotor movements such as jumping, hopping, and galloping and structured movement such as square dancing are not simple responses.

The final and most difficult response is visual-motor, which is a fancy term for "writing." However, while this task is simple for adults, it may be very difficult for some learning disabled children. Writing involves many steps: remembering the sounds and shapes of letters, selecting the correct sets of letters for words, remembering spelling rules, and using the correct motor movements. Because of its complexity, music teachers should try to avoid using this response.

Fortunately, there are many ways to avoid paper-and-pencil tasks in music. Instead of requiring children to write the names of instruments during a tone color review, give students a paper that contains the instrument or voice categories; as each number is called, have the students circle the correct answer. Give younger children a paper that has only pictures of the instruments or singers, which they circle or number. Instead of asking children to write notation that goes up or down or has contrasting durations, provide children with manipulative materials such as arrows, sticks, or sets of dark and light or short and long paper strips. The use of manipulative materials is an easier but equally effective response, as indicated in the model, and in music instruction such responses may enable learning disabled children to participate fully in classroom activities.

Summary

One of the most difficult problems with the use of labels in education is that a label tends to establish a set of expectations about individual students. Often, this labeling is a very useful tool, since it alerts the teacher to possible problems and suggests instructional adaptations before the actual teaching occurs. However, music educators must remember that *learning disability* is an umbrella term. When the label is applied to a child for classification purposes, the learning problems and educational solutions are not similar for each child with that label.

The model described in the preceding sections has evolved from clinical and diagnostic teaching experiences with children who have tested normal in intelligence but have demonstrated severe problems in learning. This model can be used in schools to diagnose learning problems of students who truly have learning disabilities. Music educators must not forget, however, that the label has become almost a catchall for any child who does not fit into one of the other precisely defined exceptionalities but who is not achieving at grade-level expectations. An attempt to fit the model to such learners may not be at all worthwhile. Only through discussion with administrators, resource teachers, and school psychologists can music educators discover how the category of learning disability is defined in their particular educational setting.

BEHAVIOR OF LEARNING DISABLED STUDENTS

The preceding section has limited the discussion of learning disabilities to experiences and abilities that relate directly to the academic school setting. Music class is often perceived by others, however, as a "social setting." Indeed, the variety of learning activities used contributes to that perception, since the activities are not the deskbound and paper-and-pencil tasks typical of the "regular" classroom. Because of the differences in teaching and learning inherent in general music classrooms, an understanding of the concomitant behavioral characteristics of some learning disabled students is as important as an understanding of the variety of possible academic learning deficits.

Strauss Syndrome

One set of behaviors that have been observed to occur in some children with severe learning disabilities is known as the Strauss Syndrome. Alfred Strauss was an educator who worked with and wrote about brain-damaged children in the 1940s and 1950s. The three components of the syndrome are hyperactivity, distractibility, and disinhibition.

Hyperactivity refers to an excess of activity, which in school settings usually results in unacceptable behaviors. In music class, where movement and changes in activities occur frequently and with regularity, hyperactivity may be much less noticeable. The behavior may occur, however, in changes between activities or during other nonstructured times in the period.

Distractibility can result from an excess of inputs, both visual and auditory. In a music classroom, children with this behavior characteristic may be distracted by the visual array of rhythm instruments that are to be used in the middle of the lesson. A learning disabled child may experience aural distractibility when repeated and noticeable sounds occur inside or outside the classroom. These can be the sounds of another class walking by or even the sound of a clock ticking inside the room.

Disinhibition implies that a child is unable to concentrate and think about present events. Rather, the child's mind is constantly distracted by events and ideas that have no relevance to the present. In music class, the child may often make irrelevant contributions in discussions and be unable to concentrate on a task.

However, the sum effect of one or more of these behaviors on learning is that learning disabled children may be prevented from focusing their attention. And the ability to pay attention is directly related to learning success or failure. Music educators can reduce hyperactive behavior with clear structure and specific directions whenever changes in activities occur. Distractibility can be reduced by eliminating extraneous sounds whenever possible and by keeping out of sight those materials not being presently used in the lesson.

A review of research literature on classroom behavior of learning disabled students (McKinney and Feagans, 1983) summarized research relating to the topics of hyperactivity and distractibility. In the reviewed studies, hyperactivity was not found to discriminate between learning disabled and nonlearning disabled children. Several research studies cited in the review do support the conclusion that learning disabled children are indeed more distractible. This finding has been documented in observational studies that record off-task behavior and student-teacher interactions.

Motor Ability

Often, children who are learning disabled may exhibit difficulty with gross or fine motor tasks. These deficits can range from an inability to ride a bike to problems with tying a shoe. In music, there are many gross motor movement expectations in primary grades, while fine motor skills, such as those needed to play an orchestral or a band instrument, develop in intermediate-age students.

Many motor expectations in kindergarten and first grade involve responding to the steady beat. Learning disabled children may demonstrate an inability to march or walk with the beat. Researchers in music education (Schleuter and Schleuter, 1985) have indicated that easier responses for primary children are speaking, clapping, or *patschen*. The use of hoops is also a way to help establish awareness of the feeling of pulse in young children with motor deficits. Include two children in each hoop and direct the students to sway together to the beat; in that way, the normal-achieving student will help the exceptional learner feel the correct movement.

If music educators can determine the simple acts that are combined into a complex motor response, then children can be taught each of the necessary components prior to the integrated task. This concept has been illustrated in music education research with learning disabled children by Janet Perkins Gilbert (1983). This researcher determined that the skills involved in striking a xylophone with a mallet included (1) motor pattern coordination, (2) eye-hand coordination, (3) movement speed, (4) range of movement, and (5) combinations of those factors. She devised a motor skills test and administered it to learning disabled and normal-achieving students ($n = 103$).

In each of the single tasks, the learning disabled children performed more poorly. However, it is of interest to note that on the tasks that combined the four single motor movements, the performance of the learning disabled children was superior to that of the normal sample. The researcher concluded that the learning disabled children may have "benefited from the sequential test item order" (p. 151). It seems reasonable to assume that the practice on each of the subskills contributed to the learning disabled subjects' competency in the task that combined those skills.

Certainly, it is unrealistic to expect a music teacher with thirty-five classes a week to teach a single child the four separate steps necessary to strike a xylophone with a mallet. However, perceptive teachers need to apply the same careful observation and attention to how a child performs motorically as were suggested earlier for cognitive activity. Attention to the demands of complex motor responses and the substitution of simpler ones may be necessary in classes that contain mainstreamed learning disabled children with motor deficits.

Although there are no accounts of learning disabled bands, there are reports in music education literature that instrumental teachers do instruct learning disabled students. One article (McCann, 1985) describes a fifth-grade student who had fine motor coordination problems. Despite his learning deficits, the student was able to become a competent clarinetist. One researcher (Ansuini, 1979) surveyed teachers who had taught these exceptional students and reported that the most common competencies were patience, knowledge of the individual and the learning disorder, ability to accept limited or no student progress, willingness to provide additional time, and ability to form personal relationships with the students.

One point of view that must be discussed briefly in this section is the perceptual-motor approach to learning disabilities as espoused by Newell Kephart (1971) and others. These educators believe that poor perceptual and motor abilities are the basis of inadequate cognitive performance. In music education, this approach is most commonly espoused in relation to possible deficits in the awareness of two sides of the body (laterality) and an inability to cross the midpoint of the body when performing motor skills, particularly playing xylophones.

A variety of tests has been devised to measure perception and motor ability, and many programs of remediation also exist. But music educators should be aware that there is serious doubt in the learning disability and reading professions as to the efficacy of the perceptual-motor model. A comprehensive review of more than 85 perceptual-motor studies is reported by Myers and Hammill (1976). These authors question the value of training activities and conclude that none of the treatments was effective in improving cognitive, linguistic, or academic readiness. Indeed, these authors question whether the activities even improve motor skills in the subjects. A meta-analysis of 180 studies of perceptual-motor training included the same conclusion (Kavale and Mattson, 1983).

Social Ability

Many learning disabled children also exhibit social behaviors that lead to poor teacher and peer acceptance. Some of these behaviors include not listening to others, not complimenting others, using an inappropriate tone of voice, and not accepting consequences for wrong-doing. Researchers investigating these behaviors use rating scales, observations, and sociograms to determine social differences.

There are numerous studies in the learning disability literature on this topic. Gresham and Reschly (1986) investigated the social behaviors and peer acceptance of mainstreamed learning disabled and nondis-abled children ($n = 200$) from the viewpoint of teachers, parents, and peers. The researchers found that the social skills of the learning disabled subjects were indeed poorer and were present at school and at home. The behaviors that contributed most to peer rejection were not accepting authority, not helping others, not expressing feelings, and having a negative self-attitude. Another researcher, Tanis Bryan (1978), has found that children describe their learning disabled peers as "untidy, not one whom one would wish for a friend, and one who tends to be ignored by other children within the classroom" (p. 127).

Since music teachers have each class for only a short interval, it could be argued that there will be no opportunity for these social behaviors to arise. But because of the less structured and controlled classroom atmosphere that most general music teachers in elementary and middle schools prefer, these social behaviors do indeed surface. They are apparent in where children choose to sit, how instruments are exchanged during a singing or playing activity, how groups are formed for movement or creating, how children line up, and even how textbooks are passed out and collected.

Teachers who are alert to the social milieu of each class will improvise ways of preventing antisocial interactions. One way to avoid the "I don't want to sit next to . . ." syndrome is to structure a musical response that involves every child as soon as he or she passes the threshold of the music room. In classes with mainstreamed students, it is imperative that teachers preselect groups for an activity in order to avoid the "we don't want Joey in our group" comment. Other social interactions, such as choosing another for a turn with an instrument, can be determined by first initials of names or by clothing colors.

Indeed, each music class can be an opportunity for musical and social success. It is a setting in which cognitive demands can be replaced by experiences with affective material and in which the entire class can become involved in the process and production of musical events. Teachers can focus on the intrinsic value of music instead of on how an individual child behaves and achieves. That is not to imply that music teachers should not have rules of behavior or have lesser expectations than other classroom teachers. Rather, it is to emphasize that in music class, the opportunity exists for all children to be equal participants—a situation that rarely occurs in other academic subjects.

LEARNING AND INSTRUCTION

Because of the heterogeneity of the population labeled learning disabled, it is impossible to describe all the possible ways that music teachers can structure successful activities and materials for these learners. Remember that each learning disabled student may have very different cognitive, motor, or behavioral deficits. Successful adaptations within the music setting, therefore, are possible only when the teacher is familiar with an individual's specific disability.

Many children who are learning disabled have difficulty with understanding *how* to learn. They do not realize that there are patterns that help one understand, relate, and remember information, and they approach each learning situation as a "fresh slate." This is especially a problem in a once-a-week class or lesson. Music teachers can assist these learners in many of the same ways suggested for educable mentally retarded students. Visual continuity can be provided by bulletin boards, prepared charts, or the inclusion of the same visual representations of sound from week to week. Verbal continuity should include the review of prior learning and clear explanations of how the present musical experiences relate to it.

Another facet of learning, memory, is also directly related to how children learn. Researchers have demonstrated that learning disabled children remember and read better when they are taught using the strategies of verbal rehearsal and visual imagery (Rose, Cundick, and Higbee, 1983). Music teachers already use verbal rehearsal when the text of a song is read and discussed before it is sung or when rhythm or tonal syllables are used prior to teaching songs, patterns, or ostinatos.

Visual imagery was suggested in Chapter 2 as a way to assist EMR mainstreamed students. Many music educators may feel that pictures are not necessary to teach a song, but for children with reading and memory deficits, pictures can be a lifesaver. Many songs with confusing verbal sequences can be clarified with the addition of pictures. Songs such as "Bought Me a Cat" and "The Old Woman Who Swallowed a Fly" will be easier for learning disabled students when pictures illustrate the word order.

Visual imagery can also be incorporated into lessons by the use of ikons. Teachers can find examples of ikons, graphic representations of sound, in all the major textbooks. These illustrations assist learning disabled students in comprehending the many abstractions of musical notation. Examples of ikons for direction, duration, dynamics, and tempo are in Figure 3-2.

Certainly, the use of textbooks in classes that contain mainstreamed learning disabled children with reading deficits must be approached

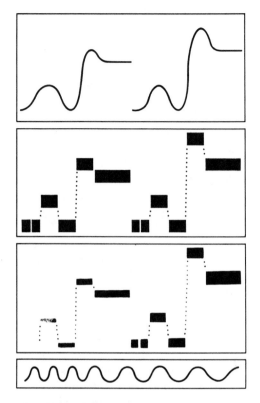

FIGURE 3-2 From *Holt Music 1988 Grade 1* by Meske, Andress, Pautz and Willman, copyright © 1988 by Holt, Rinehart and Winston, Inc., reprinted by permission of the publisher.

with care. Each page of the present music textbooks is designed to contain a great deal of information. Unfortunately, all the photographs, prints, ikons, charts, words, and musical notation often result in pages that are a visual jungle for many children.

Learning disabled readers need a clear guide so that they can find and focus on the part of the page that is important. Some children will merely need an instruction to "put your finger on the word *refrain*" or "point to the third verse." Students who are easily distracted may profit from using a reading frame, a teacher-constructed cardboard shape that is the size of the page and contains a rectangular cutout that shows only one staff line and text. The frame therefore covers up all information on the page except what is being taught. Preparing several frames and offering them to the entire class "if they need one" removes the stigma from the one exceptional child who really does need one.

Music teachers need to consider ways of adapting their teaching materials so that they will be clearer to mainstreamed learning disabled children. Decisions about such changes depend upon an understanding of the learning strengths and deficits of individual learning disabled students. A general rule to follow is to try to intensify the input being presented to students. Examples of intensification in color, size, and rate follow. Many teachers may have already used some of these ways of clarifying musical concepts.

COLOR

1. Use colored circles or beanbags to illustrate the concept of movable do and melodic patterns such as sol-mi on a floor staff. Use the same color consistently (for example, blue for mi and red for sol).
2. Use colored chalk to circle and emphasize one measure in a rhythm pattern.
3. Use a colored arrow on a page frame to cue the child as to the verse structure or where to find the word *refrain.*
4. Use colored marking pens on overhead transparencies.

SIZE

1. Put rhythm patterns on a large chart.
2. Put melodic notation on large charts with similar phrases directly under each other.
3. Draw phrase contours on charts or on the board.
4. Enlarge part of a page on a photocopier and make a transparency.
5. Use a floor staff that children can stand on.

RATE

1. Slow down your speech when giving more than one direction.
2. Teach difficult or nonsense parts of songs separately and more slowly.
3. End echo-clapping patterns with a beat of rest.
4. Pay particular attention to the tempo of recorded songs.

In addition, music teachers can assist some mainstreamed learning disabled students by consistently presenting musical concepts through a multisensory approach. One music education researcher has demonstrated the effectiveness of teaching multiplication tables to learning disabled students using melodic-rhythmic mnemonics (Gfeller, 1982). While the content has no relation to music classrooms, the use of multisensory musical approaches was very effective in the instructional experiment. The combination of auditory and visual, auditory and motor, or auditory and visual and motor inputs intensifies, strengthens, and emphasizes musical learnings. Some suggestions follow.

PRIMARY LEVEL

1. Move entire body or body parts while singing or listening and following graphic illustrations to demonstrate musical concepts of beat, pattern, meter, contour, or register.
2. Turn and face each of the four sides of the room while singing or listening to demonstrate phrase structure.
3. Include appropriate grade-level Orff activities that combine speech, song, movement, and playing.

INTERMEDIATE LEVEL

1. Use large geometric shapes, sets of children with similar and contrasting clothing, or even room furniture to illustrate the musical form of songs or listening selections.
2. Always have illustrations of specific instruments when teaching tone color.
3. Use strips of crepe paper or lengths of yarn and have students construct a representation of phrase contour, which is sung or played.
4. Incorporate Orff activities that combine speech, song, movement, and playing.

Music teachers will discover an interesting phenomenon when they incorporate these multisensory or intensification adaptations into their lessons: *All* children will learn more effectively. In addition, the puzzled looks will leave the faces of mainstreamed learning disabled students, and they will have opportunities to participate in successful musical experiences.

SUMMARY OF TEACHING SUGGESTIONS

Provide visual and verbal continuity between music classes or lessons.
Incorporate verbal rehearsal and visual imagery strategies.
Focus students' attention on the important part of a printed page.
Intensify through the use of color, change of rate, or size.
Present material through multisensory approaches.

RESEARCH IN MUSIC EDUCATION

In contrast to mental retardation, the research in music education that focuses on learning disabled children in music is quite sparse. Part of the reason, of course, is the comparatively recent identification and labeling of these students. In this section, readers are provided with summaries of the existing research. These summaries are presented in some detail so that, if necessary, they can be cited in advocating correct placement of learning disabled students.

Orff music instruction with self-contained learning disability classes ($n = 64$) was the topic of a dissertation by Harris (1976). Three classes received instruction twice a week from the experimenter, and three other classes received no special music instruction. However, their teachers did provide extra nonmusical auditory training during the 22-week experiment. The purpose of the research was to determine if Orff instruction would alter the subtest scores of the subjects on the *Illinois Test of Psycholinguistic Ability* (Kirk, McCarthy, and Kirk, 1968). The researcher reported a significant difference in two subtests, one of which was due to losses in the control classes. The conclusion of the study was that generalized music instruction is not a means of training auditory abilities. Unfortunately, the use of a nonmusical assessment measure in this study does not provide music educators with any meaningful information about learning disabled children in a musical setting.

A report by Decuir and Braswell (1978) described the administration of five subtests of the *Seashore Measures of Musical Talent* (1960) to groups defined by specificity of disability: auditory, visual, and mixed ($n = 31$). The subjects were aged 10 to 15. The researchers found no significant differences between the subgroups in any of the sections of the test but did report that the scores for each subgroup and the total sample were below the test norms. The report does indicate that the auditory group had slightly higher test means than either of the other two groups in each of the five subtests. The difference is intriguing but is not addressed by the researchers. Unfortunately, the report does not include a description of how the subjects were differentiated.

William Bell's dissertation describes the use of the *Primary Measures of Music Audiation* (Gordon, 1979) with learning disabled children ($n = 116$) in self-contained classes, grades K–5. The test has two sections, rhythmic and tonal, and is designed for children in kindergarten through third grade. The test was administered to the students by their regular music teachers in two class meetings. The teachers were instructed to take as much time as needed to be sure the children understood the instructions and stop the tape between test questions if the children seemed to have difficulty responding. The author concluded that the tonal section is appropriate for learning disabled children aged 7 to 11, while the rhythm section should only be used with 9- and 10-year-old children. However, his test sample of age 7 ($n = 4$) and age 8 ($n = 11$) subjects is an inadequate statistical basis for this conclusion.

Research with learning disabled students by the author of this text has focused on rhythmic discrimination and performance, tonal discrimination, and classroom achievement. In the initial study (Atterbury, 1982), rhythmic discrimination was investigated with 7- and 8-year-old ($n = 40$) learning disabled and matched normal-achieving readers. A significant main effect on the test means of the *Primary Measures of Music Audiation* (PMMA), Rhythm section, existed between the two groups. It is of interest to note that this difference existed despite the adaptation of the test to eliminate the paper-and-pencil response and a pretraining in the concept of "same and different." However, the mean scores of the learning disabled sample were equivalent to those for the test means. The scores of the author-constructed tests of rhythm performance indicated significant differences between 7-year-olds and nonsignificance between 8-year-olds. This finding led to a hypothesis that perhaps the amount of music instruction time affected test results. However, that hypothesis was disproved when a follow-up study (1986) of rhythm discrimination and performance (n = 56) with 9-year-olds included findings of significant differences between the two ability groups.

Tonal discrimination (Atterbury, 1986) was tested using the PMMA, Tonal section (n = 114). Results indicated a difference between the two ability groups at ages 7 and 8 but not at age 9. Again, the test was adapted to eliminate paper-and-pencil response by the subjects.

The disparate findings of these research projects certainly are a result of the existing heterogeneity of abilities and dysfunctions that the label of learning disability covers. All of this research used tests that were individually administered and that were also specifically adapted for easy response. Under these carefully constructed conditions, younger learning disabled students appear to be most at risk in ability to respond to musical inputs.

A project that investigated classroom achievement of second- and fifth-grade normal-achieving and learning disabled students was conducted by this author in 1987. The *Silver Burdett Competency Test* was administered in a class setting, and the scores of randomly selected normal-achieving students were matched with the mainstreamed learning disabled sample of twenty-five second graders and twenty-one fifth graders. Data analysis indicated significant differences at both grade levels. In addition, this project included another finding of great interest. The differences in mean scores between the two groups of fifth graders far exceeded the score differences between the younger subjects. This finding may result from the higher cognitive demands of music instruction in grade five. It may also indicate that mainstreamed learning disabled students fall further behind throughout progressive grades. It certainly is a signal that indiscriminate mainstreaming in music does not result in equal achievement.

Research tells us that for the students in these studies,

Orff instruction did not affect auditory ability.
Scores on the Seashore measure were below test norms.

Younger students performed rhythms and discriminated tonal patterns more poorly.

Both second- and fifth-grade learning disabled students demonstrated lower music achievement.

The conclusions of these research reports combine to again present a picture of children who have individual learning problems, each different from the other, and a category for whom it is impossible to generalize. Each research sample, while identified and labeled according to the federal definition, contains disparate members, which results in disparate findings among researchers. The research described in this section underscores the thesis of this chapter: Learning disabled children are a subgroup of exceptional children who cannot be described in a generalized manner. Each child must be considered as a unique individual when planning and teaching music.

CONCLUSION

A quite different and intriguing point of view regarding the category of learning disabilities is found in the writings of Sleeter (1986), Coles (1978), and Shinn, Tindal, Spira, and Marston (1987). These writers describe learning disabilities as a social construct with a shaky biological basis that has evolved as an explanation for the school failure of some middle-class children. These authors state that in the learning disability profession, the cause of learning difficulties has been placed within the child, absolving the teaching and schooling of any responsibility for the failure.

Support for this view is garnered from the changes in historical literacy standards, changes in the cutoff IQ score for mental retardation in the 1970s, and changes in the norms for standardized achievement tests after Sputnik. These factors promoted higher levels of literacy, and those children who did not meet this expectation were thus "explained" by the new label. In addition, the lack of a consistent test battery and the lack of a concise exceptionality definition are also used as support for this view. These two imprecise factors are described as the vehicles that teachers use in an attempt to homogenize their classroom, referring for placement those children who do not learn in the conventional way.

Even from this point of view, however, the result for music educators remains the same. Children who have difficulty learning in regular classrooms and who receive additional daily academic instruction are placed in music classes as though they are able to learn similarly to their peers. The interesting question for a music educator in a single school, however, is the point of view regarding the use of the term *learning disabilities.* While lip service may be given to the use of the term, teachers should be very wary when resource teachers are unable to discuss an individual student's learning strengths and deficits with the vocabulary used in this chapter.

Two approaches are necessary for music educators to meet this teaching challenge. The first is to read student files and then question classroom, resource, and special educators about how each mainstreamed student learns. The second is to incorporate this information into instructional adaptations that will enable the child to experience and learn about music.

But additionally, since P.L. 94-142 will not disappear, music educators must become more assertive about the importance of the correct mainstreaming placement for *all* children. Passive acceptance of inappropriate mainstreaming for the sake of convenience or ease of scheduling must be replaced by concerned involvement in the initial mainstreaming decision process.

QUESTIONS

1. Discuss the three sections of the federal definition of *learning disability.*
2. Describe examples of music instruction that illustrate each of the inputs from the left column of the model on page 41.
3. Describe specific ways in which verbal and nonverbal inputs and outputs are combined in music instruction.
4. Why is writing a difficult response for learning disabled children?
5. Define the Strauss Syndrome.
6. When are social skills observed in musical settings?
7. Why is an understanding of "patterns" a more effective way to learn?
8. How can textbooks be adapted for use with mainstreamed learning disabled students?

ACTIVITIES

1. Write a memo to Mrs. Johns from the resource teacher that describes Joey's learning disability using the Johnson-Myklebust model and terminology. Include specific teaching instructions and material adaptations applicable to a sixth-grade music class.
2. Observe a music class that includes a mainstreamed learning disabled student, and write a description using the learning disability model as a frame of reference.
3. Choose a call chart or a listening map from a current series and adapt it for a learning disabled student with visual perception and visual attention deficits.

BIBLIOGRAPHY

BRYAN, T. H., and J. H. BRYAN. 1978. *Understanding Learning Disabilities.* Sherman Oaks, Calif.: Alfred Publishing Co.

JOHNSON, D. J. 1971. Educational Principles for Children with Learning Disabilities. In *Educational Perspectives in Learning Disabilities,* ed. D. D. Hammill and N. R. Bartel. New York: John Wiley, pp. 133–43.

JOHNSON, D. J., and H. R. MYKLEBUST. 1967. *Learning Disabilities, Educational Principles and Practices.* New York: Grune & Stratton.

NOCERA, S. 1979. *Reaching the Special Learner through Music.* Morristown, N.J.: Silver Burdett Company.

WIIG, E. H., and E. M. SEMEL. 1976. *Language Disabilities in Children and Adolescents.* Columbus, Ohio: Chas. E. Merrill.

Gifted and Talented Students

CHAPTER FOUR

ONE MAINSTREAMING REALITY

Lakeview School

It is 2:35, and Mr. Perkins has been teaching the third-grade class about the string family. The Bowmar pictures of the four instruments are resting on the chalktray, and the class has just finished listening to a short part of the Mozart String Quartet in D Minor. There are only five minutes remaining in this week's period, and Mr. Perkins wants to conclude the period in a way that will enable him to begin next week's class talking about instrument similarities. The following exchange occurs between the teacher and a student, George Palmer.

MR. PERKINS: We've just listened to all four of these instruments play, first alone and then together. Why do we call them a family?

GEORGE: Well, it can't just be because they're the same shape. The people in my family have different shapes. Of course, they're different sizes and all use strings, but if we look at the wooden material, then why can't the oboe and clarinet be in this family also? I saw them last month at the symphony concert my Mom took me to. And also there was a wooden piccolo. And, Mr. Perkins, there were a lot of percussion instruments used at different times. They are also like these instruments. >

(Mr. Perkins thinks to himself, "Well, George has done it again! I wonder if I can possibly get the class on track before their teacher gets here. She is such a stickler about lining up quietly and leaving on time.")

MR. PERKINS: Well, class, we are almost out of time. George, you'll have to wait until next week. Can anyone else answer my question? Why are these four instruments called a family?

(Most of the children look at the clock, at Mr Perkins, and then at the door. They don't look at the pictures. They know their classroom teacher also and are no longer thinking about music. Mr. Perkins gives up and begins to line up the class.)

Return to the beginning of the dialogue and read the classroom scenario until you come to the >. Then move your eye down to the following paragraph and continue reading the scenario with the alternative ending.

> (Mr. Perkins thinks to himself, "Well, George has done it again! How can I use his ideas and help the class remember them for next week?")

MR. PERKINS: Well, George, you have a lot of great ideas there about instruments, and they all have to do with why we put them in different families. Who wants to write the class list so we can remember these ideas during the week? (*Melissa raises her hand and goes to the board.*) Let's try to sort out and make a list of things that instruments have in common. Who can tell me one? (*Different children offer shape, size, strings, and wood.*) George, tell the class why you think the strings and percussion have something in common.

GEORGE: When the men play the bass drum, the snare drum, the tympani, and the gong, they always use something to hit them with and so do the string players.

MR. PERKINS: The string instruments use a bow. Let's add that to the list for next week also. Now we're going to use these words to line up this week. Is anyone wearing any strings?

The first teacher reaction—ignoring and squelching—to the unexpected deluge of information about instruments is, unfortunately for George, often what happens in schools whose teachers are not prepared to teach classes that include mainstreamed gifted children. The second ending to this scenario will occur more often, we hope, if music educators read this text!

DEFINITION

The federal definition of this category of exceptionality is contained not in Public Law 94-142 but in Public Law 95-561, the Gifted and Talented Children's Education Act (U.S. Congress, 1978).

> The term "gifted and talented children" means children and, whenever applicable, youth, who are identified at the preschool, elementary, or secondary level as possessing demonstrated or potential abilities that give evidence of high performance capability in areas such as intellectual, creative, specific academic or leadership ability or in the performing and visual arts, and who by reason thereof require services or activities not ordinarily provided by the school. (U.S. Congress)

This definition serves as a model for state definitions, and twenty-nine states use similar or identical wording (Cassidy and Johnson, 1986). Some states, however, also either include a test cutoff or specify a percentage of the population in their definitions. For example, Florida's definition includes a statement that a gifted student's mental development is two standard deviations above the mean. In contrast, the definition used in Connecticut includes many other factors, including demonstrated or potential achievement in music, the visual arts, or the performing arts, but specifies that the term refers to the top five percent of the student population.

In some parts of the United States, gifted and talented children are the most neglected of any exceptionality. This neglect is partly due to a lack of federal mandates requiring specific services for these students, but also at the federal level, funding that existed in the 1970s has not been continued in the 1980s. The lack of federal leadership has placed the burden of specific identification and funding on the state and local levels. In addition, in some parts of our country, there still is a hostility toward highly gifted students, who often challenge educators when their thought processes and information bank are superior to those of adults. Indeed, one often-used excuse for not serving gifted children is that they will "make it on their own."

Each of the words in the phrase "gifted and talented" needs to be considered separately. The term *gifted* usually implies a high Intelligence Quotient, and the term *talented* usually is synonymous with a specific area, such as music, art, or sports. In some places, however, despite an encompassing definition, the IQ score is still the determining factor in identification. Joseph S. Renzulli and his coauthors (1981) have called this practice gifted hypocrisy.

> Gifted hypocrisy can best be described as the difference between what we say about the identification of gifted and talented students and the actual

procedures that are used to select students for special programs. In recent years almost every person writing in the area of gifted and talented . . . has lent support to the concept of the development of multiple talent and the use of multiple criteria in the selection process. And yet, the reality is that the final decision for admitting most gifted students to most programs still rests with a predetermined cut-off score on an intelligence and/or achievement test. (p. ix)

What is wrong with using such test scores as indicators of talent or giftedness? The simple answer is that the tests are one-dimensional. Intelligence and achievement tests serve to identify verbally gifted students but fail to test creativity, originality, and outstanding ability in other areas. Music educators must understand that intelligence tests really serve only two functions. The test score gives an indication of students' mental ability in relation to their peers, and the test is an excellent measure of those factors necessary for *academic* success. The most common intelligence tests, the Stanford-Binet and the Wechsler (Revised), are constructed on a premise that there is a single general intelligence factor. However, a unitary view of intelligence has been challenged by Guilford (1967) and Gardner (1983).

A model serves as a framework for assessment, discussion, placement, and instruction. The diagram in Figure 4-1 is Guilford's attempt to describe the complexity of human thought. His Structure of Intellect model provides a multidimensional way of describing intelligence that

FIGURE 4-1 Structure of Intellect Model. From J. P. Guilford, *The Nature of Human Intelligence* (New York: McGraw-Hill, 1967). Reproduced with permission.

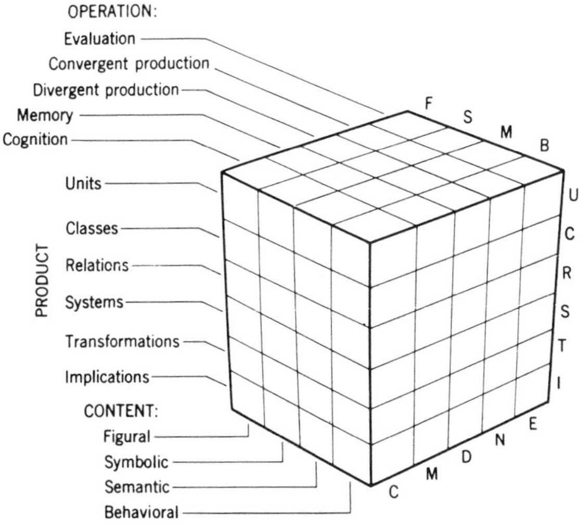

endeavors to account for the diversity of processes used in manipulating both nonverbal and verbal information.

Of particular interest are the two cells on the operations side of the cube titled convergent and divergent production. *Divergent thinking* implies using given information and generating new or varied outputs, with an additional emphasis on the quantity of responses. Many tests of creativity, including one in music by Webster (1987), measure divergent production. In contrast, *convergent thinking* produces the correct or the conventional answer and is the type of thinking measured in the standard intelligence tests.

While Guilford's point of view regarding intelligence is a more encompassing and complex one, it is not universally accepted (Cronbach, 1970). Since the model was initially described in 1961, there have been attempts to structure a test that measures the capacities in Figure 4-1. The test has been criticized in terms of norms, validity, and reliability (Clarizlo and Mehrens, 1985).

What is especially important about Guilford's model of intellect, however, is the complex view of intelligence it represents. The differentiation of convergent and divergent thinking production in this model was the stimulus for an important study of gifted students by Getzels and Jackson in 1962. These researchers demonstrated that high levels of creativity (divergent thinking) and high intelligence scores were not synonymous. The researchers studied two groups of adolescents (creative and academically successful) and reported that all students had similar achievement despite a gap in IQ scores of 23 points. The results of this study reinforce the idea that intelligence tests primarily assess cognition and memory: Gifted students who are highly creative may use a variety of other cognitive processes, including divergent production and deliberate risk taking.

How Is a Creative Student Assessed?

The thinking of creative children and youths is accented by the ability to think divergently. This ability has been tested in various ways. Getzels and Jackson used five tests to determine their two groups of intelligent and creative adolescents. The tests measured word association, uses of common objects, hidden shapes, supplying missing endings to fables, and making up mathematical problems. The common elements in measuring responses in all but one measure (hidden shapes test) were quantity and originality. The researchers described their gifted sample of students as fanciful, humorous, having an "ability to toy with elements and concepts" (p. 54), possessing an ability to take risks, and unafraid of making unusual contributions.

Numerous studies by E. Paul Torrance (1963) have also investigated the dimension of creativity through an evaluation of divergent thinking. One task that Torrance devised required children to invent ways of making common toys "more fun to play with." The children's responses were judged in terms of fluency (quantity), flexibility (different approaches or principles used), and the amount of toy manipulation by subjects. His conclusion was that a high degree of manipulation corresponded to both a high number and the flexibility of responses.

An Additional Factor in Giftedness

Another contributor in the field of gifted education, Joseph Renzulli (1981), adds an interesting and often overlooked dimension to the definition of gifted students. The diagram in Figure 4-2 illustrates the inclusion of this third factor, task commitment.

Numerous researchers who have studied highly intelligent (Terman, 1947) and highly creative (MacKinnon, 1962; Barron, 1963; and others) adults also conclude that those who are successful are task-involved, persistent, and committed to self-determined standards of excellence. The model in Figure 4-2 has, however, been criticized by others who point out that underachieving gifted students are omitted in this definition.

Musical Intelligence

Another view of human intelligence has been described by Howard Gardner (1983). This psychologist believes that there is a

FIGURE 4-2 "What Makes Giftedness." From Joseph S. Renzulli, Sally M. Reis, and Linda H. Smith, *The Revolving Door Identification Model* (Mansfield Center, Conn.: Creative Learning Press, Inc., 1981). Used with permission.

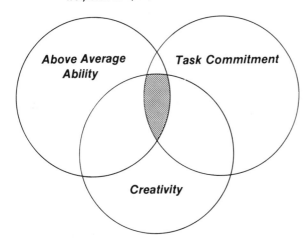

variety of intelligences, including linguistic, logical-mathematical, spatial, and musical. According to Gardner, a specific intelligence has two prerequisites: a set of skills useful in solving genuine problems and skills that enable one to find or create new problems that lead to acquiring new knowledge.

Musical intelligence as a separate construct is based upon the finding of support for what Gardner calls "signs" of intelligence in the following eight categories: potential isolation by brain damage, the existence of idiots savants and prodigies, an identifiable core operation or set of operations, a distinctive developmental history, an evolutionary history, support from experimental psychological tasks, support from psychometric findings, and susceptibility to encoding in a symbol system. Evidence for each of these categories is described and offered as support that a separate intelligence for music can be explained.

The reader can conclude from the foregoing descriptions of intelligence that the human mind is indeed an intricate "thing" and that there is no single theory that can be described as *the* gospel of how human beings learn. It is clear, however, that the unitary view of a single "g" factor of intelligence described by Spearman in 1904 has been supplanted by more elegant and elaborate explanations that attempt to account for the variety and complexity of human mentation.

LEARNING AND INSTRUCTION

The two previous chapters have emphasized that children and youth who have been identified as exceptional do not learn in a single identifiable manner. There are vast differences in the abilities of mildly and profoundly retarded children, and the learning disability label is often called an umbrella that covers a wide variety of learning deficits. A range of possible achievements and behaviors also exists in students who are labeled gifted and talented.

Despite the conclusion that standardized tests do not identify all gifted and talented children, many gifted students *are* identified by tests and demonstrate exceptional verbal and intellectual ability. These students are usually perceived by teachers as being more desirable and display an extraordinary capacity to absorb facts and principles. In describing these gifted students, teachers and parents often use such terms as *persistent, responsible,* and *highly motivated.*

But not all gifted and talented students fit into those categories. Many others are socially independent, are difficult to control in a group, and develop reputations for having silly ideas. Some gifted students are perceived as less desirable because they do not fit the teacher mold of a "good student"—one who has the correct answers. The characteristics of gifted students and the possible problems that they pose have been summarized in the table by James Gallagher (1975) shown in Figure 4-3.

The readers of this text are familiar with the recognized youthful talent of numerous musicians, both composers and performers. A recent study by Benjamin Bloom (1985) describes an investigation of the similarities between outstanding performers in several fields: concert pianists, sculptors, swimmers, tennis players, research mathematicians, and neurologists. The concert pianists were under 35, and they had won one of the major world piano competitions. The pianists, their parents, and their teachers were interviewed in depth by the researchers, and the similarities in their development are reported.

Of interest is the finding of distinct phases that were common to all pianists. One generalized finding about the early years of these talented musicians was that almost all were brought up in musical environments, encouraged to experiment with sound, and given immediate rewards and positive reinforcements, which ranged from stars to attention and praise for performance. Although their early practicing was parent-structured, the pianists all reported a time in their intermediate years

FIGURE 4-3   Source: Adapted from J. P. Rice, *The gifted: Developing total talent,* 1970. Courtesy of Charles C Thomas, Publisher, Springfield, Illinois. In *Teaching the Gifted Child* by James E. Gallagher, 1975, Boston: Allyn & Bacon.

CHARACTERISTICS OF THE GIFTED AND CONCOMITANT PROBLEMS

CHARACTERISTIC OF GIFTED	POSSIBLE CONCOMITANT PROBLEMS
Critically observes, analyzes; skepticism	Teachers feel threatened, peers censure, try to silence discussion; argumentative
Emphatic response to people; leadership capabilities	Rejection causes intense reaction (e.g., depression or hostility); may seek to dominate rather than understand others
Intellectual interests; intellectuality	Snobbishness; limited recreational outlets; boring to others; intolerance for lesser capabilities
Large vocabulary; verbal facility; high retention	Inappropriate level of communication; dominates class discussion; unnecessary elaboration
Originality	Perceived as "off the subject" by others; impracticality; frequent breaks with tradition; radicalism
Scholarliness	Anti-intellectual reaction by peers; stuffiness; pedantry
Thinks with logical systems; objective, rational problem solving	Disregard for intuitive, retrospective, or subjective solutions; rejection of belief, revelation as methods

(10–15) when they realized that they were totally committed to music, not just to piano playing.

The youthful performers in all the fields studied by Bloom are clearly delineated by the amount of parental involvement in their development in addition to their eventual deep task commitment. Clearly, as is obvious from the historical records of musical composing and performing prodigies, the development of outstanding musical talent is not a task for single music periods in a school day. Perhaps public schools cannot serve this population at all!

Instructional Adaptations

Writers in gifted and talented education have described a variety of grouping and curriculum approaches for this exceptional population. Acceleration, enrichment, independent study, and differentiated curriculum are ways of providing appropriate instruction for gifted and talented students. These approaches are described in this section, with specific suggestions for music instruction.

Acceleration. Acceleration refers to advancing the placement of students, either through early school entrance, through grade skipping, or through early college admission. This practice is one way to provide learning situations in which gifted students receive appropriate challenge. Often, highly gifted music performers are bored with the limited range of repertoire necessitated by the average ability level in school groups. While the philosophy of many schools and administrators is in opposition to grade-level acceleration, it is an alternative for music educators who recognize that the performance talent of students is not being adequately challenged by performing with their peers. In many urban settings, these students have become members of community youth orchestras. Where that is not possible, music educators should certainly advocate acceleration of gifted performers into secondary, college, or community performance groups.

Acceleration for talented musicians is also available in settings other than public schools. Many conservatories offer Saturday classes and lessons for talented public school students. A project developed at the Settlement Music School (Benigno, 1984) for superior teenage performers enabled the students to study with members of the Philadelphia Orchestra; in addition, the students received advanced solfeggio instruction and chamber music coaching at the Settlement Music School. Fortunately, the school received extensive grant funding, which paid about 95 percent of the student lesson costs; that made it possible to offer the audition opportunity to students throughout the city.

Instructional acceleration—compressing a curriculum into a shorter time or moving curriculum content to lower levels—is another means of meeting the educational needs of gifted and talented students. This approach can be employed by general music teachers who instruct self-contained classes of gifted and talented children at any level. Younger gifted children may require a far shorter readiness preparation before learning and applying musical notation, or middle-school students may acquire the skills and proficiencies usually taught in two or three years in a much shorter time and be ready for independent and challenging assignments in performance or composition. Advanced Placement courses in music theory and appreciation are a possible form of instructional acceleration at the secondary level. Individual tutoring in musical composition is another alternative for talented secondary school students.

Enrichment. A challenge for general music teachers is the main-streamed gifted and talented youngster. One approach that will help to meet the learning needs of these students is suggested by the term *enrichment,* adding greater depth or breadth to the existing instruction. For students who have the appropriate research and study skills, independent projects related to class instruction can be assigned. Such projects should focus on a topic of student interest and should include a written or spoken presentation to an appropriate audience. For example, a student who is a beginning instrumentalist may research the history and development of his or her instrument, while the inclusion of a particular listening selection may pique another student's interest in a composer and lead to an extensive investigation of the composer's life or other compositions or even a more extensive study of stylistic differences.

Enrichment activities need not only be reports. For students of varying ages, creative composing projects can be devised that provide opportunity for the *process* of creativity as described by Wallas (1926). The process contains four steps: preparation, incubation, illumination, and verification. Preparation refers to the identification of the problem and the gathering of facts and requires sustained attention from the learner. Incubation is often unconscious and is the step at which the student reorganizes the information into new forms. Illumination is the stage at which an idea or a solution occurs. Verification implies testing the idea to see if it works (Gallagher, 1975, p. 249). These four stages do not always occur in the order described or within a set time frame. However, understanding this process will assist music educators in providing alternative enrichment for gifted and talented students.

One source for individual creative composing enrichment is the Manhattanville Curriculum (Thomas) structure. Creative composition projects can range from the simple to the complex, depending upon the age and the experience of the student. The process of deciding on rhythmic, melodic, or harmonic improvisations that will accompany a poem or a story may be appropriate for a primary-age child. A complex set of instructions that specify a time length, options of instruments, and the use of creative or standard notation can be devised for older students.

Creative projects in music can also incorporate some or all of the principles devised by Osborne (1957) to stimulate new ideas, which include magnification, minification, addition, subtraction, substitution, division, and rearrangement. Questions such as the following can be incorporated into written or spoken directions:

> What will it sound like if the durations, or phrases, or sections, are longer (or shorter)?
> What sounds, instruments, rhythms, and so on could we add (or take away)?
> What instrument, melody, rhythm, or chord could we replace in this measure (phrase, section)?
> How would it sound if we rearranged the phrases (sections, instrumentation)?

These guiding principles can be incorporated into brainstorming sessions of several students or used with individuals. Brainstorming implies suggesting ideas as rapidly as possible, with no criticisms allowed during the process. Evaluation of each idea is a separate and later process.

Individual enrichment activities are also possible through computer-assisted instruction. Music educators who work in districts that have provided computers for students should not ignore this useful instructional device. Reviews of musical software have been provided in the *Music Educators Journal* by Robert W. Placek, and special issues of the journal, including December 1987, have provided up-to-date information about the latest available computer hardware.

A Gifted and Talented program for music students in Judson, Texas (Kinsey, 1988), incorporates individual and group enrichment. The carefully selected students participate in the Applied Music–Individual Study Course, approved by the state, which includes opportunities for solo performance and group enrichment. Students must perform three solos in public recitals each year, either on school-sponsored recital nights or during other public appearances, such as those offered by private instructors and by churches. The group enrichment consists of three lectures each year by professionals in various musical areas (conductors, symphony players, college professors, and so on).

The music education profession, through its local, state and national organizations, has always provided enrichment for talented musicians. District, county, and all-state performing organizations exist in every state for these students. In some areas of the country, talented musicians are served in special secondary schools for the arts. Summer is also a time when young musicians can find enrichment and challenge; the possibilities range from the most famous music camp at Interlochen to music camps at local college campuses. Music educators can also provide enrichment for talented performers through chamber music ensembles.

Differentiated curriculum. Not all gifted and talented students are performers. Music educators must find ways of meeting the needs of those students whose cognitive processes are substantially different from those of their peers. Clearly, the inclusion of a differentiated curriculum for gifted children requires overall knowledge of the structure of the subject and an adaptation of teaching approaches. Goals and objectives for these learners should be constructed to include the more complex cognitive processes found in Bloom's Taxonomy (1956); that is, analysis, synthesis, and evaluation should be emphasized rather than an extra accumulation of facts. Unfortunately, what often happens in classrooms is that when a gifted child is perceived as different, some teachers deal with the child by assigning additional work rather than by altering their own approach to the learner. Other educators prefer to ignore the reality that some gifted and talented students easily grasp the lesson content, which may result in their becoming passive spectators in the class rather than active and challenged learners.

Music educators need to structure enrichment in ways that make learning attractive to gifted and talented children. It is of interest to note that younger gifted children are often quite bored in classrooms where information is presented in small quantities, because the children prefer the complexity and challenge of larger amounts of information. The typical classroom arrangement of a daily short time span for each subject adds to the boredom of gifted children who prefer to concentrate on a task for much longer periods of time. A study by Ricca (1984) explored differences in learning preferences between a general population and identified gifted children ($n = 425$) in grades four, five, and six. The researcher reported that the gifted children had three distinct learning preferences: learning alone, tactile learning, and independent study. These three preferences certainly reinforce the suitability of exploratory, improvisatory, and compositional enrichment assignments for gifted intermediate-grade children.

It is often difficult to be a gifted child in many American school settings where teachers and peers emphasize conformity to the norm. A useful strategy for assisting these exceptional learners is the seeking out of appropriate adults (mentors) who are experts in an area of gifted child interest. Music educators have always helped parents and children find the appropriate private teacher, so that is certainly not a startling new concept. However, it can be expanded with gifted and talented children who are not performers. The literature contains suggestions for special gifted programs that emphasize song writing (Skaught, 1987) and electronic keyboard and computer use (Melillo, 1985). These programs and others may be outside the expertise of the music teacher, but there may be a community member who is knowledgeable in such special areas and who can be asked to volunteer to work with gifted students.

SUMMARY OF TEACHING SUGGESTIONS

Provide appropriate performance or curriculum challenge through acceleration.

Provide research, composition, creative, or computer-based enrichment to existing instruction.

Construct goals and objectives that emphasize more complex cognitive processes.

Structure enrichment to meet learning preferences of gifted and talented students.

Find community mentors for the gifted and talented.

Summary

The definition of the term *gifted and talented* needs to be carefully investigated by individual music educators. Schools that differentiate these students solely by intelligence or achievement scores may be eliminating both creative students and talented students—the two categories that apply most directly to musical giftedness. Once again, such situations demand that the music educator become an advocate for appropriate services for exceptional children. A clear understanding of the possible variety of gifted and talented students, the ability to articulate the complexity of cognition, an awareness of the possibility of musical intelligence as espoused by Howard Gardner, and an understanding of the differences between intelligence and creativity will assist in this advocacy. The curriculum suggestions offered in this chapter are not complete or final—they serve only as possible points of reference that may assist in the adaptations appropriate for the interests and cognitive process of individual learners

RESEARCH IN MUSIC EDUCATION

Only one researcher (Bickel, 1985) has conducted music education research with clearly defined groups of gifted and normal-achieving students. A number of other studies are summarized in this section because they pertain to creativity, certainly an important factor in musically gifted and talented students. As in the previous two chapters, the research is described in some detail to provide information that may assist in arguing for correct placements for gifted and talented students.

As an introduction to this section, the work of Donald Pond at the Pillsbury Foundation School in Santa Barbara, California, must be cited. This nursery school was founded in 1937 at the suggestion of Leopold Stokowski, who believed that young children's spontaneous music making should be studied. Pond, a composer, was hired to be the school's music director. He acquired a collection of Oriental instruments (gongs, cymbals, bells, drums, rattles, marimbas, xylophones) and some Western instruments (recorders, guitar, piano) and facilitated their use for young children. He then observed and recorded the children's music making for an eight-year period. His descriptions of the children's sound games, rhythmic development, and improvised chants and songs led him to conclude that improvisation was vital to the development of children's musicality. A record of this school exists in the monograph "Music of Young Children" (Pillsbury Foundation, 1978) and in the written documents from the school, which are preserved at the MENC Historical Center at the University of Maryland (Wilson, 1981).

Gifted and Talented

Differences between groups. The ability to conserve and judge musical duration (velocity as a function of rhythm) was assessed (Bickel, 1985) in groups of gifted children and randomly selected students in grades four and six ($n = 76$). The subjects heard two selections, each of which lasted twenty seconds, and had to determine if one of the pair took more time or lasted longer. In addition, the subjects were asked "how" they arrived at their decision. Gifted fourth graders were twice as accurate as the random sample of their age-mates, while there was a lack of significance between the scores of the sixth-grade groups. The fourth-grade difference, explained in relation to Piagetian theory, was a function of the development of time/velocity ratio. The lack of difference in the older subjects was considered a "leveling off" of the development of time/velocity understanding. At both grade levels, the gifted students gave more varied and detailed descriptions and noticed melodic contour differences.

A study by Meckley (1984) investigated the use of the LOGO computer language with four categories of learners: neurologically impaired ($n = 2$), learning disabled ($n = 3$), gifted ($n = 3$), and normal-achieving ($n = 2$). This computer language differs from others in that it does not provide a means of additional practice and drill; rather, it is a way for users to program sounds and manipulate them. Each subject's progress in the individual lessons is described in summary form, and the descriptions of the gifted subjects include the following statements:

The process of working out problems was fascinating to him and he never frustrated. (p. 99)

A single instructor-programmed example of a new command usually triggered experimentation by the subject, which in turn led to mastery of concepts. (p. 100)

Boredom and off-task behavior was frequently exhibited during the subject's first lesson. He did not enjoy working with examples and instructor-defined tasks. A significant change of behavior and attitude was evident when the subject began choosing his own projects. . . . He became intensely involved and interested in the system and worked diligently, seeing projects through to completion. (p. 109)

The researcher found that the gifted children developed quite different learning styles in their use of the computer language. One subject developed his own programming style and explored and experimented freely, while the other two were task oriented and product oriented and interested in planning and completing projects.

Existing programs. A survey to determine if existing programs include provisions for the musically gifted and talented was conducted by Sebree (1987). The researcher limited the study to cities with a population of over 50,000 in ten North Central states. Fifty-nine percent of the schools surveyed recognized *musical talent* as a facet of giftedness and included the term in their definition. However, none of the respondents reported any provision for the musically talented within the gifted programs. The programs provided for gifted students included mentorships, independent projects, honor choirs, bands, orchestras, and special schools that were provided under the aegis of music education. The researcher found that although all the school districts were making attempts to identify academically gifted children, musical talent was not being identified in the screening and identification process.

Creativity Instruction

An instructional experiment with two classes of intermediate-age children was reported by Vaughan and Myers (1971). The researchers wanted to determine if (1) musical experiences would influence the scores on a test of nonverbal creative thinking and (2) there were relationships between mental ability, creative thinking, and musical aptitude. The experimental group received instruction that focused on the four areas of creative thinking (fluency, flexibility, originality, elaboration), with an emphasis on twentieth-century music and improvisation on classroom instruments. The experimental groups excelled on an author-constructed test of creativity, but it is clear in the description of the study that the test measured what the experimental group was taught to do—improvise. It is interesting to note that the correlations between the test of music aptitude (Bentley, 1959) and each test of creativity (Torrance, 1974; Vaughan and Myers) were insignificant, indicating that perhaps the tests measure quite different abilities.

One of these authors, Vaughan, developed the foregoing test during her doctoral studies, and this process is described in her dissertation (1971). During that project, the test was individually administered to fourth graders ($n = 47$), as were the tests of Torrance and Bentley. Here, also, there were nonsignificant correlations between the author's measure and the Bentley test, suggesting that each test assesses different abilities.

Creativity Measurement

Other researchers (Gorder, Webster) have reported the development of measures of musical creativity for contrasting populations. Gorder (1980) piloted and developed a test for junior high and high school instrumentalists based on the four divergent production abilities described by Guilford (fluency, flexibility, elaboration, and originality) and one ability described by the researcher as musical originality. The test was administered to forty students at each level; content, criterion, and construct validity are reported. The test must be scored by trained judges, and the reported rescoring reliability coefficient ranges are quite vast on the tests of elaboration (.30–.63) and the tests of quality (.55–1.00). The ranges of interjudge reliability coefficients also are quite vast on all measures but the fluency test. Gorder describes the scoring of the test as requiring considerable time, effort, and expertise. Of interest, though, is the finding that the test did not correlate with music aptitude or achievement. The measure apparently taps musical abilities quite separate from those measured by current standardized music tests.

Webster's initial research (1977) in the development of a test of musical creativity was with high school students who belonged to performing organizations ($n = 77$). His individually administered test took thirty minutes and consisted of taped music improvisation activities. The test scores were correlated with scores from the *Torrance Tests of Creative Thinking* (1974), Colwell's *Music Achievement Tests* (1970), Gordon's *Music Aptitude Profile* (1965), and intelligence scores, as well as the variables of age, grade level, sex, and piano background. The dissertation includes several interesting correlations on these measures. The researcher found that students with high musical achievement also scored high on the tests of musical creativity. Figural creativity (Torrance test), which is the ability to creatively conceptualize shapes, figures, and pictures, was also significantly related to musical improvisation skill. In addition, the improvisation subscores were significantly related to the students' IQ scores.

In later work, Webster (1983, 1987, 1988) has described the development of a measure of musical creative thinking for children aged 6 to 9. The twenty-minute test contains eighteen tasks designed to stimulate young children's musical imagination, focusing on pitch, tempo, and dynamics. The test requirements are a Nerf ball; a microphone with amplifier, speaker, and small reverberation unit; a piano; and a set of temple blocks. Testing sessions are videotaped and scored for musical extensiveness, flexibility, originality, and syntax. The test has been administered to a sample of children with no previous musical background (1987) and another unmatched sample of children who had received at least two years of Dalcroze or Suzuki training. The author reports that "Children without formal music training scored significantly higher in terms of music originality than children with training and children with formal music training scored significantly higher in terms of musical syntax than children without training" (1988).

Scores on Webster's test do not correlate with *Primary Measures of Musical Audiation* (Gordon, 1979), except for musical syntax with the tonal part in the first sample only. Webster feels that the lack of correlation between the two measures is a validation of his test of creativity in an inverse way.

The 1988 report describes interscorer (ave.–.70) and internal reliability (ave.–.65) data as well as the process of establishing content and construct validity. In addition, results of that project indicated a test-retest reliability of .56 to .79 for individual factors as well as .76 for total scores (all statistically significant).

This test is titled *Measures of Creative Thinking in Music.* The guidelines, text for administering the test, scoring sheets, and criteria are available from the author for a small fee. Sample videotapes are also available. Peter Webster is a professor of music at Northwestern University in Evanston, Illinois.

Webster's test was used by Swanner (1985) in a study that explored the relationship between selected personality factors in the musically creative third grader. In addition, she administered the *Primary Measures of Music Audiation* (Gordon, 1979), the *Early School Personality Questionnaire* (Cattell, 1976), and two author-constructed evaluations of student behavior—one for parents and one for teachers. The highly musically creative children identified by Webster's measure were found to have the following common personality traits: independence, self-confidence, sensitivity, imagination, and curiosity. No significant relationships were found between musical aptitude, gender or cognitive intelligence, and musical creativity.

Is Musical Creativity Taught in Schools?

This topic was researched by Dallman (1970) with both a survey and individual interviews in which she queried the extent of composition activity in elementary schools within a 75-mile radius of Denver, Colorado. The results indicated that in grades one and two, the most frequent compositional activity was creating rhythms. In grades three through 6, creativity was fostered by composing original words to familiar tunes, creating sound pieces and original melodies, improvising, writing original words and melodies, and creating instrumental compositions. In addition, the teachers' backgrounds were investigated, and the teachers who most often included compositional activities had a strong background in creativity derived from a recent workshop experience.

Another researcher (Simpson, 1969) investigated the growth of cognitive creative behavior in students ($n = 218$) who attended various music classes in one high school, ranging from jazz workshop to music appreciation and piano class. In addition, the researcher included a control group of students ($n = 45$), who received no music instruction. All students were given five Guilford-type tests as pretests and posttests, which were scored for word fluency, divergent production of figural systems, elaboration, spontaneous flexibility, ideation fluency, and originality. Students who were members of music classes did gain more in the test scores than the control group, with the greatest effect found in members of the music appreciation class and the least effect found in students in the jazz workshop. Readers should note that these were *cognitive* tests of creativity, not musical tests.

Research tells us that in these studies,

> Gifted and talented children in the fourth grade were able to judge music duration more accurately than a random sample of their age-mates.
>
> Gifted and talented students displayed different learning styles while learning to write a computer program.
>
> Musically talented students are not served through existing gifted and talented programs.
>
> Tests of music aptitude and musical creativity seem to assess different abilities.
>
> Students in music appreciation had the greatest gain in cognitive tests of creativity.

CONCLUSION

If you are an undergraduate or a graduate student, you probably were considered at one time gifted and talented. Those words were probably applied to you because of the development of your performance skill in some musical medium. And at present, in almost all schools in the United States, students with the same types of abilities are also described as talented. However, the focus of this chapter has been the necessity for music educators to understand that "gifted and talented" means more than talented in performance.

A clear perception of the importance of developing children's divergent thinking and production abilities and the relationship of those abilities to creative musical thinking is vitally necessary for music educators at all levels and in all areas. Only with this understanding can the different learning needs of labeled and unlabeled musically gifted and talented children be met through the varied curriculum and instructional adaptations discussed in this chapter.

In addition, it is important that music educators develop an understanding of why there are differences in student answers and responses. There should not always be a single "right" answer. The "wrong" answer may indicate a thinking and reasoning process that needs to be explored and perhaps nurtured. This type of approach to student thinking is infrequently a prevailing attitude in some schools.

Once again, music educators, because of the "difference" in their subject, may be required to become advocates for students. Frequently, that will mean asserting the necessity of recognizing and accepting talent as part of giftedness. The potential and uniqueness of "gifted" or "talented" students makes this advocacy very valuable. Some of these students may not "make it on their own" any more than students who have learning disabilities or who are retarded "make it on their own."

QUESTIONS

1. Why are gifted children often the most neglected exceptionality?
2. What do intelligence tests measure?
3. Describe the difference between convergent and divergent thinking.
4. Why has the inclusion of persistence as an attribute of giftedness (Renzulli) been criticized?
5. Discuss the possible types of acceleration available for musically gifted and talented students.
6. What are the four steps in the "process" of creating?
7. Why does Howard Gardner believe there is a separate "musical intelligence"?

ACTIVITIES

1. Interview a school administrator to determine the local and state definition of "gifted and talented." Does gifted hypocrisy as defined by Renzulli exist in this definition?
2. Construct Individualized Compositional Activities for gifted and talented children in two grade levels, based on the Manhattanville Curriculum and the principles of Osborne described in this chapter.

3. Observe a gifted and talented class during music instruction or a single mainstreamed GT student. Describe the unique learning styles that these students demonstrate.

BIBLIOGRAPHY

Davis, G. A., and S. B. Rimm. 1985. *Education of the Gifted and Talented.* Englewood Cliffs, N.J.: Prentice-Hall.

Gallagher, J. J. 1985. *Teaching the Gifted Child* (3rd. ed.). Boston: Allyn & Bacon.

Music Educators National Conference. 1983. *Documentary Report of the Ann Arbor Symposium on the Application of Psychology to the Teaching and Learning of Music: Session III, Motivation and Creativity.* Reston, Va.: Music Educators National Conference.

Sisk, D. 1987. *Creative Teaching of the Gifted.* New York: McGraw-Hill.

Tatarunis, A. M. 1981. Exceptional Programs for Talented Students. *Music Educators Journal* 68 (November): 55–60.

Woodell, G. 1984. Gifted Children in General Music. *Music Educators Journal* 70 (January): 43–46.

Putting It All Together
CHAPTER FIVE

INTRODUCTION

The focus of each of the previous three chapters has been the learning differences in single exceptionalities. Each chapter has suggested instructional strategies and adaptations in order to provide a connection between abstract information about different learners and the field of music education. The present chapter provides a picture of what might really occur when exceptional students are mainstreamed into music classes. Rarely is a single child mainstreamed into a single class! A realistic description of current mainstreaming practices in music education must show the inclusion of children with very different learning abilities in single classes.

Because the preponderance of mainstreaming occurs at the elementary level, this chapter describes a fictional teacher preparing lessons for three general music classes that include mainstreamed students. However, instrumental specialists will be able to adapt the chapter's ideas for classes of either beginning or advanced students. In this chapter, you will follow the thinking process of a fictional teacher, Bill Cole, as he plans his lessons for the coming week. The planning and adaptations that are proposed are a recommended way of adjusting instruction in general music and are needed to provide mainstreamed students with successful musical learning experiences.

This planning and adaptation depends on a most important initial process, which must vary with the school, the teacher, and the administration. This step must be taken by each general and instrumental music teacher who teaches exceptional children. It is described as "finding out" about the child.

Where and how do teachers "find out" about a child? A good place *not* to do this is in the teacher's room. The reason for this "professional" suggestion is that in teachers' rooms one can certainly find out about children, but, unfortunately, most of the information tends to be negative. And as researchers have demonstrated, teachers' prior perceptions about individual children have strong effects on their interactions with those students (Aloia and MacMillan, 1983).

Previous chapters have suggested that you consult with your professional peers. Prior to any professional discussion, you should carefully read the student's file, since the information in that folder will provide a background for informed professional dialogues. If there are terms or entire sections in the file that are unclear, they can be a focused way to begin a discussion. Colleagues such as the school's resource teacher, the child's classroom teacher, the school psychologist, and teachers the child has had in previous years are valuable sources of information. A short discussion with each of those educators will be most worthwhile, since they have had prolonged interaction with the mainstreamed child that you, the music teacher, are going to teach once or twice a week.

Another place to find out about a child is in your music class! Instrumental teachers who work continually with small groups have the advantage over general teachers in this process because there are fewer students in each class. However, the finding-out process is identical in the two teaching situations. Any group must be observed and taught as a collection of individuals, not as a mass of third graders or beginning trumpet players! The individuals must be observed during each type of activity or instruction, and future instructional adaptations must be based, in part, upon the student's reactions and demonstrated abilities in previous classes. Such careful attention to individuals implies that teaching is a circular, never-ending process, which is, of course, what makes teaching so interesting and challenging.

Teachers who have become accustomed to planning one third-grade lesson for six classes or a single lesson for three beginning clarinet classes may have been mentally visualizing these classes as the cartoonist has illustrated. (See Figs. 5-1 and 5-2.) However, real classes do not contain identical-looking children, and when a class contains one or more mainstreamed students, the planning process becomes more complex. In the following scenario, the planning of our fictional teacher illustrates this process.

FIGURE 5-1

MAIN STREET SCHOOL

It is 2:00 on Friday afternoon. Bill Cole, the school's music teacher, is starting to plan for the following week. He wrote an overall year plan for each grade level in September and has that chart in front of him now. In grade one, he wants to continue to emphasize melodic direction, while in grade three, it is time to begin meter. The fifth graders need more lessons on how rhythm and harmony are used to provide repetition and contrast in both phrases and larger sections.

Bill uses the little squares in his plan book to write the musical concept(s) for each grade and what each class actually accomplishes weekly. He writes his real lesson plans for each class within a grade level on a mimeographed form that he has created, which has a space for each mainstreamed child's name and a column for writing instructional adaptations for those learners. The form has these headings:

FIGURE 5-2

GRADE _____		CLASS _____
MAINSTREAMED _____		
ACTIVITIES	MATERIALS	ADAPTATIONS

Bill has been teaching for many years and no longer feels a need to include many of the indvidual lesson-plan parts he learned in his undergraduate college methods class. However, he knows that he must plan most carefully for each year and each lesson so that he can demonstrate learning and progress to his supervisor and, much more important, to himself!

Grade One

Bill decides that the first graders are going to review descending direction before they learn a new song that contains an ascending scale line. He writes down "The Stretching Song" (*Exploring Music*, Grade One, p. 6; see Fig. 5-3) and makes a note to have resonator bells ready for children to play on the final phrase. His second review song, "My Pony" (Fig. 5-4), is from the same text (p. 148) and is a favorite of the first graders. He decides to have children play resonator bells to reinforce the descending sound on the last phrase in this song and chooses the phrase "Go and never stop" as the introduction to ascending direction. The new song, "Sky Bears" (Macmillan, Grade One, p. 108; see Fig. 5-5) has

FIGURE 5-3   From *Exploring Music 1* by Eunice Boardman and Beth Landis, copyright © 1966 by Holt, Rinehart and Winston, Inc., reprinted by permission of the publisher.

Stretching Song

Words and Music by Eunice Boardman

My Pony

German Folk Song

Trot, trot, trot! Trot, my po-ny, trot!

Where it's smooth and where it's ston-y, Trot a-long, my lit-tle po-ny.

Go and nev-er stop, Trot, my po-ny, trot!

FIGURE 5-4 From *Exploring Music 1* by Eunice Boardman and Beth Landis, copyright © 1966 by Holt, Rinehart and Winston, Inc., reprinted by permission of the publisher.

ascending scale sections in the middle but does not lend itself as easily to reinforcement with resonator bells. These phrases will need to be reinforced with movement.

The thirty-minute lesson also will include listening to music that has a clear descending and ascending pattern. Bill again plans to use the Telemann Flute Concerto (Silver Burdett, Grade 2, Record 2). Last week the children listened to the first two A sections, and they modeled Bill's

FIGURE 5-5 Appears in *MUSIC AND YOU,* Grade 1, Barbara Staton and Merrill Staton, Senior Authors (New York: Macmillan, 1988). Used by permission of Exposition Press.

movements with the descending scale passage at the end of each picture. In this lesson, Bill will include the next section, which contains clear ascending scale passages.

Finally, Bill decides on his evaluation. He writes all the specific patterns that are used in the lesson on a piece of staff paper (Fig. 5-6), which he staples to his lesson plan. He will play these on the piano in

FIGURE 5-6

different registers and have the children point large laminated arrows to indicate ascending or descending patterns.

   Mainstreamed children.   The next step in Bill's planning is always the same. He mentally reviews the mainstreamed children's names and what he knows about how they learn. Then he begins to plan how the lesson can be adapted for each of them. In Mrs. Adams's first grade there are twenty-four children, including three mainstreamed students. Two are labeled educable mentally retarded (EMR), and one is designated gifted and talented (GT).

   The two EMR students are Jeremy and Alice. Jeremy is a Down's syndrome child with mild retardation who has learned his colors and numbers to ten and can often keep the steady beat in music class. He knows many of the words to the rote songs, and his mother has asked for a copy of each new song so that she can sing it to him at home. Alice also has Down's syndrome features, but she has more severe learning problems. She has a very low voice and sings a beat or more behind the class. Alice doesn't know many of the words of the songs and has difficulty in clapping or moving to the beat.

   Todd was identified as gifted and talented in kindergarten. When he came to school, he could already read at the fourth-grade level and has a wide range of interests that include rocks, the game of cricket, dinosaurs, electricity, and historical biography. In music class, Todd has no difficulty with beat or singing on pitch, but he is very quiet and almost appears withdrawn.

   Bill Cole decides that he must plan some adaptations for both the song review and the new song for the EMR students. One way to help both Jeremy and Alice in the review of descending motion is to have partners for movement. When the class sings "My Pony," partners will face each other and perform a descending movement duet when the resonator bells are played. Bill then begins to consider how to effectively teach the new song to these learners. There is little repetition in the text of "Sky Bears," so the words need to be illustrated for Alice. He makes a note to prepare a set of pictures that will clarify the word order. Jeremy's mother will want a copy of the song, so he writes himself a reminder to photocopy the page.

The remainder of the lesson will not need any changes. During the listening selection, Bill will be modeling the ascending arm and body movements. He has a laminated large arrow, which he will use on a flannel board to demonstrate correct direction after each phrase during the evaluation.

Bill feels uneasy because he has not provided any challenges for Todd during the lessons on melodic direction. He glances around the room and sees the portable Casio he ordered this year. It is the smallest model—this is not a wealthy district—but it may entice Todd into some initial explorations in composition. The perfect time to have Todd take the Casio to the small storage room that opens on to the music room will be during the class evaluation. He will be asked to prepare some additional ascending and descending patterns and decide on a way to write them down so that he can play them for the class next week. It will be interesting to see if he tries to put them together, and the results may indicate ways to provide some extended enrichment for him in composition.

Bill's lesson-plan sheet for Mrs. Adams's class contains all the information he will need on the following Wednesday when he meets the class.

GRADE __1_____   TEACHER _Mrs. Adams_____

MAINSTREAMED _Jeremy, Alice, Todd_____

ACTIVITIES	MATERIALS	ADAPTATIONS
Stretching Song	Bells	
My Pony	Bells	Partners
Sky Bears		Sequence pictures
Telemann Flute Concerto		
Evaluation	Arrows	Todd—Casio

He takes a red pen and underlines the words *pictures* and *Sky Bears*. He will put this reminder on a separate list, to be completed during his preparation time next Monday or Tuesday.

Grade Three

Bill knows he has to decide on adaptations for the mainstreamed first graders in the other classes, but he chooses to concentrate next on the overall plan for his third graders. He decides that in this introductory lesson on meter, he will use only familiar songs and will include movement and playing activities that will emphasize the downbeats.

He decides to begin by improvising at the piano and having the children hit the floor whenever he includes a random accent. Then, gradually, he will space the accents more regularly. The next step in the introduction will be chanting familiar rhymes in 2s and 3s. He writes down "Humpty Dumpty," "Little Jack Horner," and "Oliver Twist" and decides he will have the children pat their knees for the first beat and clap softly for the other beat(s).

The songs are simple to choose, since Bill keeps a list of the songs taught this year in the beginning of his plan book. He mentally sings the first phrase of several and chooses "Who Did?" (Macmillan, Grade 3; see Fig. 5-7) and "Ain't Gonna Rain" (Silver Burdett, Centennial Edition, p. 24; see Fig. 5-8) for songs in duple meter. "Springfield Mountain" (Macmillan, p. 136; see Fig. 5-9) and "There's a Hole in My

FIGURE 5-7   Appears in *MUSIC AND YOU,* Grade 3, Barbara Staton and Merrill Staton, Senior Authors (New York, Macmillan, 1988).

Who Did?

3. Daniel, *(Daniel,)* Daniel, *(Daniel,)*
   Daniel in the li-li-li-li, *(3 times)*
   Daniel in the lion's, *(Daniel in the lion's,)*
   Daniel in the lion's den.

4. Gabriel, *(Gabriel,)* Gabriel, *(Gabriel,)*
   Gabriel blow your trump-trump-trump-trump, *(3 times)*
   Gabriel blow your trumpet, *(Gabriel blow your trumpet,)*
   Gabriel blow your trumpet loud.

Ain't Gonna Rain   AMERICAN FOLK SONG

1. The wood-chuck, he's a - chop - pin' wood,

The pos - sum, he's a - haul - in'.

My poor old dog fell off a log And killed him - self a - bawl - in'.

REFRAIN

It ain't gon-na rain, it ain't gon-na rain, It ain't gon-na rain no more.

Come on down, ev-'ry-bod-y sing. It ain't gon-na rain no more.

2. Just bake them biscuits good and brown,
   It ain't gonna rain no more.
   Swing your ladies round and round,
   It ain't gonna rain no more. *Refrain*

3. I'll tune the fiddle, you get the bow,
   It ain't gonna rain no more.
   The weatherman just told me so,
   It ain't gonna rain no more. *Refrain*

4. Oh, what did the blackbird say to the crow?
   "It ain't gonna rain no more.
   It ain't gonna hail, it ain't gonna snow,
   It ain't gonna rain no more." *Refrain*

FIGURE 5-8   From *Silver Burdett MUSIC*, Centennial Edition, Grade 3. © 1985 by The Silver Burdett Company.

Bucket" (Holt, p. 115; see Fig. 5-10) will be good examples of triple meter. He also decides that each song will have the same rhythm instrument accompaniment on the first beat and a contrasting sound on the weak beat(s). Then, after some further thought, he decides to do the four songs twice, the first time with rhythm instruments and the second time with a one-beat metallophone drone (do and sol) on the first beat of each measure.

Springfield Mountain

American Ballad

1. On Spring-field Moun - tain there did dwell
2. One Mon - day morn - ing he did go

a hand-some youth; I knew him well._____
down in the mea - dow for to mow._____

Too loo - re - ay, too loo - re - oo,

Too loo - re - ay, too loo - re - oo.

3. When he had mowed but half the field, a pesky sarpent bit his heel.

4. He took his scythe and with a blow, he laid the pesky sarpent low.

5. He took the sarpent in his hand and straightway went to Molly Bland.

6. "Oh, Molly, Molly, here you see the pesky sarpent what bit me."

7. Now, Molly had a ruby lip with which the pizen she did sip.

8. But Molly had a rotten tooth and so the pizen kill'd them both.

FIGURE 5-9 Appears in *MUSIC AND YOU*, Grade 3, Barbara Staton and Merrill Staton, Senior Authors (New York: Macmillan, 1988).

Then Bill decides how he will evaluate the third graders' under-standing of metrical organization. He writes a reminder to make a tape recording of parts of the four songs in an order different from that in the class presentation. He will have each class decide on a set of movements for 2s and 3s, and they will have to use the appropriate movement while listening to the tape.

Finally, Bill decides to make an overhead transparency of each

There's a Hole in My Bucket

Dialogue Song

With a strong accent

1. There's a hole in my buck - et, dear Li - za, dear Li - za,
2. Mend the hole, then, dear Geor-gie, dear Geor-gie, dear Geor-gie,

There's a hole in my buck - et, dear Li - za,   a   hole.
Mend the hole, then, dear Geor-gie, dear Geor-gie, mend the hole.

3. With what shall I mend it, dear Liza, dear Liza?
   With what shall I mend it, dear Liza, with what?

4. With a straw, dear Georgie, . . . with a straw.

5. The straw is too long, dear Liza, . . . too long.

6. Cut the straw, then, dear Georgie, . . . cut the straw.

7. With what shall I cut it, dear Liza, . . . with what?

8. With a knife, dear Georgie, . . . with a knife.

9. The knife is too blunt, dear Liza, . . . too blunt.

10. Whet the knife, then, dear Georgie, . . . whet the knife.

11. With what shall I whet it, dear Liza, . . . with what?

12. With a stone, dear Georgie, . . . with a stone.

13. The stone is too dry, dear Liza, . . . too dry.

14. Wet the stone, then, dear Georgie, . . . wet the stone.

15. With what shall I wet it, dear Liza, . . . with what?

16. With the water, dear Georgie, . . . with the water.

17. In what shall I get it, dear Liza, . . . in what?

18. In the bucket, dear Georgie, . . . in the bucket.

19. There's a hole in my bucket, dear Liza, . . . a hole.

FIGURE 5-10 From *Holt Music 1988 Grade 3* by Meske, Andress, Pautz and Willman, copyright © 1988 by Holt, Rinehart and Winston, Inc., reprinted by permission of the publisher.

song so that he can point out the meter signatures easily. If he has time at the end of the lesson, he will include rhythm echoes in both meters and have the children determine which meter is being used.

Mainstreamed children. Now that he has decided on the lesson content, Bill Cole begins to look at his form and think about the mainstreamed students in the first third grade he teaches on Monday. There are three exceptional children in this class also. Two, Danny and Mike, are learning disabled, and one, Mary, is EMR.

The two learning disabled children are poor readers but for different reasons. The resource teacher and the reading teacher have both talked to Bill, and each has described how Danny is still reading single words and short phrases. He has auditory memory problems and often has to be reminded of the sounds of some letters when he tries to sound out individual words. His teachers have told Bill that they consistently use visual cues to help Danny remember. Danny was able to cope in second-grade music, but he is having a very difficult time this year because Bill is using texts a great deal and because the class content involves more musical abstractions.

Mike's learning disability is also in reading, but the causes have been described as visual memory and sequencing deficits. Mike is reading whole sentences and paragraphs, but he often mixes up letters in words and the order of entire words. He reads quite slowly but has often amazed Bill by remembering everything that was done in music the previous week.

Mary, who is from the EMR self-contained class, also reads single words and short phrases. Her classroom teacher has used the words of songs for reading charts and writing experiences to help Mary succeed in music. Mary still has difficulty with a steady beat and has motor coordination problems, but her singing voice has improved since kindergarten. She no longer drones on one pitch but approximates the song contour when she joins in singing with the class.

Bill now looks at each part of his lesson and thinks about the abilities of the three mainstreamed children. He immediately makes a note to pull out the sets of sequence pictures he made for "Ain't Gonna Rain" and "Hole in My Bucket." These will help both Danny and Mary (and other children) remember the order of the words in these songs. Bill next makes a note on his form to model the correct clap-pat order in the rhymes for Mary also. She often becomes quite confused when more than one movement is used in any activity.

As Bill thinks about the four songs and the use of instruments, he realizes that Mary will be most successful if she plays on the one song that contains many repetitive words, "Who Did?" He also makes a note to have the class "help" all the instrument players by patting and clapping the beat during each song.

While looking through his Teacher's Edition of the *Holt MUSIC*, he is reminded of how that text represents meter with ikons. He makes a note to get a dark and a light shade of a single color of chalk from the supply closet so that he can use this idea on the board. He will draw some small triangles and will make the first one of each set the darker color. These pictures may help Danny understand the abstract idea of musical meter.

Bill realizes that he has been thinking only about Danny and Mary.

What in this lesson needs to be adapted for Mike? Most of the lesson is auditory, which is Mike's strongest way of learning. However, the one visual part of the lesson, at the end, is the discovery of meter signatures. Bill writes down "colored pen" so that he will remember to circle the meter signatures on the transparency. The use of color will intensify the importance of the numerals and help Danny (and others) remember their position on the song page.

The completed lesson plan for this one third grade is ready to go into the loose-leaf notebook.

GRADE _3_   TEACHER _Miss Tynan_

MAINSTREAMED _Danny, Mike, Mary_

ACTIVITIES	MATERIALS	ADAPTATIONS
Improvising accents on floor Rhymes—Humpty, Jack Horner, Oliver Twist		Model the movements
Songs		Colored chalk
Ain't Gonna Rain	Rhythm instruments	Pictures
Who Did?	2 metallophones and mallets	Mary play an instrument
Hole in My Bucket		Pictures
Springfield Mountain		
Tape of song phrases		Model the movements if needed
Transparencies	Colored pen	

Grade Five

Again, Bill Cole decides to put off his adaptations for the other third grades and begins to develop his overall plan for the fifth grades. Bill has been teaching form for two weeks, and this week he wants the fifth graders to discover how contrasting and repeated rhythm and harmonies provide variety and repetition in phrases and sections. He spends quite a long time looking through his textbooks and finally chooses two AB songs, "Going to Boston" (Macmillan, p. 15; see Fig. 5-11) and "Mineira de Minas" (Silver Burdett, Centennial Edition, p. 20; see Fig. 5-12), and a listening piece, the "Rondeau" from Mouret's *Symphonie de Fanfares* (Silver Burdett, p. 53).

His choice of the first AB song is based on its appeal to fifth graders and, more important, on the clarity of the printing. The entire class will be able to find the repeated rhythms in both sections because they are directly under each other. However, Bill also decides to make a

Going to Boston

American Sea Chantey

1. Good-bye girls, I'm goin' to Bos-ton, Good-bye girls, I'm goin' to Bos-ton,
2. Clear the way, you'll get run o - ver, Clear the way, you'll get run o - ver,

Good-bye girls, I'm goin' to Bos-ton, ear - ly in the morn - ing.
Clear the way, you'll get run o - ver, ear - ly in the morn - ing.

Refrain

Won't we look pret-ty in the ball-room? Won't we look pret-ty in the ball-room?

Won't we look pret-ty in the ball - room? Ear - ly in the morn - ing.

3. Saddle up, girls, and we'll go with them,
Saddle up, girls, and we'll go with them,
Saddle up, girls, and we'll go with them,
Early in the morning. *Refrain*

FIGURE 5-11 Appears in *MUSIC AND YOU*, Grade 5, Barbara Staton and Merrill Staton, Senior Authors (New York: Macmillan, 1988).

transparency of this song so that he can point out the use of three measures of the same rhythm in the A section. In addition, he decides to have some students play a rhythm ostinato derived from the first two measures of each section.

In the second AB song, there is a clear contrast in rhythm between the two sections. The melodic repetition is more difficult to follow for some fifth graders, but Bill had made a chart of the song the previous year, with each set of two lines combined into one. The song's harmonic accompaniment is different in the two sections and will help to illustrate one of Bill's objectives for the lesson.

The listening selection has ABACA form, and the text has two possible ways for the student to follow the music, musical notation and a call chart (Fig. 5-13). Bill knows he will have to make a modified call chart for three of his fifth-grade classes, since there are mainstreamed children in each of those classes who can neither follow the notation nor

read the text of the call chart. When he looks at the master in the back of the text, on page 374 (see Fig. 5-14), he decides that he can use this for an evaluation in the lesson because of the simple language and clear layout.

Mainstreamed children.   Bill takes a lesson-plan form and decides to begin with Mr. Moore's class. This class has four mainstreamed children; three are learning disabled and one is gifted and talented. As in the third-grade class, the three LD children—Tara, Alan, and Jeffrey—have quite different learning problems. The gifted and talented fifth grader, Robby, is new to Main Street School this year.

After writing the children's names on the form, Bill sits and thinks about Tara, who has a learning disability in reading and writing. She is reading in third-grade texts with the resource teacher, but her biggest problems are in copying from the board and writing sentences and paragraphs. This year, the resource teacher has begun to teach Tara how to type. When the song texts are simple, Tara has no difficulty following

FIGURE 5-13 From *Silver Burdett MUSIC,* Centennial Edition, Grade 5. © 1985 by The Silver Burdett Company.

RONDO FORM: REPETITION AND CONTRAST OF SECTIONS

The diagram at the top of the page will help you discover how the sections in a piece of music are put together to create a rondo form. Study the diagram and answer the following questions:

• Which section repeats?
• How many contrasting sections does the diagram show?
• Which section do you find at the end of the diagram?

CALL CHART 2: Rondo   **Mouret:** *Symphonic de fanfares,* **"Rondeau"**

This piece for trumpet, organ, and timpani is in rondo form.
Follow the chart as you listen. It will help you hear what is
going on as the music goes along.

Another time, try following the notation of the music in each
section.

1	SECTION A	TRUMPET SOLO; FOUR PHRASES— PHRASES 1 AND 3 ARE EXACTLY ALIKE, PHRASES 2 AND 4 ARE NEARLY ALIKE.
2	SECTION B	NO TRUMPET; TWO PHRASES, ALIKE IN RHYTHM AND MELODY
3	SECTION A	PHRASES 3 AND 4 ONLY
4	SECTION C	NO TRUMPET; LONG AND SHORT PHRASES
5	SECTION A	SAME AS NUMBER 1

5   NAME_____

Silver Burdett
mUSIC
Centennial Edition

WHAT DO YOU HEAR?   8
FORM: RONDO

As you hear the numbers called, decide which answer is
correct. (You are given the correct answer for
number 1.)

Listen, then circle your answer.

Mouret: *Symphonie de fanfares,* "Rondeau"

1. SECTION A	**3.** SECTION A SECTION B	
	4. SECTION A SECTION B SECTION C	
2. SECTION A SECTION B	**5.** SECTION A SECTION B SECTION C	

FIGURE 5-14   From *Silver Burdett MUSIC,* Centennial Edition, Grade 5. © 1985 by The Silver Burdett
Company.

in the books, but any evaluation that includes writing an answer is a
disaster.

Since the fifth graders are going to be using Autoharps in "Mineira
de Minas," Tara will need some additional help so that she can be
successful in this eye-hand coordination activity. If students take turns
playing on the A and B sections, Tara can be assigned to the second,
simpler accompaniment. The second section uses only two chords, so a
simple teacher hand gesture of "palms up" and "palms down" will
guide Tara in the correct chord changes.

Alan's learning disability is in mathematics. He reads at grade level
but has not progressed beyond counting and simple number facts in
arithmetic. Bill Cole has also been told that Alan has difficulty discriminating different shapes and that he is unable to tackle any word
problems that deal with abstractions. Alan participates in music sporadi-
cally. He clearly has problems with any nonverbal symbols, and he
demonstrates a negative attitude in music class when Bill is emphasizing
musical notation.

One way to help Alan understand the similarities in rhythm in the
two sections of "Going to Boston" is to intensify the notation. Bill makes
a note to himself to make an enlarged photocopy of the song and use that

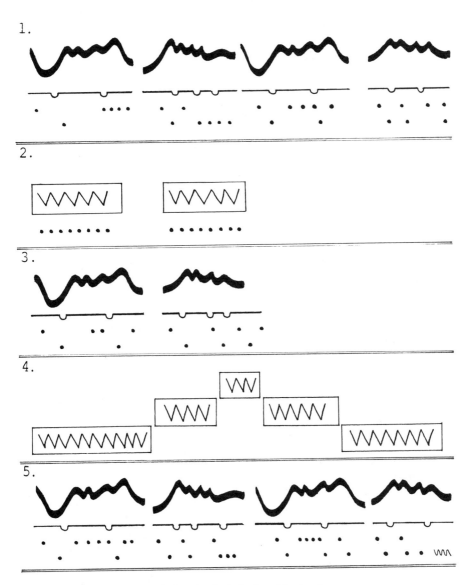

FIGURE 5-15   Graphic Call Chart for *Symphonie de Fanfares,* "Rondeau"

for a transparency. If he has two different-colored marking pens ready, he can also intensify the rhythmic contrast.

Finally, Bill thinks briefly about Jeffrey, who has a severe reading disability. Jeffrey has problems in visual discrimination and sequencing and hasn't developed a sight vocabulary. That means that when he reads, he must sound out each word. Jeffrey never volunteers in music and prefers to sit in the back and watch the rest of the class. Both of the charts in the textbook for the listening selection will be too difficult for Jeffrey to follow. Bill puts the record on and draws a simpler call chart to use in this one class. He decides to put the simplified call chart on a transparency so that he can point to the beginning of each section as an additional listening cue (see Fig. 5-15).

Then Bill's thoughts move to Robby, the gifted and talented student, who has just moved to their town. Robby has taken piano lessons since he was in kindergarten and Suzuki violin with his mother since he was 3. This year, he is also taking trumpet lessons with the other beginning fifth graders. He has told Bill that last summer he was at a science camp and three times each week he goes to the high school for advanced math and science courses. Robby is a difficult student in music because he wants to answer every question and contributes an overwhelming number of his own questions as well.

Fortunately, the instrumental teacher is not in the building on the day that Robby comes to music. That means there is a small practice room empty, where Robby can work on an enrichment project. Bill prepares an individualized assignment for Robby in which he will explore some possible combinations of rhythmic and harmonic variety and repetition to create a composition. His assignment sheet reads as follows:

In music class, we have been learning about how different elements are repeated or changed to give shape to music. This week, the class is going to be learning how rhythm and harmony help to give music its shape. During class time, I want you to explore these elements on your own. You may use any or all of the following: the Omnichord, two different rhythm instruments, the piano, your violin, your trumpet.

Your assignment is to compose a piece that illustrates rondo form—ABACA. You can use traditional notation or you may make up your own notation if you wish, but you need to notate your piece so you and possibly others can reproduce it. Each section of your composition should be at least 20 seconds long—you can make some sections longer if you wish. You should prepare to perform your composition for the class at the beginning of next period. I will include it as a class review of rondo form. If you want to have another student or two help you out or perform with you, that will be fine. You can practice in the music room during any lunch period except on Thursday, when we have chorus rehearsal.

Bill pulls out another copy of his blank lesson-plan form and fills it in for Mr. Moore's class.

GRADE <u>5</u>   TEACHER <u>*Mr. Moore*</u>

MAINSTREAMED <u>*Tara, Alan, Jeffrey, Robby*</u>

ACTIVITIES	MATERIALS	ADAPTATIONS
Going to Boston	*Rhythm instruments*	*Transparency and colored pen*
Mineira de Minas	*Chart from last year Autoharps*	*Hand signs for Tara*
Rondeau (Mouret)	*Graphic call chart*	*Regular call chart for Alan Graphic chart for Jeffrey*
Evaluation	*Silver Burdett, page 374 (prepare copies)*	

CONCLUSION

The preceding scenario is fiction. Any resemblance to living teachers or students is purely accidental! There are two clues in the scenario that indicate an unreal setting. One clue is the categories of mainstreamed students. In real life, music teachers also have many other types of mainstreamed children in their classes, not just EMR, LD, and GT. The other clue is the use of materials. Bill Cole was able to select activities from textbooks by all the publishers—a planning luxury that is very expensive. Despite those two signals that reality is not being described, the scenario does serve the central purpose of the chapter: to clarify the steps needed to adequately plan for classes that include more than one exceptional mainstreamed student. Even when students were described who had the same identifying label, vast differences in learning were described and lesson accommodations were planned based on those differences.

Similar types of adaptations could be planned for instrumental instruction as well. The three fictional fifth-grade learning disabled students could be combined in one instrumental lesson, even if they were learning different instruments. In that way, they could use larger-print pages (enlarged Xerox pages), if needed, or colored fingering charts, or they could be taught at a slower pace. In addition, such grouping would eliminate negative social reactions when these types of instructional adaptations are needed. Instrumental teachers should also consider preparing adapted simple parts for ensemble selections. Teachers can write an additional part for trumpet, clarinet, violin, or some other instrument for any piece that follows the harmonic structure but uses very basic rhythms. This type of adaptation will provide an opportunity for exceptional learners to participate in this important part of instrumental education.

How did Bill Cole know what to do for each child? You will have noted that much of the information that he had about each mainstreamed child had come from other, "special" teachers. Bill Cole spent considerable amounts of time "finding out" about the exceptional children he teaches. But you will also recognize that many of Bill's adaptations were based on his observations of individual children during previous music classes. A careful rereading of the lesson adaptations suggested in this chapter will emphasize that their purpose was to make music *learning* possible.

All music educators want students to like music, and they plan their teaching to provide enjoyable lessons. The focus of each lesson, however, cannot be on enjoyment; it must be on experiencing and learning about music. Each of Bill Cole's lessons had a clear musical focus, and each lesson contained clear examples of interesting and challenging music to illustrate the musical concept. In addition, each lesson included a way to evaluate students' learning. This type of music education planning provides a clear structure or framework for musical learning, which then can be modified as needed for individual exceptional children.

QUESTIONS

1. In any school setting, what possible sources of information about mainstreamed children are available to music teachers?
2. Discuss the possible reasons that Bill Cole planned a first-grade lesson adaptation that involved partners.
3. Describe each of the learning disabled children from this chapter in terms of the learning hierarchy found on page 41.
4. Write some additional lesson adaptations for the following exceptional children:
    Grade one—a learning disabled child
    Grade three—a gifted and talented child
    Grade five—an EMR child

ACTIVITIES

1. Reread the beginning scenarios of Chapters 2, 3, and 4. Use the lesson-plan form in this chapter and write a music lesson plan and suitable mainstreaming adaptations for each of those classes.
2. Observe a music class with more than one mainstreamed exceptional child. Discuss the children's learning strengths and deficits with their teacher and with the music teacher. Write a short description of each child and plan a follow-up lesson. Use the form in the chapter.

Hearing Impaired Students

CHAPTER SIX

ONE MAINSTREAMING REALITY

Main Street School

It is Monday morning, and Bill Cole is waiting at the music room door for Mrs. Adams's first grade. When the class arrives, Mrs. Adams is holding the hand of a newcomer to the school and introduces Tim to Mr. Cole. At the same time, she takes off a different-looking device that is held around her neck by a cord and tells Mr. Cole he needs to wear it in music. Tim is wearing a similar device.

Mrs. Adams walks away, and Bill is left wearing an amplification device that he knows nothing about and with an additional main-streamed child (now there are *four*) in this first-grade class. The lesson proceeds as planned (see p. 86), and it is not until the listening portion that Bill has an indication that everything is not right with Tim. After Bill puts the needle on the record, he stands directly over the phonograph for a short time. When he turns around, he notices that Tim's face is all twisted up. As he moves away from the record player, the child seems to relax and his face becomes normal again.

Bill Cole makes a mental note to talk to Mrs. Adams and read Tim's file during lunch that day. He knows when he needs help! He decides to have the class sing "Sky Bears" again at the end of class so that he can stand closer to Tim and listen to his singing voice. While the class is singing, he realizes that Tim has learned most of the words correctly but that he has no pitch level indications in his singing voice. Bill thinks to himself, "Now, what day does the speech therapist come? She may be able to give me some clues about how to deal with this new problem."

What Are the Mainstreaming Problems in This Class?

The music teacher was not told what function the device served.

The teacher was not informed of the degree of severity of the child's hearing impairment.

The teacher was not told how to effectively use the unit he was given to wear.

DEFINITIONS

Public Law 94-142 contains the following two definitions, which are applicable to the present chapter.

> "Deaf" means a hearing impairment which is so severe that the child is impaired in processing linguistic information through hearing, with or without amplification, which adversely affects educational performance. . . .
>
> "Hard of hearing" means a hearing impairment, whether permanent or fluctuating, which adversely affects a child's educational performance but which is not included under the definition of "deaf" in this section. (Federal Register)

These definitions use the broad term *educational performance* as a discriminator, but authorities in the education of the deaf prefer to focus on language acquisition. A more specific definition of the two terms is offered by Moores (1982), who suggests that *deaf* and *hard of hearing* are differentiated by the function of hearing in the development of language.

One additional distinction that music educators especially need to remember is the difference between listening and hearing. Listening is the ability to pay attention to sound and is a learned skill. Hearing is the physiological process by which the body perceives sounds.

HEARING

The diagram in Figure 6-1 may be familiar to readers from their science instruction. In order to adequately understand children's files and then discuss the contents with the specialists who are knowledgeable about hearing impaired students, music educators need to be familiar with the anatomy and the function of the ear. What we normally call the ear—that part that we can see—has a different scientific descriptor, the pinna, and

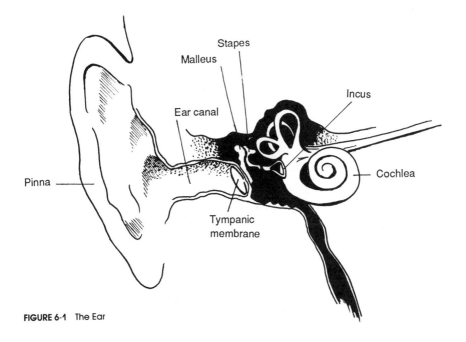

FIGURE 6-1 The Ear

acts as a type of ear trumpet, which gathers the sound waves, directs them into the ear canal, and helps us discriminate speech sounds. The middle ear begins at the eardrum (tympanic membrane) and contains three tiny bones—the hammer (malleus), the stirrup (stapes), and the anvil (incus). These tiny bones are connected to the eardrum and to each other and serve to transmit the vibrations of the eardrum to the liquids in the inner ear. The inner ear, the cochlea, has the shape of a snail shell and contains fluid, in which are found nerve endings that transmit auditory information to the brain. While this is a very simplified explanation of a most complicated process, the description is included so that readers will be able to refer to it when reading the following section, which describes the different types of hearing loss.

Types of Hearing Loss

A *conductive* hearing loss refers to damage to the outer ear, the middle ear, or both, and may be caused by accidents, ear infections, diseases, or birth defects. In small children, damage may also be caused by the insertion of foreign objects into the ear. Sound, however, can be amplified by various hearing aids, and these aids enable vibrations to bypass the outer and middle ears and be transmitted directly to the inner ear through the process of bone conduction. For some children, a conductive hearing deficit results in dissimilar acuity of contrasting (high and low) tones.

When a prospective mother contracts rubella, or German measles, there is a great risk that her child will be born with a hearing loss. This type of congenital loss is usually *sensorineural*, which means that there is a loss of sound as the result of damage to either the inner ear or the auditory nerve. Besides different types of prenatal infection, genetic inheritance can be a cause of sensorineural hearing deficits.

A third classification that music educators may read in files is *mixed* hearing loss. This term implies that the student has both conductive and sensorineural hearing deficits.

Assessment

Hearing is tested and reported in terms of frequency and intensity. *Frequency* is the cycles per second of air vibrations and is described in hertz (Hz), the standard unit for measuring frequency of sound. While humans can hear from 20 to 20,000 Hz, the most important frequencies for speech are 500, 1,000, and 2,000 Hz. *Intensity* is measured by decibels (db) with 0 db being the least sound pressure to which healthy young people can respond. Hearing loss is described in decibels above zero. A child's hearing threshold level for each frequency (Hz) is described for each ear on audiograms, which are graphlike charts prepared by audiologists. These results are often available in the files of hearing impaired children. A Pure Tone Audiogram for a child with a conductive hearing loss is illustrated in Figure 6-2 (Gerber, p. 29).

There are degrees of hearing loss, which are classified according to severity. These categories are described in terms of decibels, and one authority (Ling, 1984) lists the following groupings:

Mild: 20–55 db
Moderate: 55–70 db
Severe: 70–90 db
Profound: 90–110 db

While hearing loss is measured with pure tones, hearing impaired children are also tested and described in terms of decibels of speech reception. Speech reception thresholds are measured with the child using his or her individual hearing aid or amplification device.

Hearing Aids

Music educators should be aware that there are different hearing aids for different types and degrees of hearing losses. The determination

PURE TONE AUDIOGRAM

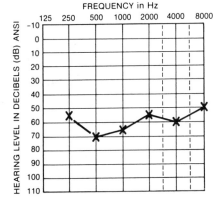

FIGURE 6-2 Pure Tone Audiogram. From S. E. Gerber and G. T. Mencher, *Auditory Dysfunction* (San Diego, Calif.: College-Hill Press, 1980). Used by permission of the authors.

of the appropriate means of managing the amplification and reception of sound is made after extensive assessment by qualified personnel. Therefore, some student will have aids that are worn at ear level, while others will use portable FM systems, which are worn on the body.

Personal ear-level aids may be fitted behind the ear or in the ear. These devices contain microphones that may be either directional or omnidirectional, and some aids may contain both types (Ross, 1982). Because the ears are still growing, in-the-ear aids are not economically viable for young children, but some music educators may teach adolescents who have been fitted with this type of aid.

Portable FM systems include units that are worn by both the teacher and the student. The teacher's unit contains a microphone and a transmitter, while the student's unit contains a receiver and a hearing aid. Music teachers must remember that the microphone is in the unit *they* are wearing, and if another class member answers a question, the teacher needs to repeat the answer so that the FM receiver can be activated. In addition, if a student is reading, performing, or in any way producing sounds to which the remainder of the class is expected to respond, the producer of the sounds should be wearing the teacher's FM unit.

Music educators who teach students wearing hearing aids will need to investigate a number of important factors in order to provide an adequate educational experience. A most important question to pursue is, What can the student hear? Does the student's hearing device amplify only limited frequencies, and will that limitation affect musical perception? A second question that must be asked is, What must the teacher do so that the student can hear? If the student wears a personal hearing aid, what is the range of the unit? A hearing aid that is effective within eight feet demands teacher behaviors different from those required for an FM training system. Personal hearing aids with a short range require teachers to continually adjust their movements so that when they speak, they are close to the hearing impaired child. When a teacher is out of optimum range, speech reaches some hearing aids as low-intensity signals: The quieter speech sounds (*s, f, th*) are lost, and speech signals are more easily masked by other classroom noise.

Teachers need to be very sensitive to the level and the sources of ambient noise in their classrooms. Noise from heating systems, overhead projectors, and instrument or music distribution can mask or interfere with the student's reception of speech or musical sounds. The management of extraneous sound within a class clearly depends upon the teacher's knowing the capabilities of the amplification being used by an individual student.

In addition to being continually aware of classroom conditions, music educators must also be aware that the degree of room reverberation can interfere with the effectiveness of hearing aids. In rooms that have little or no sound absorption qualities—such as lunchrooms and gymnasiums (and some music rooms)—it is difficult for a hearing impaired child to effectively discriminate speech from other sounds.

Readers should be aware that advances in digital technology have resulted in the invention of hearing devices that filter out distracting background noise (Today's Hearing Aids Get Smaller, Smarter, Costlier, *Portland Press Herald,* Feb. 26, 1988). However, these aids are expensive and must be individually adjusted for each wearer after extensive tests. How adaptable they will be for young children is yet unknown.

Clearly, all hearing impaired students are not similar, since degrees of hearing loss can range from mild to profound. And although students with a similar label may wear devices that improve their hearing acuity, these devices also differ from student to student. The possible variables underscore how important it is that the teacher of a mainstreamed child be as well informed as possible before beginning to adapt music instruction.

LANGUAGE

Definitions of language include several facets: It is a form of communication; it is based on a set of organized rules; those rules (grammar) are learned without being specifically taught. Most readers of this text communicate with others through spoken or written language, but signing is also a means of communication. For the hearing impaired, therefore, an alternative modality or channel (Fischer, 1982) may exist for communicating with others. For normal-hearing infants, language acquisition is a process that occurs through continual interactions with parents or other caregivers. Young children gradually learn that the sounds they are receiving have meaning and that they can express similar meaning. Through language, children are eventually able to refer to present and absent persons, places, and things.

One language theorist, Noam Chomsky, has hypothesized that infants have an innate predisposition to learn language, which accounts for the rapidity and the complexity of language acquisition during the preschool years. This predisposition explains the ability of young children to quickly learn how to expand single-word utterances into grammatical combinations for which they have not heard a spoken model.

A differing point of view is that of Jean Piaget, who described children's interactions with their environment by the concepts of assimilation and accommodation. It is through those processes that organized patterns, or schemas, are developed. Piaget believed that young children develop internal schemes of things, relationships, or situations, upon which their speech is based.

Whether one accepts Chomsky's theory or that of Piaget, all authorities in hearing impairment agree that the acquisition of spoken language by children with hearing deficits depends primarily upon the degree of hearing loss. Other variables that affect language learning include the age at onset of hearing loss, the amount of speech training, the age at which hearing impairment is discovered, the type of language input (English or American Sign Language), and the type of language output (spoken or signed).

Varied Means of Communication

The variety of communication modes used with and by the hearing impaired population is documented in a study conducted in 1978 by the Office of Demographic Studies of Gallaudet College (Jensema and Trybus). The authors reported the types of language communication used by parents and teachers of 657 hearing impaired children. Eighty percent of the parents used speech, either by itself or in combination with signs, finger spelling, writing, and gestures. About half of the teachers reported using speech as the single mode of communication. The population in the study ranged from children in residential schools for the deaf (profoundly deaf) to children mainstreamed into public schools. These findings indicate an important variable—how meaning is transmitted—that music educators must investigate when hearing impaired students are mainstreamed into music.

One manual communications mode is American Sign Language (ASL). This system is described as a language because it has a grammatical structure different from that of English. The use of hand shapes and positions combined with various facial and body movements produces a visual and spatial form of communication.

There are other manual systems used in educational settings, including Signing Exact English (SEE) and Signed English. SEE signs are produced in the order used in English, and words for which there are no signs are finger-spelled. Finger spelling involves a separate hand movement for each letter. Signed English uses ASL signs within the order of the English language. Each of these types of communication places a heavy load on visual and spatial memory—a load that is not a part of normal-hearing children's language acquisition. Music educators should note that there have been descriptions of ways to incorporate signing into music classroom and performance groups. Articles by Darrow (1987) and Knapp (1980) in *Music Educators Journal* have addressed this topic. In addition, an article in *Soundpost* (1987) reported a general music teacher's integration of signing into her instruction.

Other forms of communication include spoken or oral English, either by itself or in combination with gestures or cues. Some early-intervention programs (Ling, 1984) use only speech in conjunction with amplification devices and are most successful when the hearing impairment is determined in infancy. At that time, language can be taught in ways similar to the way in which hearing infants acquire speech. Total Communication is a term that describes the use of both oral and manual communication and may include the "use of residential hearing, speech, speechreading, fingerspelling, and signs" (Moores, p. 10).

Hearing impaired children who are not fortunate enough to be identified and receive amplification and speech training at the age when normal-hearing children acquire language are usually handicapped in English or spoken language development. And since most schooling depends on the use of spoken and printed language, the academic progress of hearing impaired children is also impeded. Quigley and Paul (1984) note that few deaf children become skilled readers and explain the various factors that contribute to successful reading acquisition.

> Where the typical hearing child brings to the reading process a substantial knowledge base resulting from a wide variety of infant and early childhood experiences which have been internalized through the spoken language acquired by interaction with parents and significant others, the deaf child typically brings to the same process a very impoverished knowledge base. This is not always due to lack of exposure to early experiences, but often to the lack of a fluent language and communication system with which to signify and internalize those experiences in some manipulatable code. (p. 137)

Another facet of cognitive and academic success is memory. Language is heard and processed in sequence, and children who rely primarily on visual and spatial forms of communication do not develop the degree of temporal mnemonic ability that will enable them to be as successful as their peers in the academic tasks that use sequential memory—namely, reading and writing.

Therefore, although some hearing impaired children may appear to have cognitive or learning deficits, the differences are probably the result of a lag in language development. A survey of profoundly hearing impaired students (Shellem, 1982) included the finding that students whose primary means of communication was speech had higher reading and language ability than those who used speech and sign language or sign alone. A language deficit also contributes to the difficulty of assessing the academic ability of hearing impaired children, since there is a lack of appropriate language-free evaluation measures. However, perhaps spoken English should not be the goal for hearing impaired children. Many within the deaf community advocate the use of ASL in residential settings, rather than the reliance on spoken speech in mainstreamed settings. It has been estimated that two-thirds of the 80,000 deaf students are presently mainstreamed, and the educational results seem fairly inadequate. "The average 12th grade deaf student reads at a fourth grade level and does arithmetic (his best subject) at a sixth grade level" (Lane, 1987).

Many linguists believe that ASL is as efficient a communication mode as English. Lane (*New York Times,* July 16, 1987) suggests that the "least restrictive environment" for a deaf child is not isolation within a class of hearing peers but placement in a setting where all interactions—communication, education, and social—are constantly possible by means of a common signed language. Indeed, it has been suggested (Quigley and Paul, 1984) that perhaps in the future, information can be imparted to users of sign language through signed videotapes instead of the traditional printed page.

HEARING IMPAIRED STUDENTS IN MUSIC

Music teachers who meet classes that contain mainstreamed hearing impaired children must, of course, become knowledgeable about the topics discussed thus far in this chapter: the degree of hearing loss, the type and capacity of the amplification used by the child, and the child's means of language communication. That information can be found in file folders and through conversations with resource teachers, speech therapists, parents, and classroom teachers. Only after the teacher has acquired that information can competent mainstreaming adaptations occur.

Many general suggestions are found in the literature that will help mainstreamed hearing impaired children to be successful participants in music instruction. One that is easily incorporated into general music classes is the use of visual aids and nonauditory cues to support and emphasize spoken speech. Some visual aids for primary grades already exist in the form of large charts prepared by each textbook company. Teacher-prepared charts can illustrate song language and verse sequence, and these charts can be made even if the teacher is not an amateur artist. The teacher can find pictures in magazines, newspapers, and coloring books that will provide visual cues for a mainstreamed child. Other charts can be prepared to visually illustrate musical concepts: Steady beat can be easily illustrated with straight lines or repeated pictures of objects as found in the Thresholds to Music Charts (Richards, 1964); melodic direction or register can be illustrated with line drawings, as can the phrase contour and the form of musical selections.

In addition, teachers must remember that the simplest visual aid—the blackboard—can provide a way of helping hearing impaired children in music class. Placing the new vocabulary, page numbers, and any other general directions for a lesson on the board will assist these learners. If teachers write on the board during class, they must remember to write without speaking and *then* turn and speak to the class.

There are other ways, of course, to assist these exceptional learners in a music class. Many hearing impaired children try to lip-read in addition to using amplification devices, and teachers can help these students by standing still in a place where light falls on their face when they do speak to the class. When teachers want to ask a question of a hearing impaired child, they should cue the child first by calling the child's name to get his or her attention and then ask the question.

Music teachers must also monitor hearing impaired children for nonverbal cues that they are confused. Directions or instructions that incorporate unfamiliar vocabulary may need to be rephrased in simpler language, but this type of monitoring can be accurate only when it is based upon a prior knowledge of the hearing impaired child's language development. Unfortunately, some hearing impaired children become "nodders" or "smilers" and use these behaviors for both understanding and lack of understanding. Thus, teachers must use carefully constructed evaluative techniques to determine a child's comprehension.

In some schools, profoundly hearing impaired students may be mainstreamed into music class. This category accounts for approximately one-fourth of the hearing impaired students in public schools. In a survey of mainstreaming practices with this population, Shellem (1982) reports that half of his sample was achieving at least two grade levels below their normal-hearing peers in academic courses. The majority of these students were educated in self-contained classes, although 79 percent were integrated into art and music classes. Of those students who were mainstreamed into music and art, only 38 percent received interpreting services.

The researcher does not discuss this finding, but it certainly is of interest to music educators. These hearing impaired students are the most severely impaired in this exceptional category and therefore the most in need of additional aids and services. One wonders if the 62 percent who did not receive interpreting were able to participate fully in music instruction. The findings in this survey certainly alert the reader to the possible difficulties (achievement, language, comprehension) that a mainstreamed hearing impaired student with a profound degree of hearing loss may have.

In music classes for older students in middle, junior high, or secondary schools where note-taking is a facet of daily music classroom instruction, hearing impaired students may need special consideration. One suggestion is to select a student who is a careful notetaker and provide either carbon paper or special note-taking or duplicator paper. Teacher-prepared outlines are another way of providing mainstreamed students with clear and complete study guides.

Instrumental teachers may also adapt any of the foregoing strategies when teaching mainstreamed hearing impaired learners. Teacher modeling of fingerings, hand positions, and correct embouchure can be very effective instruction in addition to or in place of spoken directions. Page numbers for the day's lesson or the next week's assignment should be noted visually in addition to being spoken. Most important, children with hearing impairments should not be automatically eliminated from consideration during the recruitment period by an instrumental music teacher. Those students who have the desire and motivation can be taught the musical skill of listening while being taught the techniques of instrumental playing similarly to their peers.

A report by an elementary instrumental instructor (Folts, 1977) describes the successful beginning integrated instruction of five profoundly deaf children on flute, clarinet, and trumpet. Correct fingerings on the wind instruments were indicated visually, and the trumpet player was taught to differentiate the correct pitches for similar fingerings by holding the bell of the trumpet and discriminating different vibrations. The instructor used physical motions to indicate durations and placed the students where they could see their peers to assist in rhythmic accuracy.

A successful instrumental program at a residential school for the deaf (where hearing impairments are usually much more severe than in mainstreamed children in public schools) is described by Robbins and Robbins (1980). These authors suggest that the three requirements for learning an instrument are similar for both a hearing and a hearing impaired child: good teaching, consistent practice, and positive support. They stress the importance of having hearing impaired children wear their aids during instrumental practice so that the physical motor and auditory experiences are continually reinforced.

Each hearing impaired child should be considered as an individual with particular strengths and weaknesses, and it is the music teacher's job to adapt instruction accordingly. This statement applies to both general music classes and instrumental instruction. A student with this exceptionality may need little or no consideration during class. On the other hand, he or she may require moderate adaptations or, in some extreme cases, a great deal of adaptation.

SUMMARY OF TEACHING SUGGESTIONS

Use visual aids and cues to emphasize spoken language.
Assist students who lip-read by standing still and in proper light.
Cue a hearing impaired student before asking a question.
Monitor for confusion and comprehension.
Assist older students who need accurate notes.
Provide a visual model of instrumental techniques.

The joy and pleasure that music offers to all humans can be and must be made accessible to hearing impaired students. A teacher in Maryland, Teri Burdett, described what happened when a fifth-grade hearing impaired student was mainstreamed into her music class after attending a state school with no music instruction. "I remember the first time we used the Autoharp and he held it up against himself. With all of the vibration going into his sternum, his eyes jumped out of his head! His reaction couldn't have been louder" (*Soundpost*, 1987). While this individual's musical reaction was not the typical response to which music teachers are accustomed, it was certainly an authentic aesthetic reaction—which is, after all, the ultimate goal in all of music education.

RESEARCH IN MUSIC EDUCATION

While music educators might assume that subjects with hearing deficits would not be the subjects of music research, the inclusion of this section indicates the opposite. There is not a large body of research with hearing impaired children, but there are a few studies in which rhythmic and melodic abilities have been investigated. In view of the statistics reported in the survey by Shellem that 79 percent of his sample of profoundly impaired students were mainstreamed into music, the research applicable to music education is summarized in detail in the following sections. Readers may, at some time, need to refer to these findings in discussions about proper placements of hearing impaired students.

Rhythm

Korduba (1975) compared normal and deaf (inability to hear under 85 db) third graders ($n = 30$) in tasks that measured the ability to keep a steady beat and to reproduce a rhythm pattern. The patterns were presented visually, kinesthetically, and aurally on a bass drum, and the children imitated the patterns on a snare drum. Independent judges later reviewed the tapes, and the researcher reported that the ability of the hearing impaired children to keep the beat was *better* than that of the normal-hearing subjects. However, she also reported that a metronome was used during the testing. The sound of this device may have interfered with accurate reproduction by the hearing subjects. There were no significant differences between the two groups in the ability to reproduce rhythmic patterns. The researcher describes the strategies that the deaf children employed. These included keen attention to the examiner and visual and motor attending to the production of the patterns on the bass drum. In addition, the deaf subjects counted beat impulses and attended to and imitated the body impulses of the researcher. These strategies developed during the research task and resulted in improvement in the reproduction of later and more complex rhythm patterns. This research is of interest, since the findings indicate that adequate adaptations made similar rhythmic responses possible for all subjects.

Another researcher (Kracke, 1975) also compared groups on a rhythm reproduction task. Her groups included profoundly deaf, receptive aphasic (language deficient), and normal-hearing (n = 36) and were matched for age, sex, and nonverbal intelligence. The research task involved discriminating same and different rhythm patterns that were presented both aurally and through vibration applied to fingertips. There were no statistical differences between the deaf and the normal-hearing groups.

Darrow (1983) compared the rhythmic responsiveness of normal-hearing and hearing impaired students (n = 62) using Kaplan's *Test of Rhythmic Responsiveness* (described in Chapter 2). The ages of the subjects ranged from 9 to 16, and the normal subjects were matched by age and sex. In addition, the researcher investigated the suprasegmental features of speech—rate, rhythm, pauses, and inflection. The music test was administered to the hearing impaired subjects through a portable speech audiometer (the device usually used to measure hearing loss), and directions were given by the researcher using signs.

No differences were reported between groups in the tests of steady beat, tempo change, response to metric accent, and rhythm pattern ostinato. There were significant differences between the two groups on the subtest of melodic rhythm duplication and imitation of rhythm patterns. The researcher hypothesized that the hearing impaired children's lack of musical experiences contributed to unfamiliarity with the songs used for melodic rhythm duplication. No discussion is included regarding the difference in imitation of rhythm patterns.

While these findings are of interest to the present chapter, readers must note two factors. Kaplan's test was based on the rhythmic content of textbooks for primary-age children and was constructed for children of that age. Therefore, findings of no group differences on several subtests might be due to the relatively simple rhythm content of the measure. In addition, the hearing impairment of the subjects ranged from mild to profound, and results are described not in terms of similarity of impairment but in terms of age. However, in the researcher's conclusion, she does state that "The present study found hearing status to be related to specific rhythmic skills. Degree of loss was significant only for subjects designated profoundly hearing impaired" (p. 72).

Aptitude

The same researcher (Darrow, 1987) administered the *Primary Measures of Music Audiation* (Gordon, 1979) to hearing impaired children (n = 28) in grades one through three. All the subjects had severe or profound hearing loss and attended the Kansas School for the Deaf. The test was administered through a portable audiometer, and directions were signed. Test means, reliability, standard deviations, and standard error or measurement and difference were compared with the norms provided by Gordon in the test manual. Data analysis indicated lower scores for the hearing impaired subjects on all comparisons. However, mean scores did increase by grade level, and the researcher hypothesizes that hearing impairment delays development of musical aptitude. Readers should note that this research was conducted with subjects who did not attend public schools.

Pitch

A study by Cypret (1963) used a researcher-constructed test that evaluated musical discrimination (rhythm, melody, and timbre) in a matched sample (n = 30) of hearing impaired and normal-hearing students. Subjects were required to indicate if two musical phrases were the same or different. Results indicated significant differences between the groups in all tests except the timbre measure.

Another researcher (Ford, 1985) investigated the effect of school music programs and age on the ability of hearing impaired children to distinguish same and different pitches. All subjects (n = 39) had sensorineural loss that was congenital or prelingual, and all attended residential schools. The researcher individually administered a test of pairs of complex tones during which the subjects compared the first tone with the second and made decisions of same or different. The test was given at both 250 Hz and 500 Hz. One school had a music program, but the researcher found no difference between the two groups in pitch discrimination, even though one group had had musical instruction. In addition, subjects were compared by age groups (younger mean was 8.4, older mean was 11.11), and no differences were found.

The specific intervals that the students were able to discriminate are itemized in this study; 61.5 percent were able to discriminate minor thirds and larger intervals at both Hz settings. The researcher suggests that the range from B below middle C to a twelfth above may be the optimal range for sounds with hearing impaired students (p. 90). In addition, Ford states that hearing impaired students may benefit from early experiences in discriminating large changes of pitch and that nonverbal responses, such as hand levels, body movements, and visual aids, should be used to illustrate contrasts in register.

Training

Ford's finding that her subjects could discriminate intervals even with no instruction corresponds to the finding by Gengel (1969). This researcher investigated the effect of practice on the ability to discriminate different pitches. Three groups of children were assessed: deaf, hard-of-hearing, and normal-hearing (n = 34) who ranged in age from 10 to 17. The subjects participated in three test sessions, and both hearing impaired groups made significant improvement in pitch discrimination as a result of the training. The researcher reports that half of the hearing impaired subjects discriminated differences of 4 percent (a change of a semitone equals 6 percent at these settings) at both 250 Hz and 500 Hz after limited practice. While the researcher was primarily concerned with speech discriminations, the finding that pitch discrimination improves with practice is of interest to the music educator of hearing impaired children.

An investigation of musical ability in hearing impaired children was reported by Klajman, Koldej, and Kowalska (1982). The researchers tested musical ability in 130 hearing impaired students attending schools for the deaf in Poland. Twenty-five students who received the highest musical scores received three months of musical training and then were retested. The researchers report significant improvements in test scores in this group and conclude that the musical abilities of hearing impaired children can be improved. Unfortunately, the report does not differentiate subjects by age (range 7–19) or degree of hearing impairment, and it does not indicate the researchers' training content.

Research tells us that for the hearing impaired and normal-hearing students in these studies,

> All students kept a steady beat and performed rhythm patterns similarly.
>
> The two groups performed steady beat, tempo changes, metric accents, and rhythm ostinatos similarly but differed in melodic rhythm and rhythm pattern reproduction.
>
> The hearing impaired sample had lower music aptitude scores on the PMMA.
>
> The two groups differed in the discrimination of rhythm and melody but not timbre.
>
> Music instruction did not affect pitch discrimination.
>
> Training improved pitch discrimination.

Summary

Other researchers (Darrow, 1979; Rileigh, 1971; Squires, 1982; Sterritt, Camp, and Lipman, 1966) also report the assessment of differences in hearing impaired and normal samples, but the tasks and findings are not applicable to classroom instruction of mainstreamed students. Because each of the aforementioned research projects tested contrasting populations and used different measures, it is impossible to generalize findings of musical ability in this exceptional population. It would appear (Korduba, Kracke) that when adequate adaptations are made for hearing impaired subjects, they can process musical inputs similarly to their peers. The development of pitch discrimination appears to be possible with hearing impaired subjects also. These research findings again alert music educators to the complexity of a single exceptionality label and the possible abilities that individuals with that label may possess.

CONCLUSION

The contents of this chapter clearly illustrate the limitations of our own language. The single term *hearing impaired* may indicate a child with a mild, moderate, or severe conductive loss or a student with a profound sensorineural impairment. Each descriptor will have quite different implications for the type and the number of adaptations necessary in music instruction. The implications of the degree of impairment must be addressed in combination with an awareness of the type, range, and strength of amplification available to the child. This information will help the music educator plan physical instructional adaptations. An investigation of the student's language level will provide the knowledge needed to adapt or reword questions, directions, content, and assignments.

Most students with hearing impairments do benefit from music instruction. A report (Cleall, 1983) of a young deaf musician in England included some of the subject's own words.

> I have found that low, loud noises are felt through the legs and stomach: high, loud sounds are felt through the throat and chest. The noises are either very high and loud or big, booming noises which one feels all over the body. If children were taught to feel and understand vibrations at an early age, I am convinced that this would help them to communicate, as well as making music fun. The satisfaction of feeling vibrations, and being able to communicate through music, gives deaf children the greatest pleasure. (p. 101)

These words are the best possible argument for providing appropriate and adequate music instruction for hearing impaired students. Music provides all of us with inexpressible feelings, and our job as music educators is to provide opportunities for *all* students to participate in musical perception and reaction experiences.

The research cited in this chapter does indicate that some hearing impaired children may not differ in their melodic or rhythmic responses to music. Unfortunately, anywhere from 25 to 40 percent of the children born with hearing impairments also have other handicaps. Most often, those handicaps are retardation, cerebral palsy, or both. These children, then, provide a further challenge when mainstreamed into music classes, since the hearing handicap requires specific modifications in instruction and since other handicaps may add to the adaptations needed for one child. Planning for these individuals must take into account the suggestions offered in various chapters of this text, and teachers must select those that will be most feasible for the student in their individual music class.

The focus of this chapter is on hearing impaired children who are mainstreamed into music classes. Readers who are looking for information about teaching self-contained classes of hearing impaired children will find help in the texts by Edwards (1974) and Robbins and Robbins (1980) and in the articles by Atkins and Donovan (1984); Darrow (1985); and Perkins (1979). In addition, a dissertation by Sposato (1982) describes the factors that should be considered when planning a music curriculum for the hearing impaired.

QUESTIONS

1. What is the difference between "deaf" and "hard of hearing"?
2. Describe the physical deficits that may cause each of the categories of hearing loss.
3. How are auditory pitch and loudness in hearing impaired individuals measured and described?
4. Discuss the possible sources of extraneous noise that could interfere with speech reception for a hearing impaired child in (1) a general music class and (2) an instrumental class.
5. What are the types of manual communication, and how do they differ?
6. List the reasons that may explain poorer academic achievement by hearing impaired children.

ACTIVITIES

1. Reread the section in Chapter 5 on first grade, and discuss the lesson adaptations in relation to the child, Tim, described in the opening scenario of this chapter. What additional knowledge will the teacher, Bill Cole, need to plan for this child's inclusion in music?
2. Interview a school speech therapist about the hearing impaired children in one school. Focus questions on the types of impairment, variety of hearing aids, and interpretation of audiograms in children's files.
3. Observe a hearing impaired child in a music class and discuss the ways the teacher assisted the child's audition. Describe other possible adaptations of instruction for the child based on the chapter content.

BIBLIOGRAPHY

Bess, F. H., B. A. Freeman, and J. S. Sinclair, eds. 1981. *Amplification in Education.* Washington, D.C.: Alexander Graham Bell Association for the Deaf.

Moores, D. F. 1982. *Educating the Deaf, Psychology, Principles, and Practices* (2nd ed.). Boston: Houghton Mifflin Co.

Nix, G. W. 1976. *Mainstream Education for Hearing Impaired Children and Youth.* New York: Grune & Stratton.

Ross, M. 1982. *Hard of Hearing Children in Regular Schools.* Englewood Cliffs, N.J.: Prentice-Hall.

Sposato, M. A. 1982. Implications of Maximal Exploitation of Residual Hearing on Curriculum Planning in Music Education for Hearing-Impaired Children. Ed.D. diss., State University of New York at Buffalo.

Stern, V. 1975. They Shall Have Music. *Volta Review* 75 (November): 495–500.

Swaiko, N. 1974. The Role and Value of an Eurhythmics Program in a Curriculum for Deaf Children. *American Annals of the Deaf* 119:321–24.

Visually Impaired Students

CHAPTER SEVEN

ONE MAINSTREAMING REALITY

Main Street School

Bill Cole is standing at his doorway waiting for Miss Tynan's third grade to come to music. As he hears the sound of the class coming up the stairs, he looks back into the music room and realizes that he has rearranged the room since last week's lesson. Three Orff metallophones are in a direct line from the door to where the children sit on the rug. Last week, there was a new mainstreamed child, Anna, in this class (now there are four in this class also!), and he learned during the week that the furniture placement needs to be consistent from week to week for her.

When the class gets to the door, Bill moves to Anna's side and leans over to her. "Anna, I have put out some instruments for us to play today and they are in your path, so I will help you walk around them." As the class moves into the room, Anna lightly holds the teacher's arm, and the pair walks around the obstacles.

Bill begins his planned third-grade lesson (see p. 93), and Anna has no difficulty in showing the accents during the lesson introduction. However, when he introduces the rhyme activity, he demonstrates the patting and clapping and does not verbally describe what the class is to do. During this activity, Anna only claps and does not pat the unaccented beats. Bill realizes that Anna is confused. He is unsure what to do to help her, and he doesn't want to single her out too much in her second music class.

After the class has sung the first song with rhythm instrument accompaniment, Anna raises her hand to volunteer and looks eager to participate. Before the class begins "Ain't Gonna Rain," Bill hands her a pair of finger cymbals. He picks up his guitar and gives the class the starting pitch, but Anna is not ready to play. Bill is in a quandary: Should he ignore Anna's problem and hope she'll get it sorted out by herself, or should he stop and help her hold the finger cymbals correctly? He decides to ignore her problem and has the class sing the song.

Later in the lesson, the class is offering suggestions for possible movements for 2s and 3s. Anna appears to listen carefully to the class discussion, which includes statements such as, "We could do this, Mr. Cole," "How about this movement?" and "I know what we could do." Bill concludes the class discussion by saying to the class, "Let's use Tom's idea for 2s and Tammy's idea for 3s." He then gives the class the directions for the evaluation part of the lesson. Students are to listen to a tape of phrases from the four songs in a mixed order and show the correct movement for meter in 2 or 3. During this activity, Anna stands when the class is told to stand but does not participate in the movements.

After the class leaves the room, Bill Cole makes a mental note to discuss Anna's participation with the resource teacher before she leaves the building at 12:30 that day. At lunch, Bill describes Anna's problems in music class to the resource teacher. She has only one comment: "Did you *tell* Anna how to hold the instrument and what the movements were?" Bill looks abashed and immediately realizes that future lessons for Miss Tynan's class will need very careful planning and quite different adaptations.

DEFINITIONS

The definition of this handicap in Public Law 94-142 is as follows:

> "Visual handicapped" means a visual impairment which, even with correction, adversely affects a child's educational performance. The term includes both partially seeing and blind children. (Federal Register)

The definition of legal blindness is more specific.

> A person is legally blind in the United States if: 1) vision is less than 20/200 in the better eye with corrective lenses or 2) the field of vision in the better eye is less than 20 degrees in diameter, even if the central vision is 20/200. (Kraut, 1988)

Other statements define visual impairment in relation to the ability of the person to function in society.

Partially sighted indicates that, without special aids, a person is unable to perform tasks that normally require detailed vision.

Blindness means that, without increased reliance on other senses, a person is unable to perform tasks that normally require gross vision. (Jan, Freeman, and Scott, 1977, p. 23)

Each of these definitions includes some reference to the variety of handicapping conditions found within the single chapter heading. Whether the condition is called low vision or partially seeing or refers to differences in acuity, refraction, or field of vision, readers will have already realized that, once again, a single label or category includes a variety of possible handicapping conditions. There is clearly more to visual impairment than blind and not blind.

SEEING

The diagram in Figure 7-1 may be familiar to readers from their science or biology instruction. To adequately understand children's files and then discuss the contents with specialists in the education of the visually impaired, music educators need to be familiar with the anatomy of the eye. Since the function of the eye is to receive and convert light stimuli, a loss of vision is the result of an obstruction in this process, which can occur anywhere from the cornea to the brain.

The very simplified explanation of the anatomy of the eye begins with the outermost and transparent eye covering, the *cornea*, which is frequently compared to the lens of a camera. The comparison is made because, like a camera lens, the cornea initially bends, or *refracts*, the received light rays to form an image. The colored portion of the eye is the *iris*, which surrounds the round black opening, the *pupil*. After light has passed through the cornea, it passes through the pupil and then through the lens to the retina. The *retina* has often been compared to the film in a camera, since it is the surface on which a light image is formed (Harley and Lawrence, 1984).

In normal-seeing persons who have normal refraction, the eyes are able to focus reflected light rays from twenty feet away on the retina. Some visually impaired children, however, have a refractive error, such as myopia, hyperopia, or astigmatism. *Myopia* is the inability to see objects clearly when they are far away. Students with this visual impairment may need special attention as to their seating placement when charts or the chalkboard are used in music class. In addition, some students need large print (or large notation). *Hyperopia* is the inability to see objects clearly when they are close. Some children with this visual deficit may "gaze out the window to rest their eyes, or wrinkle their foreheads and seem to strain to see their books" (Harley and Lawrence,

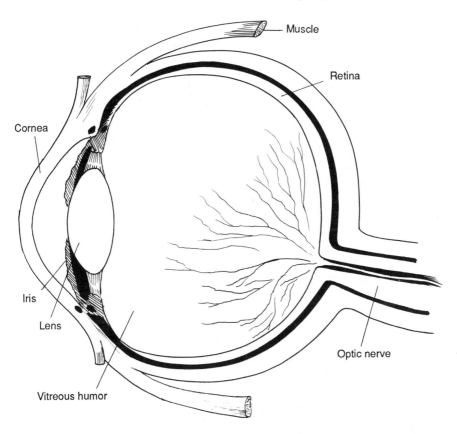

Muscle

Retina

Cornea

Iris

Lens

Vitreous humor

Optic nerve

FIGURE 7-1 The Eye

p. 122). *Astigmatism* is an uneven curvature of the cornea, which results in the reception of blurred or distorted images. Each of these refractive deficits can be corrected with lenses, and music teachers must be aware of the importance of wearing glasses to a student who has one of these visual impairments.

In education, visual deficits relate to specific academic tasks—reading and writing. The impairment is defined in terms of whether the student is able to cope with normal print or whether he or she will learn to read using the Braille system. The term *partially sighted* implies ability to use print, while *residual sight* refers to inadequate vision to read print but more vision than just light perception.

One of the terms defined on page 123 and often found in educational files and discussions is *legally blind*. This term is applied to facilitate the provision of special services for an individual, child or adult. When one is defined as legally blind, the conditions stated in the definition in terms of vision tests are met. However, some legally blind individuals may still be using vision for daily functioning.

The numerals in the definition, 20/200, are derived from the eye examination, which all readers have taken at one time or another, that uses the chart developed by Snellen in 1862. The chart was devised to measure visual acuity, the ability to distinguish the smallest possible formed retinal image. If one reads this chart and has 20/20 vision, or normal acuity, one can read the letters designated number 20 at the distance of 20 feet. If a child has 20/200 vision, he or she can read the largest letter—200—at a distance of 20 feet. The initial numeral can be changed also as in a score of 5/200, which means that the chart had to be read at a distance of 5 feet. The term *partially sighted* has been defined as covering those individuals whose Snellen test scores range from 20/70 to 20/200 in the better eye after correction (Napier, 1972, p. 103).

In addition to sharpness or indistinctness of sight as related to distance (acuity), there are also visual handicaps in which the area that the eye scans, or the field of vision, is severely impaired. It is very possible to have 20/20 vision and still be "legally blind" if adequate peripheral vision does not exist. If the periphery angle is 20 degrees or less, the condition called tunnel vision is defined as legal blindness. There are also visual handicaps in which the opposite situation (good peripheral but poor straight-ahead vision) occurs.

Music educators must note that in addition to impairments in acuity, refraction, and field of vision, there can be impairments in vision for color. Color blindness is hereditary (X chromosome), and about 8 percent of the male population have red-green blindness (Harley and Lawrence, p. 83). While not as debilitating as some of the other conditions, it must be taken into consideration by music educators who prepare graphic adaptations or visual referents that rely on color to intensify information.

Another common term that music educators may meet in reading the files of visually handicapped children is *amblyopia*, the inability of the two eyes to track together. If this condition is uncorrected, a child will overcome it by learning to ignore the visual image from the weaker eye. The weaker eye, through disuse, becomes even weaker, and blindness can occur. Fortunately, this is one visual impairment that can be corrected by either nonintrusive or surgical treatment.

VISUALLY IMPAIRED STUDENTS IN MUSIC

When one begins to consider the inclusion of visually impaired students in music classes, there are two misconceptions that might arise. Music educators might think that since a visual handicap does not affect a child's aural perception, few adaptations in music instruction are necessary. However, as demonstrated in the opening scenario, that is not at all the case. Another common misconception about visually impaired persons is that they have an unusually strong auditory ability. Auditory acuity must be developed in blind and visually impaired children—it is not a compensation that is genetically provided in lieu of sight.

There are three ways that visual impairment affects learning: limited range of experiences, restricted mobility, and fewer environmental interactions (Lowenfeld, 1973). Each of these factors has an impact on the rate and degree of cognitive development. Each factor will be discussed and then related to instructional strategies in music education.

Experience

The language development of some visually handicapped children may not be equal to that of their age-mates, since much language development occurs through visual experiences. Infants gradually learn that objects and persons have verbal labels. But this development is highly dependent on some very specific visual factors, including eye contact, gaze direction when looking at more-distant objects, and the development of gestures to communicate demands (Urwin, 1984). The lack of such prelingual experiences contributes to the slower development of language in severely visually impaired children.

Children with severe visual handicaps may have had a very limited variety of experiences with objects, which will affect their language development and conceptual understandings. It is not possible to learn details, size, or relationships from aural clues, because audition gives an idea of direction and approximate distance only. However, children who are blinded by accidents may retain visual memories of objects and size relationships, which will assist in their cognitive development. For that reason, it is most important for music educators to learn the age of onset of a student's visual impairment.

Tactual experiences adequately compensate for the inability to see most small objects, but this sense is limited. It is obviously insufficient for large objects or abstract ideas, such as valleys, helicopters, colors, or even snowflakes. In some children, the lack of adequate concrete experiences leads to what is called verbalism—a use of "empty" language (that is, lacking a clear understanding of meaning).

Therefore, music teachers must be very aware of their own vocabulary, the texts of songs, and other instructional language when teaching visually handicapped children. Asking children to move like an elephant or a falling leaf may be one fine way to have students illustrate musical contrasts. However, this direction may be meaningless to a mainstreamed child who has never seen either one and who therefore has no idea of what movement is expected.

Good teaching in music implies that no song is ever sung if the students do not understand the words they are singing. The acceptance of this common-sense rule, therefore, implies that in a class that contains a mainstreamed visually handicapped child, there will be careful consideration of song vocabulary. Words and abstract ideas that seeing children have acquired from experience or television viewing may not have been equally accessible to sight-impaired youngsters. Music teachers may need to consult the child's resource or classroom teacher every week to determine which words will need explanation or a possible concrete experience either before or in class.

Instrumental experience. Visually impaired students should not be ignored or eliminated during an instrumental teacher's recruitment time. Some visually impaired students may want to participate in instrumental lessons and ensembles with their age-mates. Certainly, the work of Suzuki in Japan has demonstrated the efficacy of instrumental experience without the need for notation. Sight-impaired youngsters can learn to play instruments, when they are interested and motivated, similar to their peers. Sending a tape of the lesson along with the child is one helpful adaptation. You may need to investigate the possibility of having materials magnified or brailled for the child and determine the availability of existing music in bold-note notation or in Braille from the Library of Congress. The National Library Service for the Blind and Physically Handicapped will send you appropriate catalogs at no cost upon request (see addresses at the end of the chapter).

A project was conducted in 1968 (Levine) in which music for five instruments (clarinet, flute, alto saxophone, cornet, and trombone) was recorded in three ways for study and use by blind students. For each instrument, two pieces were recorded at a reduced tempo without accompaniment, at the recommended tempo without accompaniment, and at the recommended tempo with accompaniment. The "Recorded Aid for Braille Music" was a set of materials that contained not only these three recordings but also a Braille transcription, a large-print copy, and the publisher's print edition. The music selected was of Grade II difficulty, described by the author as early junior high level. Unfortunately, these materials are no longer available from the Library of Congress. However, instrumental music educators could provide similar recorded aids to accompany the existing Braille editions of solos or instrumental methods texts. Additional suggestions can be found in an article by McReynolds (1988) in *Music Educators Journal*.

Mobility

Many authorities consider the most debilitating factor of severe visual impairment to be the restriction in mobility. In order for a child to become physically independent while in school, he or she must develop a mental map of space that includes such details as placement of doorways, desks, and other objects. The mental map must also include a way of remembering the distance from class to a bathroom or the library or the office. In the opening scenario, Anna had begun during the previous week to develop her mental map of the music room. Without Bill Cole's warning about the placement of the instruments in what she remembered as an open space, there could have been an accident to both Anna and the metallophones. Music teachers of mainstreamed visually impaired students must find time to allow the development of this mental spatial map. A student can explore both the room and musical materials either before class, during study hall, during recess, or during lunch.

The lack of mobility may affect children's sense of independence and their self-confidence. Often, well-intentioned adults, through their desire to protect, do not allow visually impaired children the freedom to explore and interact with their environment. Music educators must assume that mainstreamed children will be able to follow any instructions that direct independent body movement within a controlled space. Movements that require the entire class to move through the room must be structured so that the visually impaired child has a partner who will provide a spatial and body guide.

The educator most responsible for emphasizing the importance and incorporation of movement into music instruction, Émile Jaques-Dalcroze, realized that the blind would especially benefit from eurhythmics experiences. His chapter (1931) on the education of the blind contains descriptions of two of his students who used his method with blind classes. In addition, he lists many mobility training exercises that would enable more independent movement for those without sight.

It has been found that many blind individuals are able to perceive large objects or obstacles that are in their path. Researchers have discovered that this obstacle perception is the result of high-frequency sound waves reflected off the objects. This perception is inoperable, however, if there are noises (such as rain or traffic) that drown out the sound waves or if there are surfaces that absorb the sound waves. Children with no vision may appear uncannily accurate while walking through halls, but when the additional sounds associated with music class are present, their ability to avoid obstacles will be greatly reduced or nonexistent. The development of a device called the Sonicguide

(Jose, 1983) may facilitate mobility in the future even more for individuals with restricted vision. This head-mounted device employs an ultrasonic beam to locate objects within the environment and to translate their presence through an auditory signal to the wearer.

Environmental Interaction

The third limitation that affects educational performance of visually impaired children is the inadequacy of audition as a reliable and accurate environment scanning device. A loud crash in the lunchroom will turn everyone's head, but once the culprit is determined, no comment may ever be made about cause and effects. The visually impaired child who has attended only to the noise is left with an incomplete understanding of events. Similar situations occur daily in music classrooms when books, objects, or instruments are dropped. Teachers need to be alert to the implications of unusual noises, incorporating into their ordinary speech an explanation for the mainstreamed child.

The environment for visually impaired children also includes unseen objects and affective facial expressions. Sighted children enter the music room each week and immediately scan for lesson clues: A row of instruments, a new bulletin board, an open record player, or an open Big Book on an easel all have immediate meaning to the seeing child. In addition, the sighted child can easily read welcome and acceptance in a teacher's face without a word being spoken. The visually disabled child does not enter a room and immediately experience any physical lesson orientation, nor is the child able to attend to facial affective communication. Music teachers need to carefully consider both of these factors. A visually handicapped child may need a classroom orientation before every class, or a teacher may casually but carefully include statements in the lesson opening that describe the new aspects of the physical setting. Music teachers must remember also to include spoken statements of affect in addition to facial expressions.

The visually impaired child may need a verbal cue during questions so that he or she will understand if the question is directed to one child or to the entire class. In class settings, sighted children will often follow the teacher's eyes and wait for the response of the student who is the focus of the teacher's gaze. Visually impaired children need cues and clues as to what is happening during those times.

Improving the environment.   Several types of environmental adaptations are available to the music educator who teachers mainstreamed visually impaired children. The inclusion of magnification, adequate contrast, correct lighting conditions, and Braille labels will depend, however, on an understanding of the severity of each child's deficit.

Magnification is a type of adaptation often used for sight-impaired children and can include the use of both larger print and larger music notation. When preparing materials, music educators must also consider the clarity of contrast on the page or chart. The greatest contrast is black print on a yellow background, and the use of a buff-colored paper can also reduce glare for some students. Teachers must be very careful not to use mimeographed sheets with faint or purple print, since these may only provide frustration for a visually impaired child.

There are many different types of devices used for print enlargement, including the photocopier, hand-held and stand-type magnifying glasses, large-print typewriters, and electronic magnifiers that interface with computers. Music teachers should investigate the type of technology being used to assist visually impaired children and determine if there are ways of using the equipment to prepare music class materials.

Teachers should also consult with resource or special educators of visually impaired children to determine the most efficacious lighting for the music room. Children with poor vision can benefit if adequate brightness is provided and if conditions that produce glare are eliminated. The type of natural and artificial light used may need to vary depending upon the weather conditions and the number of windows. A simple action such as never standing in front of a window while teaching will be beneficial to some sight-impaired children, since natural light through a window can also produce a glare.

Braille.   At one time, Braille was used with children who had poor vision as a way to "save" their sight. That is no longer an educational practice, since it has been determined that sight does not dissipate through use. Braille is now taught only to children whose visual impairment prevents them from reading print.

Braille is a system of reading by touch that was invented in 1829 by Louis Braille, who was blind. The system uses combinations of six dots in a group or cell, some of which are raised or embossed. For example, the first three letters of the alphabet are as follows:

a	○ •	*b*	○ •	*c*	○ ○
	• •		○ •		• •
	• •		• •		• •

In addition to single-letter designations, there are combinations for letter sounds such as *ch* and for common words such as *and* or *the*, and there are also combinations for contractions, which save time in tactual reading. There is also a special form of Braille that can be used for music.

Examples of this system (Krolick, 1979) are as follows:

Double Bar ○ •   ○ •   *Fermata* ○ •   ○ •
              • •   • •   ○ •   ○ •
              • ○   ○ •   • ○   ○ •

Braille notation is never taught unless Braille reading has already been mastered, because it is a very complicated system with separate sets of symbols for the left and right hands. In addition, to use Braille notation, one must memorize the symbols before producing music—a complex memory task that is not required of sighted musicians.

Mainstreamed blind children who are learning to read using Braille should be accommodated in music instruction whenever possible. It may be possible to have materials brailled for the child by volunteers, or it may be possible to gain access to a Thermoform Brailon Duplicator machine, which makes Braille copies of music symbols. The Braille symbols for xylophone bar or Autoharp key letter names can be made using braillabel sheets (clear plastic with an adhesive back), which are used in a brailler.

Children who use Braille as their means of reading are not at risk in their early education, since all children read fairly slowly for the first two or three years. However, Braille reading is three to four times as slow as print reading (Jan, Freeman, and Scott, 1977). Therefore, once a student has mastered the initial task of reading, other technologies are commonly used to provide a faster reading or learning pace. These include tapes of "talking books" and the Optacon. Talking books are recordings or cassettes that are prepared by the National Library Service for the Blind and Physically Handicapped, part of the Library of Congress.

The Optacon is a portable machine with a hand-held scanner, which the reader slides over a print page. The machine transforms the print into a tactual form, one letter at a time, and this tactual form is regular print, not Braille. The use of this device by legally blind students in reading music notation has been described by Bruscia and Levinson (1982).

Students with low vision will not require Braille adaptations, but there are other ways that a music teacher can assist these children in obtaining maximum use of their vision. One suggestion is to use pieces of yellow acetate, which can be purchased at office supply stores, and place one over a printed page to increase contrast and print darkness (Todd, 1986). Another classroom suggestion is to use a reading frame with a window cut out, which the child slides down a page to expose one word or line at a time. This instructional adaptation has been previously suggested for some learning disabled readers (see p. 50). Advances in computer technology have also resulted in new (but expensive) equipment to magnify print from a printed page onto a television screen.

Sensory Adaptations

Auditory adaptations. Because of the importance of audition to the blind or visually impaired student, music teachers must be very sensitive to the aural input that they provide. Our auditory environment has increased in extent and intensity during the past few decades. Bennett Reimer (1970) has described the omnipresence of sound as "aural molasses," but for many environments, that is now a mild descriptor. In homes where television and radios provide a constant sound barrage and in shopping malls and restaurants, which provide a continual musical accompaniment to every activity, visually impaired persons must ignore the ever-present sound for survival's sake! Unfortunately, this constant bombardment of sound does not provide environmental clues but, rather, masks them. In addition, constant sound may result in visually impaired children (as well as nonimpaired children) who become nonlisteners.

The act of listening consists of three subskills: attending, identifying, and assigning meaning. For visually impaired children, as for all children, these aspects of listening must be considered in music planning. Directing children to listen to a song or a record with no specific reason is just poor teaching. Students of any age with or without a disability are able to daydream if they are not directed to attend and respond to a specific aspect of music.

Identifying sounds and assigning meaning can be continually incorporated into music instruction and may occur at very different levels within a single lesson. Simple examples include: "Say the name of the person next to you and then pass the ball with the beat of the music," or "Play the cymbal when we sing the word *day*." Much more complex examples involve attending and understanding the significance of musical interactions and experiencing an aesthetic reaction. In classes that include visually impaired students, all listening must be accompanied by very clear directions so that selective and meaningful listening will occur.

But students must be given something to listen for. As illustrated in the opening scenario, a music educator must be especially alert to demonstrations of movements and activities without verbal descriptions. This type of instruction leaves the visually impaired child without any clue as to how to participate. Teachers need to incorporate the articulation of directions while showing them to a class in order to provide necessary but unobtrusive adaptations for the visually handicapped child.

Haptic adaptations. Children with severe visual impairment are not born with a keener sense of touch than their peers but, rather, are taught to use the haptic sense as a means of increasing their knowledge of the environment. A mainstreamed blind learner in music will need opportunities to hold each rhythm instrument and associate the shape, material, and texture with the sound it produces. This learner will also need special opportunities to feel vibrating surfaces, whether they be strings attached to an Autoharp or bars on a xylophone.

The use of graphic representations in sound (ikons), which has previously been described, is a useful intermediate step between experience and notation for young children. These illustrations can be translated into appropriate media for sight-impaired youngsters also. Representations of steady beat, metrical grouping, register, phrase contour, or form can be made with textured materials such as string, yarn, cotton, pipecleaners, and fine sandpaper, or they can be created by using a tracing wheel on aluminum foil. Musical concepts can also be illustrated by the use of manipulative objects ranging from rods or Popsicle sticks for steady beat to sets of varied felt shapes for form.

Many of the series texts include listening maps to direct students' attention to specific musical events in a piece of music. These maps can be adapted for visually impaired students through enlargement and reproduction on a copying machine and the subsequent attachment of different textures. These additions can intensify the direction and sequence of events and the musical highlights.

SUMMARY OF TEACHING SUGGESTIONS

Consult resource teachers about abstract song vocabulary and movement directions.

Tape music lessons.

Investigate the need for magnified or brailled materials.

Provide a consistent placement of objects in the music room.

Structure partner movement activities to provide a guide for visually impaired students.

Include explanations of unusual noises.

Consider the auditory environment.

Provide haptic experiences with instruments, textured notation, and listening map representations.

Adapt the visual environment through magnification, clarity of contrast, use of appropriate technology, and consideration of lighting conditions.

Have materials, labels, or directions brailled when appropriate.

Summary

The term *visual impairment* is used in this text and in public education to describe children with a wide range of handicapping conditions. The educational implications and adaptations for a child who has absolutely no usable vision are very different from those required for a child who has the ability to see at a distance of a few feet. Inasmuch as about three-fourths of the visually impaired children in public schools do have some usable vision (Barraga, 1976), the application of the suggestions in this chapter must certainly be on an individual basis.

The investigation of a visually impaired student's deficits must include attention to the student's prior experiences, language level, and degree of mobility. The environment in music can be adapted for this student in many ways, depending upon the degree of disability. For students with usable vision, magnification and an attention to adequate contrasts in visual material may be sufficient. For students with no sight, a variety of Braille adaptations will be necessary. All visually impaired students will benefit when careful attention is paid to their two senses that are intact: the auditory and the haptic.

RESEARCH IN MUSIC EDUCATION

The research included in the final section of this chapter is indeed meager. There is one study of rhythm, one of musical ability, and one of mental imagery associated with sounds. In addition, a cognitive assessment developed for use with the visually impaired is summarized. Graduate students who are looking for a fertile research area should consider musical ability, aptitude, or achievement in the sight impaired as possible topics.

A research study by Rosenstein (1957) included a group of ten blind children in addition to equally matched sets of normal, deaf, and aphasic children, ages 11–13. The deaf and the blind subjects attended residential schools for their disabilities. The researcher administered the rhythm test from the *Seashore Measures of Musical Talent*, which requires discrimination of same and different patterns, and all respondents used a tactual form of response. The mean of the blind subjects was significantly better than the means of the other three groups. This finding, of course, should not be surprising, since the subjects must have had extensive tactual training while learning Braille and thus had a sharpened sensitivity, which differentiated them from the other subjects.

The musical ability of blind children was compared with a matched group of sighted children ($n = 220$) by Pitman (1965). The researcher administered the *Wing Tests of Musical Ability* and used an alternative method of response for all subjects. The overall scores for the blind group were significantly higher than those for the control sample. The subtests in which the exceptional population excelled were as follows:

Test 1, in which the student estimates the number of notes in a chord; Test 2, which involves detecting the direction of a note change in the second playing of a chord. On two other subtests, the visually impaired scored slightly better. Those were Test 3, which is a melodic memory test, and Test 5, in which the student expresses a preference for harmony when the melody is replayed with a different harmonization. These results are partially attributed to an increased concentration on aural input during general instruction.

The researcher concluded that despite the overall statistical superiority of the blind sample, the scores were affected by the greater deviation within the group. This conclusion is supported by a reference to the range of scores. The researcher also indicated that the musically talented blind children in the sample had received concentrated aural training and this additional prior musical experience skewed the scores on the tests.

However, since the test was administered to the sighted sample in the same manner as to the blind children, the advantage of the blind sample may also have been due to a familiarity with a tactual response mode. This possibility was noted by the researcher, who stated that since there were no differences between the groups in a test of English using the same tactual response, the superior musical results of the blind sample must be due to within-group skewedness. Readers of this text, however, will remember the earlier discussion of slower language acquisitions in visually handicapped students. The two groups simply may not have been adequately matched.

Walker (1985) replicated an earlier study that investigated mental imagery associated with sound by means of the visual externalization of four pure tone sound components: frequency, amplitude, duration, and timbre. The response sheet used with 224 sighted subjects in 1981 was transformed into Braille, and 11 subjects (ages 8 to adult) were asked to indicate which of four shapes corresponded to the sound in the test. The responses of the earlier test indicated that pitch was matched with vertical movement, loudness with size, duration with horizontal movement, and texture with wave shape. The blind subjects in this study did not differ significantly in their responses from the earlier sample.

The development of a cognitive assessment for therapists' use with young children is described by Browne (1984). The test is based on a test developed by Rider (1981), designed on a Piagetian model, and can be used with blind, visually impaired, and nonverbal children, ages 2–7. The Auditory Perception Cognition Profile (APCP) measures fifteen behaviors, including two-beat imitation (spoken, clapped, played on a drum); matching instrument sounds; imitative imagery (using bells, Autoharp, drum to imitate an animal moving); tempo, duration, and loudness discrimination; and conservation of rhythmic pulse, auditory beats, tempo, and duration. The APCP was administered to both non-handicapped (n = 250) and handicapped (n = 65) children, and interobserver, test-retest, and intertester reliabilities are reported at about 90 percent. Those teachers who have the services of a music therapist in their school may wish to investigate the use of this measure and incorporate the results into the IEP development.

Research tells us that some

> Blind children discriminate rhythm patterns better than a matched population when a tactual response is used for all subjects.
>
> Blind children score higher than sighted children in musical ability when a tactual response is used for all subjects.
>
> Blind children do not differ from sighted subjects in their mental imagery of sound.

CONCLUSION

Teachers of self-contained classes for blind children will find additional information and instructional suggestions in the chapter by Graham (1975), as well as in articles by Herlein (1975), Kersten (1981), Lam and Wang (1982), and Mooney (1972) in *Music Educators Journal*. Of interest to some teachers may be a study by Cormier (1980), which describes music for the deaf and blind student. A description by Manion (1986) of teaching piano to two blind adolescents is applicable to private teachers.

Music educators who use handbells in classroom instruction may want to read the account by Lewis (1974), who developed a simplified Braille notation for blind students. The author describes other strategies that supported successful participation in this ensemble. Each student played within only one octave and always played the same bells. The conductor provided cohesion during initial rehearsals of a piece by providing an auditory steady beat, which assisted in unifying the rhythm.

A teacher of a self-contained blind class or a teacher in a residential school might be especially interested in owning a copy of the dissertation by Kersten (1979). This impressive document contains detailed descriptions and analyses of materials and methods for the visually impaired from 1891 to 1978. Teachers of mainstreamed visually impaired children also might be interested in this document because of the extensive lists of method books and texts that are available in Braille or large print. For example, the fourth- and fifth-grade books in the *Silver Burdett MUSIC* series have been brailled and are available from the Johanna Bureau for the Blind and Visually Handicapped in Chicago.

The *Belwin Brass Method* in Braille can be obtained from the American Printing House for the Blind in Louisville, Kentucky.

Music educators who teach mainstreamed visually handicapped children are faced with a challenge that requires continual monitoring of language, directions, and materials. To provide adequate music instruction for mainstreamed learners of any exceptionality, teachers must assume the stance of a diagnostician—using one adaptation, judging its success or failure, and deciding what to try next. In this way, an appropriate music education can be provided for these students.

One researcher (Bishop, 1986) investigated the characteristics of mainstreaming success with visually impaired students as noted by teachers, parents, principals, and the students themselves. One important conclusion was that successful mainstreaming depends on the continual collaboration of the many professionals who have daily contact with the child. Some of the mainstreaming suggestions in this chapter are just not realistic possibilities, considering any single music teacher's daily schedule. Providing successful music instruction for a mainstreamed visually handicapped student requires the assistance of other professionals, aides, and perhaps community volunteers. Other important factors that contribute to mainstreaming success for visually impaired students included an accepting and flexible teacher, peer acceptance, available support personnel, and adequate supplies and equipment. A music educator may have to advocate strenuously for the last two, but the 304 respondents of this researcher's survey felt they were important variables that contributed to mainstreaming success.

Each child, with or without handicaps, deserves the opportunity to participate fully in musical experiences throughout his or her public school education. The job of music educators it to accept every student as an individual and find the ways to make musical success possible. Most of the ways will be within the classroom—some may be outside the music room. A teacher who fully understands the disability of each visually impaired learner and what is necessary for that student's musical success will be prepared to adapt his or her own instruction and advocate for additional help when it is needed.

QUESTIONS

1. Discuss the difference between legal blindness and blindness.
2. Describe the different types of visual handicaps.
3. Provide examples of how experiences with objects can be incorporated into music classes that include mainstreamed visually handicapped learners.
4. Discuss why it is important that music educators monitor their language when teaching visually impaired students.
5. Describe the types of adaptations possible for music notation.

6. What strategies will contribute to success in instrumental music instruction for visually handicapped students?
7. Why will visually impaired and blind children require differing movement considerations in music class?

ACTIVITIES

1. Prepare lesson-plan adaptations for the visually handicapped child, Anna, who was described in the opening scenario of this chapter.
2. Observe a music class that does not contain a mainstreamed visually impaired child, and describe the ways that the environment and the instruction provide implicit nonverbal cues that would need to be made explicit for a visually impaired student.
3. Observe a music class that includes a mainstreamed visually impaired child, and describe the instructional adaptations and the child's musical participation.

BIBLIOGRAPHY

GRAHAM, R. M., ed. 1975. *Music for the Exceptional Child.* Reston, Va.: Music Educators National Conference.

HARLEY, R. K., and G. A. LAWRENCE. 1984. *Visual Impairment in the Schools* (2nd ed.). Springfield, Ill.: Chas. C Thomas.

JAN, J. E., R. D. FREEMAN, and E. P. SCOTT. 1977. *Visual Impairment in Children and Adolescents.* New York: Grune & Stratton.

KERSTEN, F. 1979. An Analysis of Music Education Methods and Materials for the Visually Impaired Synthesized from Documents Written between 1891 and 1978. D. Ed. diss., Pennsylvania State University.

SCHOLL, G. T., ed. 1986. *Foundations of Education for Blind and Visually Handicapped Children and Youth: Theory and Practice.* New York: American Foundation for the Blind.

SOURCES

American Printing House for the Blind, Inc.
1839 Frankfort Avenue
P.O. Box 6085
Louisville, Kentucky 40206

Johanna Bureau for the Blind and Visually Handicapped, Inc.
30 West Washington Street
Chicago, Illinois 60602

Library of Congress
National Library Service for the Blind and Physically Handicapped
Washington, D.C. 20542

Recording for the Blind
215 East 58 Street
New York, New York 10022

Physically Handicapped Students

CHAPTER EIGHT

ONE MAINSTREAMING REALITY

Iroquois School

The music teacher, Miss Phelps, has just closed the door to her room and has settled the twenty-seven fourth graders into an organized seating pattern on the bottom three risers. Her room contains five carpeted risers, which are initially level with the door and which then move down to a small flat space in which the piano and the phonograph are kept. The door opens noisily and a wheelchair is pushed into the room. The aide locks the wheels and leaves the child, Donna, seated at the back of the room. Miss Phelps does not acknowledge the presence of an additional class member and continues to assign book monitors for the day.

The lesson for these fourth graders is on meter and the two contrasting rhythm patterns in "Hill an' Gully" (*MUSIC and You*, Grade Four, p. 121; see Figure 8-1).

The resonator bells for a pentatonic scale are already placed on a music stand, and Miss Phelps begins with a review of last week's lesson, which emphasized the particular sound of this scale. After a discussion of omitted notes and a comparison of the sounds of two scales, major and pentatonic, Miss Phelps evaluates the ability of the class members to differentiate the scales by asking the children to raise one hand whenever she plays the pentatonic scale. After each scale is played, Donna tries to lift her arm but cannot succeed in the short response time. The teacher does not acknowledge Donna's attempts to participate.

140

After the class has learned the new song, Miss Phelps follows the lesson plan in the teacher's book. The children discover the two types of meter signatures at the beginning of the song, and Miss Phelps then has the class echo-clap the two eighth-note patterns in the first line. Donna barely has her hands together when the activity is finished. Then Miss Phelps assigns rhythm instruments for the even eighth-note pattern and F resonator bells for the last measure of each line. Donna is not given an instrument, since Miss Phelps knows that she cannot hold instruments without dropping them.

Ten minutes before the class is finished, the door opens and the aide returns to take Donna to lunch. Her self-contained class has lunch at the same time as the second grade, so she never stays for the entire music class. Neither the class nor Miss Phelps pays any attention to the child in the wheelchair as she leaves.

Why Is Donna in This Class?

The decision to place Donna in this fourth-grade music class was made by the principal, who is following a district ruling. The superintendent instructed all administrators that every exceptional child was to be mainstreamed into music, art, and physical education classes. The teachers at Iroquois School are not consulted as to appropriate placement but receive, during the first week of school, a list of mainstreaming decisions, which are obviously based on schedule convenience.

Several factors prevent Donna from receiving an adequate musical education. One is the physical arrangement of the music room. A teacher who is instructing twenty-seven informally seated children does not want to move up the risers and thus be out of eye contact with the entire class very often. A second factor is lack of knowledge about the individual mainstreamed learner. Donna is the only child at Iroquois who is in a wheelchair, and the art and music teachers have not received any instructions or information regarding her abilities or disabilities. Obviously, when mainstreaming decisions are made without teacher cooperation, a lack of concern for the education of these children is implicitly conveyed to the teaching staff.

DEFINITIONS

There are two laws that affect the education of children with physical disabilities in public schools. The first, Public Law 94-142, contains the following definitions:

> Orthopedically impaired means a severe orthopedic impairment which adversely affects a child's educational performance. The term includes impairments caused by congenital anomaly (e.g. clubfoot, absence of some member, etc.), impairments caused by disease (e.g. poliomyelitis, bone tuberculosis, etc.) and impairment from other causes (e.g. cerebral palsy, amputations, and fractures or burns which cause contractures). . . .
> Other health impaired means limited strength, vitality or alertness due to chronic or acute health problems such as a heart condition, tuberculosis, rheumatic fever, nephritis, asthma, sickle cell anemia, hemophilia, epilepsy, lead poisoning, leukemia, or diabetes, which adversely affects a child's educational performance. (Federal Register)

In addition, Section 504 of the Rehabilitation Act of 1973 addresses accessibility for the handicapped in public buildings and facilities.

No otherwise qualified handicapped individual in the United States, as defined in section 7(6), shall, solely by reason of his handicap, be excluded from the participation in, be denied the benefits of, or be subjected to discrimination under any program or activity receiving Federal financial assistance. (U.S. Code and Administrative News)

Physical Handicaps

The term *physically handicapped* has the immediate implication that the extent of a student's movement capabilities or stamina is restricted. The condition may be temporary—such as a broken limb caused by an accident—or permanent because of a birth defect. As will be clear in this chapter, the term covers a wide range of conditions, from the treatable (diabetes) to the more complex (cerebral palsy) to the terminal (Duchenne muscular dystrophy).

Most teachers have coped with the student who has a temporary physical handicap. Usually, the student is excused early from music class with an accompanying peer to get to his or her classroom safely, whether by stairs, by elevator, or just through the halls on one level. Temporary accommodations include using a music stand for a textbook holder for a child with a broken arm or providing a chair for a choir member who has a broken leg. These physical disabilities are the easiest for music educators to cope with because the student's mental and physical capabilities were known before the accident occurred.

Students with physical disabilities since birth present a different impression to teachers because of the difficulty in thinking of the student as an individual separate from the disability. Teachers must remember that any physically handicapped student is first and foremost an individual, not a handicap. This chapter contains a plethora of information about varying handicaps, but music educators must not be overwhelmed by all this information. There is still only one approach that will ensure success for each mainstreamed physically handicapped student: Determine the learning capabilities of the individual and adapt instruction for that individual.

This approach is nicely described in two personal accounts, one by a music educator and one by a physically handicapped student. In an article in *Music Educators Journal* (1972), Clark Eddy describes how he adapted instrumental instruction for a fourth grader who wanted to play clarinet. The child had only one intact digit, her left thumb, and only stubs for fingers. The writer discussed alternative instruments with the child and her mother and finally decided that she might be able to press the buttons on a mellophone. He also describes her later successful instrumental experiences playing the French horn. The author movingly describes his feelings when he realized that the child had no fingers.

Barbara said excitedly, "Mr. Eddy, I don't think you understood me this morning. Do you think I will be able to play a clarinet?" She put her little, outstretched hands into mine. When I looked down at them, my heart came up into my mouth. For almost a full minute, I was unable to speak. (Eddy, p. 61)

The student's point of view is found in an article by Mike Teplitz (1985). The 15-year-old author has cerebral palsy and is a member of a marching band. In the article, he describes the most exciting day in his life—when he "marched" in the Tournament of Roses Parade in his wheelchair, to which were attached a tambourine, a cymbal, and a triangle. His band director also accommodated his chair during the band's performances at football games. He found a stationary position for Mike in the percussion section during their regular halftime shows. The student has played percussion instruments and participated in band since elementary school. He expressed his feelings about marching in this famous parade as follows: "It was so special for me because I wasn't really 'special.'"

Most educators are unable to articulate their feelings as clearly as Clark Eddy when they are faced with permanently physically handicapped students, and, certainly, few students write articles about their musical experiences for national magazines. Indeed, such articulation is not a necessary process in music teaching or learning! But music educators need to understand that a child who "appears" different often causes feelings in the teacher that may not be immediately recognized. The opening scenario of this chapter presents one reaction—to completely ignore the student's presence. (That is not a fantasy scenario— the author saw it happen in a music class.) It is hoped that readers of this chapter and this text will be able to recognize their own initial feelings and immediately move beyond them to the task of musically educating the individual student.

Finding appropriate instructional strategies for these students depends upon the use of the same approaches described in previous chapters. Music educators must first understand the general causes, characteristics, and degrees of disabilities. Then they must determine the specifics that apply to the mainstreamed student. The final step involves adapting, whenever necessary, instructional materials and activities to enable the student to learn successfully. Each of these topics is covered in the remainder of this chapter.

Characteristics of Various Disabilities

Cerebral palsy. Individuals with cerebral palsy demonstrate movement and posture disabilities that are the result of damage to the motor areas of the brain or the spinal cord. Such damage usually occurs prior to or during birth. There are three important factors that differentiate students with cerebral palsy. Through professional discussion and reading files, music educators should determine the type, the part of body that is affected, and the degree of impairment. After determining those important aspects, teachers can begin to contemplate individual instructional considerations.

Three classifications of cerebral palsy are spastic, ataxic, and athetoid. About half of all children with cerebral palsy have the *spastic* type: They move very stiffly and expend a great deal of energy and effort in controlling their muscles. *Ataxic* individuals have injury to the nerves that are involved in equilibrium and will experience difficulty with their sense of balance. Students with *athetoid* cerebral palsy demonstrate excessive motion whenever they try to move and even speak. It is also possible for students to be diagnosed as having more than one type of palsy; this is called *mixed.*

The second descriptor identifies which body parts are involved and uses the terms *monoplegia, hemiplegia,* and *quadriplegia* (Fraser and Hensinger, 1983). It is quite rare for only one limb of the body (monoplegia) to be affected by cerebral palsy. Hemiplegia denotes involvement of only one side of the body and implies that the muscles of both arm and leg are involved. This classification fits the self-description of the boy who participated in the Rose Parade. Quadriplegia indicates dysfunction of the muscles of all four extremities, and often the head and the trunk as well.

The most important classification, however, is the term that describes the degree to which the child is handicapped. These terms— *mild, moderate,* and *severe* (Bowley and Gardner, 1972)—indicate more clearly the types of instructional strategies needed for individual learners. A child with mild cerebral palsy can walk and talk but may have some awkward movement patterns. Students having a moderate degree of impairment may have an unsteady walk, indistinct speech, or problems in controlling their hands. Those with severe cerebral palsy are nonambulatory and often have severe speech impairment.

In addition, many children with cerebral palsy have other disabilities that will affect their learning. About half of the students with cerebral palsy are also retarded, and another 15–25 percent may have other problems (Apgar and Beck, 1972), which include hearing or visual impairments, epilepsy, and speech deficits. While those are sobering percentages, readers must remember that the same statistics indicate that it is also possible for a child with cerebral palsy to have normal or above-normal intelligence.

Spina bifida. This term describes the unusual formation of the spinal column that occurs prior to birth. The normal spinal column consists of hollow vertebrae, which contain nerves. In spina bifida, one or more of the vertebrae fail to form a complete circle and the nerves do not develop and grow through these bones—the term literally means "cleft spine" (Edgington, 1976).

Children with spina bifida do not have a singular motor disability. Some children may have slight damage, while others may be totally nonambulatory. In addition to damage to the motor nerves, effects may include loss of sensation to pain and lack of bladder and bowel control. Children with spina bifida often also develop hydrocephalus (excess fluid in the brain), but this is now routinely treated with a bypass operation (Apgar and Beck).

Readers will note that the foregoing description discusses only motor damage. When severe, spina bifida certainly affects the child's mobility, but unless the hydrocephalus has not been treated in time, it may not affect the child's intellectual functioning at all. Also, because of the location of the spinal damage, there is usually not any damage to the motor functioning of the individual's arms and upper trunk.

Muscular dystrophy.   The type of dystrophy most often met by educators in school situations is that which affects young males, Duchenne dystrophy. This genetic disease is progressive, and boys who have it usually die by their midteens. The attendant motor problems develop progressively. Initially, there is difficulty climbing stairs and a lack of stamina. As the disease progresses, the child may wear a back support to enable him to remain upright while using a wheelchair. The last muscles to be affected are the finger muscles, and they are usable long after the child has been confined to a wheelchair.

Certainly, this disability is the most affecting of any described in this chapter. Adults who teach any student with a terminal disease must struggle not to display pity or feelings of inadequacy. What these children need from music class is similar to what all children need—opportunities to participate equally in expressive musical experiences and occasions to experience musical perception and reaction.

Cystic fibrosis.   Children with cystic fibrosis are less noticeable in public schools because they are ambulatory. However, the condition affects one's ability to participate in activities in a normal manner, and the student with this diagnosis must be carefully considered in instructional decisions. Cystic fibrosis is a genetic disorder in which an enzyme needed by the body is not produced. This enzyme affects the production of mucus and saliva. Secondary effects include the body's inability to resist respiratory infections, and often the excessive mucus produced by the body also interferes with food digestion (Apgar and Beck, 1972).

There are several attendant problems that a teacher must be aware of when children have this medical diagnosis. One obvious effect is a persistent cough, which is not contagious and which is the body's reaction to the unusual mucus collection in the lungs. In addition, children with cystic fibrosis have reduced stamina and may be absent from school a great deal. Since their digestion is affected by the enzyme imbalance, these children may have unusual appetites (presumably not noticeable in music class), which may result in the need for abnormal restroom use.

Other physical impairments. *Juvenile rheumatoid arthritis* is an inflammation of the joints, with varying degrees of severity and resulting impairment (Miller, 1982). The inflammation is treatable (usually with aspirin), and most children eventually outgrow the disease. When the joints become acutely inflamed, the child may use a wheelchair or crutches. Even after the disease has become inactive, excessive straining or jarring of the joints must be avoided.

Limb deficiency may be congenital or may be the result of amputation necessitated by disease or accidents. Children with these physical handicaps must be considered on an individual basis in terms of physical abilities. Obviously, any adaptations must fit each particular deficit.

Juvenile diabetes is a chronic but controllable disorder with few implications for the music educator who teaches the child once or twice a week. It is important to recognize that a child with this disease may occasionally display insulin reactions, which can result in unusual behavior or a lack of attention (Christiansen and Hintz, 1982). Uncommon behaviors should be immediately described to the child's classroom teacher or to the school nurse so that the student's medication level can be checked by qualified professionals.

Other physically handicapping conditions can be the result of asthma, hemophilia, heart disease, and sickle-cell disease. Each of these, and any other physical disorder, should be thoroughly investigated by reading records and by holding discussions with parents, classroom teachers, and school health personnel. The music educator who has a clear understanding of a child's abilities will be in a position to adapt instruction to accommodate a child's disabilities.

You may have noted that many of the foregoing individual labels cover a wide range of disabilities from mild to severe. The presence of such a possible range within each of the terms, as well as within the term *physically handicapped,* is vitally important to remember when a child with one of these conditions is mainstreamed into your music class. Merely knowing the label that denotes a physical handicap will not provide a music educator with the information needed to adequately adapt instruction.

LEARNING AND INSTRUCTION

Students who are physically handicapped often differ from their peers in outward appearance, and they may also lack similar prior movement, play, or speech experiences. Children who have been nonambulatory since birth have had vastly inferior interactions with the physical environment. Children with severe cerebral palsy who are unable to easily grasp objects have not had the multiple play experiences that enable children to develop object and spatial comparisons. Youngsters who have poor motor control that involves the speech apparatus may not have been motivated to continue to try to produce communicative sounds when their huge amount of effort seems to receive no response from others.

Children without physical disabilities who begin school at age 5 bring to school a wide background of physical and mental interactions, upon which later cognitive learning is based. Many physically handicapped children are lacking in these important early experiences. Understanding that these limitations may be present in the learning background of some physically handicapped students is an essential part of providing adequate instructional adaptations.

Children who are physically handicapped have an additional difference in how they learn. The singular disadvantage for these students is that they always have a barrier in their lives that cannot be removed. That barrier is their inability to negotiate freely in their environment. When normal children meet a barrier of any kind, they use either speech or movement to negotiate the obstacle. Physically handicapped children cannot negotiate barriers easily.

Another way that physically handicapped children may differ from their peers in their learning is in their need for time. Many physically handicapped students take a great deal of time to accomplish what is done quickly by their age-mates. Some may need extended time just to articulate a response. Recognizing that need and providing opportunities for the students to respond and participate is an important facet of competent mainstreaming accommodation.

Other possible learning differences have been researched in children with cerebral palsy (Sears, 1985). Some children with spastic cerebral palsy may have disturbed tactual perception and discrimination. Students with ataxic palsy may lack an awareness of their body movement in space, may have a poor body concept, and may have poor spatial relationships. In addition, there is a greater incidence of visual and auditory problems in these children than in the general child population. Mainstreaming children with multiple handicaps implies that the music educator must consider the child's learning from several viewpoints and adjust and adapt instruction accordingly (see Chapter 11).

Adaptations

Adaptations for nonambulatory students.   Mainstreamed students who are confined to wheelchairs will need some special consideration. These learners are usually able to independently maneuver their chairs through the spaces found in the school. The music teacher's responsibility is to ensure that the child has adequate space to move the chair in the teaching area. Some children in wheelchairs may need assistance in manipulating the leg rests. On some chairs, the leg rests can be released and swung toward the back of the chair, while on others, the leg rests are lowered and then folded up. The most important fact to remember about a wheelchair is that it must be locked when it is stationary, especially if the child is getting out of or into the wheelchair. Young children may need constant reminders to lock their chairs until the act becomes a habit.

Because of federal legislation, new school buildings must be wheelchair-accessible. Unfortunately, many older buildings, including some places to which teachers may take students on trips, are not. Most music teachers take large groups of students to various musical functions outside their own building. When one of these field trips is planned and a nonambulatory student is included, the teacher must check ahead of time for wheelchair access. If the trip is to an auditorium, the teacher must find out if there are steps into the concert space. Other factors to be considered ahead of time include the accessibility of toilet facilities, a place for a wheelchair to be placed during the concert, and the availability of a bus with a wheelchair lift, if the student needs one.

An important decision that must be reached by the music teacher and other school personnel is what procedure to follow if the nonambulatory child is in music and there is a school emergency. While the undergraduate reader might think that this is a rare occurrence, practices for this eventuality occur many times throughout the school year. In most states, there is a legally required number of unannounced fire drills each year. The procedure for safe movement of a wheelchair-bound child from the music room to the outside of the building must be discussed and established at the beginning of the school year.

Some important steps for lifting and carrying physically handicapped children may apply to emergencies. These include the following (adapted from Landecker, 1980):

LIFTING

Establish eye contact.
Speak to the child.
Allow the child to respond and offer you physical help.
Ask the child to help.
Lift the child gently.

PREVENTING TEACHER INJURY

Bend knees and keep back straight.
Avoid twisting, lift directly in back or in front or to the side of the child.
Keep the child's body as close to yours as possible.
Give the least amount of help needed.
If possible, walk the child backwards or sideways rather than carrying him or her.

Because one of the five activities generally recommended and widely accepted as necessary in elementary music instruction is movement, adaptations for nonambulatory students must be a part of the planning process by music educators at this level. Directions for creative movement can be given to include the body parts that a physically handicapped child *can* manipulate easily. Children who are very proficient at maneuvering their chairs may be able to participate in slower structured dances or circle movement activities. Others may need to have their chairs pushed by a classmate.

At times, however, it may be necessary to plan alternative activities for a class member who cannot move as quickly or in an intricate pattern. It may be possible for a primary student to move a puppet or a rag doll similarly to his or her classmates. Whatever alternative is planned, the activity should always reinforce the musical learning rather than simply be a way for the child to "feel included."

Each of the three published music series includes suggestions for mainstreamed students. One example that suggests a movement alternative for physically handicapped fifth graders (by the author of this text) is found on page 208 of the teacher's edition of *MUSIC and You* (Macmillan, 1988). The lesson begins with movement to introduce the dotted-quarter and eighth-note pattern. The mainstreaming suggestion reads as follows:

> When planning the activity to "set the stage" for this lesson, consider the physical abilities of the students in your class. If movement is not possible for any student, plan to use rhythm instruments to reinforce the difference in sound between the even and uneven rhythms and have any physically handicapped student(s) play these instruments.

Adaptations of materials.   In addition to planning movement alternatives for physically handicapped students, there are many other types of adaptations that will enable mainstreamed children to participate more completely in musical activities. Some of these changes are quite simple; others are more complex and may be found in the student's classroom or resource room. It is not possible to suggest an adequate adaptation for each of the physical disabilities described earlier in this chapter. What follows are a number of suggestions that can be incorporated into classroom instruction, depending upon the type and severity of a mainstreamed student's physical impairment.

A number of suggestions for helping children grasp a pencil can be adapted to assist children in grasping and holding different rhythm instruments. For example, some rhythm instruments that are shaken may be fastened to children's arms or hands with Velcro strips. Other ways to make it easier to grasp a maraca or a jingle clog or a drum beater include expanding the handle by wrapping it with clay, masking tape, or rubber bands. An instrument handle can also be placed through a rubber ball or a foam rubber hair curler.

If the instructional activity involves using a piece of paper for an evaluation, some physically handicapped students may need assistance in keeping the paper in one spot on their writing area. Two simple but effective suggestions are to use tape and to attach the paper to a clipboard.

An excellent source for instrument adaptations is the paperback by Clark and Chadwick entitled *Clinically Adapted Instruments for the Multiply Handicapped,* published by Magnamusic-Baton (1980). This compilation includes sections that describe how to adapt picks, beaters, shakers, and wind instruments. In addition, the authors describe ways to construct stands and frames for students who cannot hold any instrument. While the book is primarily directed to music therapists, it contains helpful and effective suggestions for music educators of students with severe physical deficits.

Many other types of furniture and equipment are available for handicapped students that may be used in instructional settings other than music. One of these is a standing table—a waist-level table containing a circular cutout that enables the student in a body brace or a wheelchair to work more comfortably. Students may also use automatic page turners, special typewriters, computers, or electronic communication boards. The type of equipment available depends on the particular needs of the student and, of course, on the financial ability of the school district to supply this equipment.

It may be possible to incorporate each piece of equipment into the student's music instruction. The first part of the music teacher's inquiry, therefore, is to determine *what* the child uses in other school locations. The second step is to decide if these additional aids will really help the learner overcome physical obstacles in music instruction. This determination must be based on careful consideration of the learner and the nature of the music class content. Music teaching depends upon involvement in music making at all levels, but, fortunately, our aural art depends very little on the modes of instruction prevalent throughout most of the other subject areas—the extensive reading of texts and the constant written assignments.

Other adaptations. It may also be necessary to adapt language input or response with a physically impaired child. Alternative ways of communicating with students whose cerebral palsy has affected the motor speech apparatus will have been established by parents and other teachers. For example, some students may use a series of established gestures, while others may use a communication board. This device contains pictures, symbols, or words that the child can point to, and the content is changed as the child grows. An electronic communication board not only has the symbols or words but also provides the speech output (Fraser and Hensinger, 1983).

Instrumental teachers must also adapt the same three strategies as classroom teachers when recruiting beginners and a physically handicapped child is in that grade level. An awareness of the cause of the disability and the instructional implications are two preliminary steps. Considering the possible adaptations for the student will depend both on teacher observation and on discussion with the child's parents and other teachers. Earlier in the chapter, there was a description of how one instrumental teacher helped a student choose an appropriate instrument (mellophone) for her physical disability (incomplete extremities). The teacher's written description implies a rather quick and, fortunately, an accurate judgment call.

A contrasting approach is contained in a report from Germany (Probst, 1985) that describes the training of instrumental teachers to work with the handicapped. The teachers motivated student interest and observed the students during a three-month period prior to actual instrument selection. One facet of this instruction was the use of games, during which the teachers observed the motor and sound-producing abilities of physically handicapped students. In addition, the three months of preinstruction were centered on the instruments the students could choose. The instruments taught ranged from trumpet to guitar to accordion.

The two preceding approaches achieved the same result! Children who were physically handicapped learned to produce and experience music in a manner they and others thought was not possible because of

their disabilities. Instrumental teachers need to provide such an opportunity for *all* motivated students whenever possible.

SUMMARY OF TEACHING SUGGESTIONS

Provide adequate space for wheelchairs.

Investigate concert locations for wheelchair accessibility.

Plan fire drill procedures for a class that includes a nonambulatory student.

Adapt movement activities to emphasize functional body parts for handicapped students.

Include students in wheelchairs in structured dances.

Plan alternative activities for nonambulatory students that reinforce musical learning.

Incorporate appropriate adaptations for holding instruments or for paper-
and-pencil tasks.

Investigate the applicability of special furniture or adaptive equipment
and technology.

Adapt instructional language or response modes when necessary.

RESEARCH

This section will include research from both music education and the
general field of education that may assist readers in future discussions of
mainstreaming. There is only one music education research report that
included this handicapped population. It is hoped that readers of this
text will be interested in filling the research gap and will seize the
opportunity to investigate this exceptional population. Perhaps such
future projects will provide the profession with additional information
that will assist in improving instruction for physically handicapped
students.

A report by Moog (1979) describes the rhythmic testing of three
groups (*n* = 75) of 10- and 11-year-old children who were either
physically disabled (with normal intelligence), of low intelligence, or
nonhandicapped. The assessment of rhythmic similarities and differences included three difficulty levels. Subjects did not use a paper-and-
pencil response but, rather, raised either a green card for "same" or a
dissimilar-shaped red card for "different." The researcher reports significant differences between the scores of the physically handicapped and
the nonhandicapped subjects. In fact, Moog concludes that "Limitations
of movement since earliest childhood reduce perception of rhythmic
forms in all test parts nearly to the extent of low intelligence" (p. 77).

One nonmusic area that has been researched is the self-concept of
physically disabled students (Harvey and Greenway, 1984). The 9- to
11-year-old subjects (*n* = 51) included three groups: a physically

handicapped group attending a normal school, a physically handicapped group attending a special school, and a nonhandicapped control group. The instrument used was the *Piers-Harris Self-Concept Scale for Children*, an individually administered scale that contains statements that the children either agree or disagree with. Examples of these statements are: "I am a happy person," "I have pretty eyes," and "I am strong." The researchers report no differences between the group of physically handicapped that attended a normal school and the group that attended a special school. There was a finding of a lower self-concept in the total handicapped group when compared with the control group. "The presence of the physical handicap was associated with a lower sense of self-worth, greater anxiety and a less integrated view of self" (p. 280).

Another social topic that has been pursued by researchers is the attitudes of nonhandicapped peers toward the physically handicapped child. A review of the literature (Westervelt and Turnbull, 1980) includes a description of the three techniques used in this research: viewing pictures of nonhandicapped and handicapped children and answering a question such as "Which child do you like best?"; viewing pictures and answering questions (Social Distance Questionnaire) that do not involve ranking, such as "Would you want this person in your class?"; and sociometric techniques—used when a physically handicapped child is a member of the class and in which children list the class members they would choose as friends.

This review includes findings that children as young as 5 and 6 preferred nonhandicapped to handicapped in the assessments that used pictures. Several studies are summarized that included similar rejecting attitudes. However, one project that used a sociometric measure found no differences in the number of friend choices in a junior high school classroom. It is unclear whether the younger children in these research studies had experienced any actual interactions with physically handicapped peers. This factor may differentiate students' reactions.

Summary

Students with physical disabilities may have poorer rhythmic abilities than their age-mates because of a lack of prior movement experiences. Students who are physically handicapped may also have a poorer self-concept and may not be socially accepted by their peers. For some of these exceptional students, music may provide one of the few settings for social acceptance and success if classroom interactions are carefully structured by the teacher.

CONCLUSION

Readers of this chapter are now aware that many types of physical handicaps can be found in student populations. Within each category, there exists a range of possible conditions from mild to severe. This multitude of possibilities makes it impossible to generalize how a physically handicapped student will be able to participate in music. Only when teachers have an understanding of a student's deficits and abilities will they be able to structure adequate musical learning experiences.

The importance of assessing the individual attributes of main-streamed students is suggested by the findings of researchers (Center and Ward, 1984) who identified the characteristics related to academic and social success in a group of cerebral-palsied children. The students were identified as having mild, moderate, or severe disabilities and were administered a battery of fourteen tests. Neither academic nor social success was related to the degree of the handicapping condition. Rather, academic success was most strongly related to cognitive ability, and social success was strongly related to a high level of self-esteem.

Musical success for individual students may also be highly dependent on these two factors. Cognitive ability and self-esteem are individual attributes over which a music teacher has little control. The facets of instruction that can be modified by a music teacher relate to physical accommodations, understanding individual differences, and accepting students who do not look the same as their peers. Successful main-streaming in music certainly will be possible if teachers determine what the student *can* do. Music educators need to structure and experiment with different instructional adaptations to find the ways that individual students can experience music to the maximum extent possible.

The information in this chapter should provide a base upon which music educators can develop an open and accepting attitude for physically handicapped students. Teachers must remember that funny-looking or different-looking kids who move differently or hold an instrument awkwardly are individuals who deserve to have the same valid and valuable musical education as their peers. While their physical abilities may be less, their cognitive abilities may be equal to or even superior to those of many of their peers.

Many barriers in education have been overcome for these students. Doors have been widened and ramps built. Computers have been purchased and rhythm instruments adapted. Students in wheelchairs have participated in circle dances or have learned to play an instrument. But one possible barrier remains. That barrier is found within an individual teacher who does not believe that physically handicapped students can learn music similarly to their classmates. This attitude can be tacitly communicated to students, and it will form a barrier that an exceptional student can never overcome. Communication of acceptance and positive feelings will not allow this barrier ever to be erected in a music room. It is hoped that this chapter has pointed out ways for teachers to eliminate all possible future barriers to music learning for mainstreamed physically handicapped students.

QUESTIONS

1. Why do teachers have different perceptions of students with temporary physical handicaps and those with permanent physical handicaps?
2. What are the three possible ways that students with cerebral palsy may be differentiated in school records?
3. Which physical handicap descriptors indicate a possible range of disability?
4. What aspects of instruction can be changed for students who are confined to wheelchairs?
5. Describe additional possible adaptations for instruments or materials that might be used in music instruction of physically handicapped students.
6. Discuss the one barrier that physically handicapped students cannot overcome.

ACTIVITIES

1. Write a lesson plan for the opening scenario that includes specific adaptations for the mainstreamed child.
2. Interview two experienced music teachers and discover the number and types of physically handicapped children they have taught. Include questions that focus on specific instructional and material adaptations used by the teacher.
3. Physically handicapped students may have obvious learning differences, and some also have less obvious experiential deficits that affect learning. Describe three music teaching situations and discuss how both types of learning deficits could be accommodated for physically handicapped youngsters.

BIBLIOGRAPHY

APGAR, V., and J. BECK. 1972. *Is My Baby All Right?* New York: Pocket Books.

BLECK, E. E., ed. 1982. *Physically Handicapped Children: A Medical Atlas for Teachers.* New York: Grune & Stratton.

COATES, P. 1986. Piano Sessions for the Handicapped. *The American Music Teacher* 36 (September): 27.

EDGINGTON, D. 1976. *The Physically Handicapped Child in Your Classroom*. Springfield, Ill.: Chas. C Thomas.

ELLIOTT, B., et al. 1982. *Guide to the Selection of Musical Instruments with Respect to Physical Ability and Disability*. St. Louis: Magnamusic-Baton.

ERICKSON, L. B. 1973. Keyboard Fun for Children with Osteogenesis Imperfecta and Other Physical Limitations. *Inter-clinic Information Bulletin* 12 (January): 9–17.

FRASER, B. A., and R. N. HENSINGER. 1983. *Managing Physical Handicaps*. Baltimore: Paul H. Brookes Publishing Company.

LIEBMAN, J., and A. LIEBMAN. 1973. On Stage *Every*body, Music Theatre for Physically Handicapped Children. *Music Educators Journal* 60 (October): 45–46.

MICHAL, E. T. 1987. Teaching Piano Skills to Handicapped Persons through Use of Systematic Instruction: A Proposal. Doctoral dissertation, Ohio State University, D.A.I. 48/05-A, 1051.

Emotionally
Disturbed
Students
CHAPTER NINE

ONE MAINSTREAMING REALITY

Unity Lane School

It is Friday afternoon, and the music teacher, Miss Pauls, is preparing to enter the last class she must teach this week. (Unity Lane had a music room until last year, when it was needed for a "new" third-grade class.) Her cart with phonograph, instruments, and books is beside the door, and she is waiting for the signal from the classroom teacher that the second-grade children are ready for music.

Miss Pauls checks her watch again and begins to get concerned when the door is not opened several minutes after the assigned time. She can hear the teacher's loud voice and the movement of desks and chairs and knows that she has not been forgotten. Finally, eight minutes late, the classroom teacher opens the door with the words, "Sorry, Miss Pauls, but some of us had a hard time with Friday." The classroom teacher mutters on her way out, "They're all yours!"

The group of second graders is sitting quietly on the carpet, and Miss Pauls begins to pass out the textbooks. As she looks around, she realizes that there is a new student in the class. She leans over and in a whisper asks one child what the new boy's name is. The child, Jason, is not sitting with the group but is sitting in the "time-out" chair with his face to the wall. One of the children hands Jason a text, but he knocks it from the child's hand.

Miss Pauls ignores this interaction and asks the class if anyone can remember what happened to the sounds of the "Hot Dog" song (*Holt*

MUSIC, Grade 2, p. 44) when they sang it last week. One student identifies the upward and downward direction of the melody, but no one remembers the correct term. The teacher takes out the eight resonator bells, and the children wave their hands, wanting to be chosen. Jason does not raise his hand.

After the scale review, Miss Pauls follows the text lesson plan (pp. 54–55) and begins to teach the children to recognize scale notation. Jason begins to hum and make occasional screeching sounds during this part of the lesson. The children tell Miss Pauls that Jason did this earlier and that is why he is sitting alone. She walks over to Jason, picks up his book, opens it to the correct page, and asks him to turn his chair around so that he can follow the lesson. Jason moves his chair and holds the book but does not stop humming.

Miss Pauls returns to the front of the class and begins again to emphasize the melodic structure of "One Potato, Two Potato" by using the bells and the notation. As she continues, she realizes that Jason's sounds have stopped. She looks back to where he was sitting. The chair is empty! Jason is crawling on the floor between the legs of the many desks and chairs.

She continues to teach the rhythm of the song and selects eight children to play the accompaniment. As the children stand in front of the class, Jason crawls out from under the nearest desk and silently watches the bell players. At that moment, the door opens and the classroom teacher comes in, sees Jason, and takes him back to the "time-out" chair. The entire class watches Jason and their teacher, who retrieves her plan book from her desk, softly says, "Sorry, Miss Pauls," and leaves the room.

Miss Pauls returns, once again, to the lesson and takes her packets of matching numbers and notation phrases from her cart. She gives the children careful instructions about selecting a partner they can work with. Jason turns around in his chair, and she asks him if he would like to play her game. Jason nods his head. The class is completely paired off, so Miss Pauls walks back to Jason's chair and tells him she will be his partner. After she sings the first phrase, Jason takes one of the cards and throws it in the air. She picks up the cards for that packet and returns to the front of the class. Jason sits silently during the rest of the lesson.

The following Monday.   Many times when a child transfers from a school in one community to a school in a different town or state, the transfer of school records does not occur with the same speed. Jason is a new transfer student from a town several hundred miles away. His records did not arrive at Unity Lane until after this Friday music class. When Miss Pauls goes to the office before school on Monday to read his file, his classroom teacher is just reading it for the first time. The two teachers read that Jason has been tested and has been found to be emotionally disturbed. The school psychologist and his previous classroom teacher had been following a carefully structured behavior modification plan with Jason. His time-out was always limited to one minute, and he received a reinforcement every time he demonstrated a positive classroom behavior.

The classroom teacher looks at Miss Pauls and says, "I'll see Dr. Douglas at lunch today, and by the time you come on Friday, perhaps we can have a working plan so we both can teach. I hope I never have another week like last week!"

DEFINITIONS

The definition of seriously emotionally disturbed found in Public Law 94-142 is as follows:

> The term means a condition exhibiting one or more of the following characteristics over a long period of time and to a marked degree, which adversely affects educational performance.
>
>   A. An inability to learn which cannot be explained by intellectual, sensory, or health factors
>   B. An inability to build or maintain satisfactory interpersonal relationships with peers and teachers
>   C. Inappropriate types of behavior or feelings under normal circumstances
>   D. A general pervasive mood of unhappiness or depression
>   E. A tendency to develop physical symptoms or fears associated with personal or school problems
>
> The term includes children who are schizophrenic or autistic. The term does not include children who are socially maladjusted, unless it is determined that they are seriously emotionally disturbed. (Federal Register)

A definition of emotional disturbance that attempts to encompass all aspects and clarify meaning is offered by Newcomer (1980).

> Emotional disturbance is a state of being marked by aberrations in an individual's feelings about him- or herself and the environment. The existence of emotional disturbance is inferred from behavior. Generally, if a person acts in a manner that is detrimental to him- or herself and/or others, he or she may be considered in a state of emotional disturbance. (p. 6)

Readers will note that, like each of the previously described exceptionalities, this handicapping label is heterogeneous. A careful reading of the list in the federal definition shows that there is great ambiguity in that definition; indeed, of all the other definitions cited in this text, only the definition of learning disabilities (Chapter 3) may be more vague. Certainly, it will not be as easy to recognize an emotionally disturbed student as it is one who is visually, hearing, or physically disabled. But as illustrated in the introductory scenario, often the unusual behavior of a student will alert music teachers to the fact that the student may require careful attention in the planning and execution of instruction.

MODELS

In addition to the imprecision of the language found in the definition of emotional disturbance, there is the added confusing factor that more than one model is used to diagnose, treat, and control students. These models are the medical (based on disability or biology), the psychoanalytical (based on personality disturbance), and the behaviorist (based on deviance or conduct). Music educators need to be familiar with these disparate points of view, since the model adapted in a school for diagnosis and treatment strongly affects not only the individual learner but also each teacher who interacts with the student.

If emotional disturbance is defined from a medical perspective, there is a specific diagnosis of an illness by a medical doctor (psychiatrist), which affects and implies the type of treatment that will be used. These diagnoses include such terms as *schizophrenia, psychosis, neurosis, psychopathy,* and *autism.* The patient is informally observed (usually not at school but in a clinical setting), diagnosed, and treated by the doctor, and often there is very little communication with interested educators. The medical approach is based on finding ways for the individual to adapt rather than be cured, and the approach often includes a heavy reliance on drug therapy (Newcomer, 1980).

Closely related to the medical model is the psychodynamic or psychoanalytical model. This approach is based on the premise that changing overt behavior is less important than dealing with the underlying causes of the behavior. Implicit in this approach is the working out of anxieties and the development of a healthy ego. The therapist does try to change the patient, since the underlying conflicts are initially unconscious: Subsequent resolution of these previous disturbances provides the needed insight for change. If this diagnosis is made by a psychologist, the child is tested with a battery of standardized measures (intelligence, perceptual-motor, auditory, visual, personality development) to ensure that the child's problem does not stem from other factors. This approach relies on the psychological theories of Freud and others, and its use with children has been described in the writings of Redl (1966) and Morse (1976).

The behaviorist model of emotional disturbance is based solely on the observation of maladaptive or disruptive behaviors that affect learning. This model is used by educators, not medical personnel, and a student's overt behavior is measured and compared through careful (often timed) observation and record keeping. Behaviorists believe that all behavior is learned (and thus can be unlearned) and that the only behaviors that are important are those which can be observed, quantified, and compared. This model is based on stimulus-response learning theory expounded initially by Pavlov and later by Watson, Thorndike, and B. F. Skinner.

Of these three models, only one is education based—the behaviorist model. The other two approaches depend on the testing or diagnosis of either psychiatrists or psychologists, and medical treatment is provided by those specialists. Unfortunately, sometimes in educational settings, there is little or no interaction between concerned teachers and the medical specialist. Some music teachers may discover that a student is receiving such outside assistance only through chance conversations with the student or the parents.

BEHAVIORS

Emotional disturbance is the one handicapping condition that is primarily defined by one's behavior, and, in fact, many readers may live in states or areas where the more socially acceptable term *behaviorally impaired* is used to describe the same handicap. Some behavior generalities that are used to describe this exceptional population include atypical, deviant, aggressive, anxious, inattentive, and neurotic. As can be imagined, such vague terms make it much more difficult to determine who is truly emotionally disabled, since most students, at one time or another, display some degree of deviance, aggression, anxiety, and so on.

Emotional disability is a complex handicapping condition, and music educators should be aware that many of the behaviors exhibited by these students will arouse negative reactions in the teacher; these students rarely arouse feelings of pity or inadequacy. It is much more likely that teachers will feel bewildered by and often quite hostile toward students whose behaviors disrupt instruction.

The following list (Newcomer, p. 107) indicates the possible range and variety of behaviors that emotionally disturbed students may exhibit.

1. Attention to classroom activities (inattention, daydreaming, withdrawal)
2. Physical activity (restlessness, hyperactivity, noisemaking)

3. Reaction to tension (emotional upsets)
4. Appropriateness of behavior (telling tales, collecting objects)
5. Meeting work requirements (self-criticism, giving up, not working)
6. Interest in work (playing, doodling, drawing)
7. Getting along with others (name-calling, fighting, passivity)
8. Consideration for group needs (impatient with others, interrupting others, talking out loud)
9. Response to teacher requirements or instructions (arguments, rudeness, disobedience)
10. Degree of independence (seeking praise, attention, support, currying favor)
11. Regard for school rules and conventions (swearing, smoking)
12. Regard for general rules (truancy, tardiness, destroying property)
13. Integrity (cheating, tattling, stealing)

At this point, readers, especially those who have never taught, may begin to feel overwhelmed. Do remember that each child will not exhibit all thirteen behaviors! Also remember that each school includes resource teachers, a psychologist, guidance counselors, and a principal, all of whom are concerned with providing educational structure and success for the mainstreamed child. All these personnel will be willing and able to help a music teacher who teaches a mainstreamed emotionally disturbed student.

At the same time, it should be clear to readers that it may not be a simple matter to teach classes into which emotionally disturbed students are mainstreamed. Such classes may require considerable amounts of teacher patience, effort, and persistence. Additional competencies include objectivity, flexibility, organization, energy, resourcefulness, and common sense—all descriptors of competent teachers. There are some specific strategies that will facilitate more successful teaching and learning in music classes that include these students; those strategies are described in the following sections.

Consistency

For itinerant teachers who interact with the child only once or twice a week, the most important factor in classroom management is providing consistency. If the teacher is a "cart pusher," the rules and behavioral expectations within the regular classroom must be followed during music. If the teacher has a room or a space to which individuals or classes come for instruction, the behavior expected of the emotionally disturbed child must remain identical to that expected of the regular class. Of course, this consistency can be provided only if the music teacher knows exactly what rules and consequences are utilized by the student's teacher.

Music teachers may also need to provide consistency from week to week or from period to period within their own class. Many factors can contribute to a stable learning environment for an emotionally disturbed child. Physical order, an absence of distractions, or the same arrangement of chairs may be very important. Teachers who follow the same routines in passing out materials or in lesson format may supply needed structure for the student. Teacher language also needs to be very carefully structured. Major choices or important decision-making opportunities should not be directed to students who are incapable of dealing with uncertainty.

Providing Choices

Beginning teachers often have difficulty differentiating between asking and telling. Telling implies no choice, whereas asking indicates that the class, or an individual, has at least two alternatives. Common statements used by inexperienced music teachers include "Did you like that song?" and "Would you like to sing (listen, dance, play instruments) now?" The teacher has not thought ahead to the possibility that the students will say no and how the teacher will then respond.

Teachers of classes with mainstreamed emotionally disturbed students must carefully consider when to give choices and when to give commands. The following are a few examples of when to give an option: (1) when either choice is acceptable and the true intent is to accept either choice; (2) when dealing with a student who is extremely emotional and noncompliant; (3) in situations for which no follow-through for noncompliance has been established; (4) when the child is more reliable and compliant and the goal is independence and maturity (adapted from Browning, 1983, p. 52).

Teachers should monitor their teaching and understand that providing options may cause negative behaviors in some disturbed students. Such a simple direction as "find a partner" or "make a group of four people" or "choose another child to play the drum" can cause a possible disruption. Planning and listing groups or assigning each student a number, a letter, or a shape, and clearly stating how combinations or choices are to be made, will help to eliminate many possible problems.

Behavior Modification

Because of the prevalence of the behaviorist approach in the education of the emotionally disturbed, music teachers should have an understanding of operant conditioning and know the terminology used by those who employ this theory. Basic to this point of view is the belief that all behavior is learned and can be modified through the use of reinforcement. Some of the terminology that may be used by resource or classroom teachers and with which music educators should be familiar include the following:

> *Reinforcement:* Any occurrence after a response that increases the possibility of recurrence of the response. Examples of reinforcers are food, tokens, praise, stars, and free time. Reinforcement can be positive or negative.
>
> *Praise:* Praise must sound pleasing and exciting to the child. It must be very clear and refer precisely to a specific behavior.
>
> *Reinforcement schedules:* How often the reinforcer is used. Some possibilities include after each response (continuous), every few seconds or minutes (fixed), or after a certain number of responses (fixed ratio).
>
> *Shaping:* A procedure in which a complex skill or behavior is separated into incremental small steps and the successful completion of each step is reinforced.
>
> *Extinction:* Removing a reinforcer to decrease the frequency of the behavior. For example, when a teacher ignores a student's constant tattling, there is no reinforcement (teacher attention) for the behavior.
>
> *Time-out:* Removing the child from any opportunity for reinforcement.

Many teachers and parents use the time-out procedure as a discipline device. If it is used within the confines of behavior modification and suggested as a discipline device for the music educator, several factors must be remembered. The child should know in advance the specific behaviors that will result in time-out, as well as how long the time-out will last. The time-out should be quite short (one to five minutes), since the child may quickly forget what occurred before the punishment was given. The teacher must assign time-out with as little attention and emotion as possible and must use it *every* time the undesired behavior occurs. If the student does not follow the time-out, there must be a clear knowledge of the possible consequences. Finally, when the time-out is finished, there should be no attention given to the return, and a reinforcement for a positive behavior should occur as soon as possible (adapted from Hall, 2, p. 39).

A complete and quite concise description of behavior modification can be found in two small pamphlets published by H & H Enterprises, Box 3342, Lawrence, KS 66044. The titles are "Managing Behavior 1" and "Managing Behavior 2," and both are by R. Vance Hall. Readers are strongly urged to invest in these or in another description of this approach if it is used in the management of emotionally disturbed students where they teach.

A note of caution must also be inserted at this point. There is not universal acceptance of behavior modification, and, indeed, there are some very serious criticisms, which music educators should be aware of. As should be clear after reading the foregoing section, the focus is on very simple behaviors and the principles listed may not be useful when applied to more complex problems. Proponents of the approach appear to reject the importance of any affective or cognitive aspects of learning, are often overcommitted to the behaviorist model, and are often unable to consider alternative approaches (Apter, 1982).

LEARNING AND INSTRUCTION

It is clear that children who are emotionally disturbed may present special behavioral problems in music class. These students have been described as "behavioral misfits at school, likely to cause the consternation of teachers, and almost certain to be avoided or rejected by their peers" (Cullinan, Epstein, and Kauffman, 1984, p. 18).

Will students who are labeled emotionally or behaviorally disordered also exhibit learning differences? Readers will remember that the federal definition indicates that educational performance is affected by the emotional disturbance. There are mixed research findings that describe attendant academic deficits in this exceptional population. Different researchers have concluded that from "one-third upward to 80 percent" (Cullinan, Epstein, and Lloyd, p. 256) of behaviorally disordered students also had academic problems.

Other researchers have compared exceptional students to learning disabled groups. Scruggs and Mastropieri (1986) concluded that the academic performance of behaviorally disordered primary students was slightly below average and quite similar to the performance of a learning disabled sample. Epstein and Cullinan (1983) concluded that intermediate-age behaviorally disordered students had higher academic performance than their learning disabled peers. The type and degree of severity of academic deficits is yet another variable that must be investigated by music educators who teach any group that includes a mainstreamed student.

Mainstreamed students with academic and emotional or behavioral problems are an important reason for music educators to pay careful attention to the *how* of teaching in conjunction with planning the *what*. Most of the adaptations for these exceptional students must be completed during the planning phase. When preparing for class activities, performance rehearsals, or instrumental lessons, music educators must decide what is to be taught, how the students will learn, and how the teacher will decide that they have learned. This process is certainly nothing new—all readers will probably have practiced these steps in writing objectives for methods classes or in actual classrooms. However, when thinking and writing out goals and objectives for a group that contains a mainstreamed emotionally disturbed child, the teacher should try to pinpoint and forecast the times when the child may be unable to cope with the class expectations and should plan alternative strategies.

What are these times? In general music classes that involve several activities, the times between sections of the lesson need to be carefully thought out. These include any or all of the following transitions: between sitting and moving, between exchanging instruments, when passing out materials or texts, when choosing a partner or forming a group, and when entering or leaving the room. In instrumental lessons or performance classes, these transitions include the setup time before instruction, the transitions between rehearsal selections, and the times when the teacher is directing his or her attention to one student or one section.

How should a teacher's planning address these transitions? The most important aspect is acknowledging, prior to teaching the class, that it is during these occasions that the child may be unable to cope. For example, teaching children that there are five steps to follow before an instrumental lesson (sitting down, opening the case, assembling the instrument, putting music on stand, putting practice sheet on stand) and listing the steps on a bulletin board provide a clear structure, as opposed to the general direction "Get ready while I fix this saxophone for Wendy."

General music teachers must plan the unstructured times in their lessons also. Writing a musical term on a poster and placing it on an easel outside the door can provide a focus for organized entry into the room (for example, lento, presto, piano, forte). Or a set of preparatory steps similar to those in the instrumental lesson may be posted. Clear directions must be planned so that students continually know what is expected of them. A direction such as "Put the instruments away," which provides an opportunity for chaos, should be replaced by a specific direction such as "Will the drummers quietly put their instruments on the bottom shelf (or cart) while we open our books to page 26." The end of a general music class is often a very unstructured time, and emotionally disturbed children may lack the needed control to follow the vague direction "Line up quietly." Clear alternative directions should be provided, such as "Children with red shirts (or whose names begin with *P* or whose birthdays are in March) line up now."

Two of the assets and appeals of music instruction are the variety of activities and the continual opportunity for direct involvement in music making. The inclusion of movement reinforces musical learning in a needed concrete manner, especially during primary grades. Providing opportunities for students to experience the process of creating music is another important aspect of music teaching. A movement activity may be a structured dance or an individual or group response to a rhythm, a phrase, or an entire musical selection. A composition project may be assigned individually, to partners, or to small groups and may include choices of instruments and opportunities for movement within the classroom. Either type of activity requires carefully planned directions so that the mainstreamed child will not lose control and will be able to successfully participate in the musical experience.

Planning for a class or group that includes an emotionally disturbed child should also focus on consequences. What will the music teacher do if the child does not follow directions? The best advice and the most effective suggestions will come from the teacher who is responsible for the child during most of the school day. In addition, a simple set of posted rules and consequences will help the music teacher avoid prolonged and unnecessary interruptions. Again, these suggestions are not new or specific to teaching this one exceptionality. However, preparing for the possibility that a child may "lose it" is a wise and necessary planning step.

While it is obvious that there is a wide range of possible problems within this exceptionality label, readers must also remember that each individual educator has a varying degree of overall tolerance for deviance. Indeed, that tolerance level may vary depending on the day, time, and season! Most teachers have been found to be least tolerant of outer-directed or potentially disruptive behaviors. These include those described as negative aggressive (teases or torments classmates) and poor peer cooperation. Children with equally severe disturbances who demonstrate failure anxiety or who are socially withdrawn do not interfere with others and thus are more tolerable (Safran, Safran, and Barcikowski, 1985).

Teachers should also be aware that some mainstreamed children prefer the attention they receive for unacceptable behavior. One study (Maag and Rutherford, 1986) included the finding that both behaviorally disordered students and their teachers perceived their inappropriate behavior similarly. Students seemed to be aware of their misbehavior but decided to not follow rules because either the reward for doing so was not great enough or the attention received from undesirable behavior was greater (p. 15). Music teachers must carefully monitor their reactions to the behaviors of emotionally disturbed students and be sure that their own response does not serve as a reinforcement for inappropriate behavior.

Many emotionally disturbed children are highly distractible, and interruptions in the daily or class routine may be intolerable for them, causing distress and unusual behaviors. Some distractions can be controlled by music teachers, while others are unavoidable. Visual distractions can include instruments or charts that are not going to be a part of the lesson. Planning should include a teacher note to store these before teaching a lesson or class with a mainstreamed distractible child. Interruptions from the office often come by means of a wall speaker or a fire drill siren, and those cannot be controlled by the teacher. When such interruptions occur, it may be necessary to provide a physical reminder to the student that you are nearby. Looking at a student or moving to his or her side while answering a wall speaker summons or holding a child's hand during a fire drill are ways to deal with interruptions and the mainstreamed child simultaneously.

SUMMARY OF TEACHING SUGGESTIONS

Provide consistency in behavioral expectations, physical order, and teaching routines.

Plan opportunities for student choice making.

Investigate and study operant conditioning if it is used in your setting.

Plan effective strategies for lesson beginnings, transitions, and endings.

Carefully direct movement or composition activities.

Establish clear rules and consequences.

Monitor your own response to deviant behavior.

Control distractions whenever possible.

Summary

Successful mainstreaming of emotionally disturbed students is indeed possible in music classes. As with all mainstreamed children, the emphasis needs to be on providing adequate opportunities for participation. Success for these youngsters may require teachers to adapt materials if the students have severe academic deficits in addition to paying careful attention to lesson structure. Music teachers must be aware of the rules and consequences that the student is following and incorporate them in music class whenever possible.

A survey of music teachers (Davison, 1972) included a section that queried the professional and personnel assets that the teachers felt they possessed and that assisted in their work with emotionally disturbed children. Respondents reported that their academic training, experience, creativity, and endurance were most valuable. "The ability to anticipate potential problems and prevent them from occurring overtly was also mentioned" (p. 34). While this is a standard approach to planning a musical rehearsal through careful score study, classroom music specialists do not usually anticipate and plan for possible problems. This approach, however, is highly recommended for teachers of classes that include mainstreamed emotionally disturbed students.

RESEARCH

Unfortunately, there is no music education research with this exceptional population. Here, again, is a fertile area that awaits the interest of future graduate students. The research that is summarized here comes from the literature of music therapy, and as in previous chapters, those reports contain conclusions that are applicable to public school music teaching and that may be useful in mainstreaming placement discussions.

Steele (1977) described her five-year project of consultations with teachers of behaviorally disturbed students and offered suggestions that could be useful to both classroom and instrumental teachers. The techniques applicable to teaching classes containing mainstreamed students include recording the number of encouraging statements made during the lesson, as opposed to statements of criticism or instruction; the possible difference of voice tone during praise and criticism; and noting the effect of close proximity as opposed to distance. At the end of the program, the teachers reported that the following teaching techniques were effective in their setting (p. 26):

1. Being firm is not synonymous with being negative.
2. Consistency and patience are essential.
3. Look for and praise successive steps toward the desired goal; don't wait for perfection.
4. Some behavior is best ignored.
5. Emphasize the positive.

Another music therapy program was designed to assist in treatment so that emotionally disturbed children could be mainstreamed into regular classes (Presti, 1984). The program involved an extensive behavior modification approach in which cooperation and work with others was taught and reinforced by successive steps in group therapy sessions. For example, the first step involved teaching the students to play an instrument (rhythm, melody, harmony) only when cued. The students received reinforcement for the correct response, while inappropriate responses were ignored. The following cooperative group behaviors were the focus of the final levels, since these would be necessary for success in an integrated music class: "(a) accepting and/or relinquishing an instrument . . . without verbal and physical interruption; (b) refraining from talking, singing, or playing instruments during another student's turn; and (c) participating throughout an activity and completing the task with the group" (p. 121).

A nonstructured approach was used by music therapists (Merle-Fishman and Marcus, 1982) in an investigation of spontaneous music making by emotionally disturbed and normal children ($n = 16$) who ranged in age from 7 to 10. During seven individual weekly sessions, the children's preferences and behaviors were recorded by data collectors. Group differences were found in rhythmic, verbal, and vocal behaviors.

The emotionally disturbed children had a higher incidence of impulsive rhythmic behavior and produced a larger number of tonal or rhythmic sounds in response to the therapist's improvisation.

Giacobbe (1973) described a project that compared the responses of emotionally disturbed and normal boys, ages 9–11 (n = 40), in their evaluations (happy–sad, like–dislike, good–bad) of 50 thirty-second musical selections. The researcher found differences on only 6 out of 204 possible variables and concluded that all subjects agreed in this type of musical evaluation.

Rhythm response in emotionally disturbed students (n = 24), ages 11–15, was evaluated with a task in which the subjects were asked to reproduce on a conga drum the rhythm they heard on a tape recording (Gibbons, 1983). Subjects were differentiated by their "need for external structure to control behavior" and defined by their teachers as requiring either a mild, a moderate, or a severe degree of structure. The researcher's report of the six weekly rhythm-testing sessions indicates that the students described as the mild structure group scored significantly better than the other two groups (moderate and severe). The conclusion includes a hypothesis that "perhaps rhythm response success or failure is related to the internal behavior controls which provide the organization required to perform the rhythm task" (p. 101).

Research tells us that

Cooperative group behaviors can be taught through music instruction.

Some emotionally disturbed children have a higher incidence of impulsive rhythmic behavior.

Emotionally disturbed and normal boys evaluate short musical selections similarly.

Rhythmic response was best for emotionally disturbed students who needed a mild degree of external structure.

Summary

Only one of the aforementioned reports (Presti) was conducted in a public school setting; nevertheless, the conclusions from therapists in other settings contain findings that have application for public school music teachers. First, teaching techniques in classes with mainstreamed students may have to be carefully self-monitored to ensure that both verbal and nonverbal interactions with these students are positive and supportive (Steele). Second, rhythmic ability in some emotionally disturbed students may not be similar to their peers (Merle-Fishman and Marcus; Gibbons), and rhythmic activities for these students may need very careful planning and structuring.

CONCLUSION

Music educators who are fortunate enough to work in schools that employ a therapist will be familiar with the assistance that these professionals provide for individual students. While a therapist's primary focus is not teaching *about* music or teaching large groups, he or she is a superb resource with regard to a disturbed child's behavior and should be the first resource person consulted if an emotionally disturbed child is mainstreamed into music class.

A mainstreamed emotionally disturbed child may present a real challenge to the music teacher. The challenge may be the disruption of a lesson, a display of inappropriate behavior, or a lack of involvement or participation. Following the recommended steps of reading files, talking with psychologists, resource, and guidance teachers, and observing the child's behavior during instruction are, again, the necessary precursors of successful adaptive instruction. All these steps are necessary to provide instructional adaptations for an individual student within any music setting at any level.

In a chapter titled "The Orchestration of Success," which addresses the teaching of emotionally disturbed students, Frank Hewett has written the following:

> I have always been intrigued with the excitement for learning seen among kindergarteners. One of the aspects of kindergarten curriculum that accounts for its reinforcing properties is that just completing a task is fun since qualitative judgments of grading, accuracy, and comparisons with others' work are often minimized at this level. Another aspect is that emphasis in the curriculum is often on multisensory stimulation and movement. Looking, listening, touching, tasting, and moving are powerful reinforcers for insuring the child's active participation. (Hewett, 1977, p. 84)

The writer then suggests that similar curricula throughout successive grades provide the best environment for mainstreamed emotionally disturbed students. Music educators should reread the preceding excerpt and substitute the word *music* for the word *kindergarten*. What the reader will find is that the description (except for tasting) fits music classes exactly. We have all the necessary elements already in place in our curriculum. The important factor that needs to be added to music instruction for these mainstreamed students is a more careful teacher self-monitoring prior to and during actual instruction.

Readers must remember that the emotionally disturbed student does not come to school every Friday and decide to deliberately "get the music teacher." These students are often truly unable to control their own behavior. An emotionally disturbed child, like all children, needs the structure and limits provided by adults. Providing the ways to practice self-control for a mainstreamed child is as essential in music as it is in any other class. However, music teachers must never lose sight of their basic purpose with these children, which is the same as that for all students—to provide opportunities for participation in musical activities and ways to experience the joy of musical reaction.

QUESTIONS

1. Describe each of the three models used to diagnose and describe emotional disturbance.
2. Why would parents prefer that their child be described as behaviorally disordered?
3. Discuss how music educators can provide consistency for emotionally disturbed students.
4. Provide examples of statements that illustrate the difference between asking and telling.
5. What are the important facets of the time-out procedure?
6. Why are transitions during lessons or rehearsals the most difficult times for emotionally disturbed students?

ACTIVITIES

1. Write a lesson plan for the opening scenario. Include some appropriate mainstreaming adaptations for Jason.
2. Observe a music class, rehearsal, or lesson that includes a mainstreamed emotionally disturbed student. Describe the student's behavior during structured and unstructured instruction time.
3. Write a rehearsal plan for an instrumental or choral ensemble. Describe rehearsal transitions, and indicate suggested modifications for a mainstreamed emotionally disturbed ensemble member.
4. Investigate the psychological literature describing one of the theoretical models of emotional disturbance. Prepare a written or an oral summary that describes the strengths and weaknesses of the model in relation to education.

BIBLIOGRAPHY

APTER, S. J. 1982. *Troubled Children Troubled Systems.* Elmsford, N. Y.: Pergamon Press.
BROWNING, E. R. 1983. *Teaching Students with Severe Emotional and Learning Impairments.* Boston: Allyn & Bacon.
NEWCOMER, P. L. 1980. *Understanding and Teaching Emotionally Disturbed Children.* Boston: Allyn & Bacon.

NOCERA, S. 1979. *Reaching the Special Learner through Music.* Morristown, N.J.: Silver Burdett Company.

PAPPANIKOU, A. J., and J. L. PAUL, eds. 1977. *Mainstreaming Emotionally Disturbed Children.* Syracuse: Syracuse University Press.

REDL, R. 1966. *When We Deal with Children.* New York: Free Press.

Putting It All Together
CHAPTER TEN

It is now 2:30, and Bill Cole, at Main Street School, is partway through his planning for next week (see Chapter 5). He needs to decide how he will adapt his first-, third-, and fifth-grade lessons for the rest of the sections of these grades that include visually and hearing impaired, physically handicapped, and emotionally disturbed students.

INTRODUCTION

Only through the magic of print can we return to this fictional teacher and follow his thoughts and decision-making processes as he prepares to teach classes which include other mainstreamed children. The purpose of this narrative is to summarize Chapters 6–9 by describing how one teacher plans for the types of exceptional children described in those chapters. In this way, the reader may more clearly understand the planning process necessary for successful mainstreaming.

Although it may seem that every exceptionality possible has already been described, that is not the case. Public Law 94-142 includes two other definitions. One is that of speech impaired students. These children may have articulation disorders, may stutter, or may have voice disorders and receive remediation from speech therapists in public schools. These deficits rarely affect children's participation or success in music. Students with severe language or communication disorders are fairly rare in mainstreamed or public school settings. Therefore, a separate chapter on speech impairment has not been included. The other exceptionality—multiply handicapped students—has been alluded to briefly in the preceding chapters and will be discussed more fully in Chapter 11.

The amount of background, music teaching, and research information included in this text cannot be retained by teachers for long (but do hold on to it long enough to pass all your exams!) simply because of the memory capacity humans possess. After a student leaves the class in exceptionalities and gets a teaching job or returns to the classroom, what are the most important points to remember about teaching exceptional children? How does a teacher of fourth-grade clarinetists, fifth- and sixth-grade trumpeters, five third-grade general music classes, and junior high band use the information this book contains?

One simple suggestion is to use the text as a future reference. Leave the book on your desk, and three years from now, when a hearing impaired student wants to learn to play the tuba or is mainstreamed into your seventh-grade general music class, reread the applicable chapter. If you presently teach children who fit some of the categories described in the text, use the book as a reference during your planning. When we were young students, we believed the teacher knew everything! Now that you are teachers (or are on the way), the reality is that you know where to go to find what you can't remember. The information you use daily is going to be retained more easily than that which is used infrequently.

Throughout each of the previous chapters, a process has been described as the appropriate approach to mainstreamed exceptional students. The steps in that process include investigation, discussion, observation, and adaptation of materials and instruction. Each step implies the consideration of individuals while planning and teaching large groups. An individualized approach is not a common part of college music methods curricula, but planning for individuals is necessary when classes include exceptional students. As you now know, many mainstreamed students have unique patterns of learning, which must be accommodated in music instruction so that these students will also be successful class participants.

The introduction to Chapter 5 contains specific suggestions about how to "find out" as much as possible about each mainstreamed child. Many teachers resist this step, explaining that they do not want to rely on other teachers' beliefs and perceptions but prefer to do their own observing and diagnosing. But a music teacher has the constant pressure of time. We rarely teach classes every day, and when we do, as in a rehearsal, we are dealing with very large groups. A prime thesis of this text is that any music teacher who sees a student for only an hour or less each week should spend some time investigating student file content. Then he or she needs to discover what other teachers know about the exceptional child to prepare adequate adaptations of music instruction.

When we describe our symptoms to a medical doctor, we expect that this professional either has read about those symptoms or has had other patients with similar problems. A good doctor, we know, will consult a specialist. We do not expect or pay the doctor to wait and watch and see what will happen next! Skilled music educators need to act in a similar professional capacity and accept the necessity of acquiring as much information as possible prior to planning for and instructing groups that include mainstreamed exceptional students.

"But I don't have any extra time in my schedule! I teach thirty-two classes a week! I have seventy-nine beginners and two bands! I teach in four different buildings!" Rarely is music teaching the ideal situation with five classes, a daily prep period, and a lunch period without any duty. But the bottom line is that we do what we do because we love music and we want future generations to love music also. The love and appreciation of music must be equally available to every member of the future generation, even those who don't learn the same way or look quite the same as their peers. This may indeed mean that music educators have to spend some extra time preparing to teach these students or spend precious time discussing students' learning differences with other staff members. However, with practice, such preparation will become second nature and will not be an imposition.

MAIN STREET SCHOOL

Grade One

Bill Cole has quite a number of pieces of paper scattered on the top of his desk by 2:30, and he has finished planning each of the lessons for the seven grade levels he teaches each week. He looks again at his plan for first grade, takes a clean lesson-plan sheet off his pile, and writes in the teacher's name, Miss Zimmerman. Then he begins to plan how to adapt the lesson on melodic direction for Amy, who is visually impaired, and Lloyd, who is physically handicapped. The first-grade lesson begins with a review of descending stepwise sounds, using resonator bells on the final phrase of "The Stretching Song" (Fig. 10-1). A second review song, "My Pony" (Fig. 10-2), is being used both as a review of descending direction and as an introduction to ascending direction. The next part of the lesson will be teaching a new song, "Sky Bears" (Fig. 10-3), and focusing the children's attention on the upward scale sections in the middle of the song. Each of the upward and downward phrases is also going to be reinforced by instruments or movement or both.

The other two sections of the lesson involve listening to recorded music and to short phrases played on the piano. During the recorded

Stretching Song

Words and Music by Eunice Boardman

Telemann Flute Concerto, Bill plans to model movements for the students, and after playing each of the short evaluation phrases, he plans to model the correct answer with a large arrow.

In Miss Zimmerman's first-grade class, there are twenty-five children, including the two mainstreamed students. Amy is legally blind, and Lloyd has cerebral palsy and is confined to a wheelchair. Neither child has any other learning deficits. Amy has been blind since birth, and although she can distinguish very large shapes and light and dark, she is being taught to read with Braille symbols. Amy has a different classroom

My Pony

German Folk Song

Trot, trot, trot! Trot, my po - ny, trot!

Where it's smooth and where it's ston - y, Trot a -long, my lit - tle po - ny.

Go and nev - er stop, Trot, my po - ny, trot!

FIGURE 10-2 From *Exploring Music 1* by Eunice Boardman and Beth Landis, copyright © 1966 by Holt, Rinehart and Winston, Inc., reprinted by permission of the publisher.

partner each week. The partner's job is to answer Amy's questions when she cannot see what the teacher is doing. Mr. Cole is quite accustomed to hearing these intermittent, whispered interruptions during music class, but he still tries to plan the directions for his activities so that Amy will understand what she must do next.

Lloyd has severe quadriplegic spastic cerebral palsy and speaks very slowly. He maneuvers his chair by himself and can grasp instruments, although he cannot coordinate two finger cymbals or hold a drum

Key: C   Starting Pitch: G   Scale Tones: *do re mi fa so la ti do'*

Sky Bears

Music by Milton Kaye
Words by Elizabeth Pliant

Oh, it snowed last night, snowed last night. The

sky bears had a pil - low fight; They tore up ev - 'ry

cloud in sight and tossed down all the feath - ers white. Oh, it

snowed last night, snowed last night. _____

FIGURE 10-3 Appears in *MUSIC AND YOU,* Grade 1, Barbara Staton and Merrill Staton, Senior Authors (New York: Macmillan, 1988). Used by permission of Exposition Press.

and play it simultaneously. Lloyd tries very hard to be self-sufficient and independent, so each week Bill Cole tries to find ways to adapt the classroom instruments and materials for him.

Each of the two review songs is going to include tone bell playing and movement. Amy will not be able to see the bell, but she has good tactual and kinesthetic abilities, so Bill decides he will give her an Orff instrument mallet that has a larger head and a shortened handle. In the third drawer of his desk is a tone bell mallet that has been prepared previously for Lloyd. The handle is wrapped with masking tape and has a very thick middle section. Lloyd has held this mallet very successfully during previous lessons.

The movement activities are also going to require some adaptations. Bill makes a note that he must remember to not only demonstrate but also verbalize the directions for each movement activity. Then Amy will know how to participate with the class. The echo partner movement activity he planned for the two Down's syndrome children in Mrs. Adams's class will be a good idea, but the children will need to hold hands in this class. Lloyd cannot move his arms easily, but if he has some help raising them, he can lower them during the music. Bill underlines the word *movement* in red and adds *Lloyd next to the word.

Next, Bill thinks about teaching the new song to these children. Amy will need some help! Bill makes a note to bring in some feathers for her to hold so that she will understand what they are and that they are as light as snow. He thinks about the lack of repetition in the words and immediately remembers the sequence pictures that he plans to prepare for Jeremy in Mrs. Adams's class (Chapter 5). The pictures could be reduced on the photocopier and made into a small textured chart for Amy that would have cotton texture on the clouds, satin cloth on the sky bears, and lots of feathers.

The next part of the lesson also includes movement as a response to the recorded music. The same careful directions for Amy and the individualized help for Lloyd will be needed during this part of the lesson. During the evaluation, the children are to point their arrows in the correct direction when Bill plays a phrase that they have moved to previously in the lesson. He looks at the pile of laminated 8-inch arrows he has used in other classes and decides to add some texture to the pointed end of one arrow for Amy to use.

Bill Cole feels that these adaptations for Lloyd and Amy will help them succeed next week. He begins to fill out the lesson-plan sheet.

GRADE __1__   TEACHER __Miss Zimmerman__

MAINSTREAMED __Amy, Lloyd__

ACTIVITIES	MATERIALS	ADAPTATIONS
Stretching Song	Bells	Special mallets for Lloyd and Amy
		Movement partners
My Pony	Bells	Mallets
		Movement partners
Sky Bears		Feathers
		Textured sequence chart
Telemann Flute Concerto		Help Lloyd move
Evaluation	Arrows	Textured arrow for Amy

Bill Cole adds the words *textured sequence chart* and *textured arrows* to the materials list that he will prepare during his prep period next Monday. Then he pulls out another clean lesson-plan sheet.

Grade Three

The third-grade lesson is lying on top of the pile of papers in front of him. He reads it quickly and simultaneously thinks about the two mainstreamed children in Mr. Neil's class—Todd, who is hearing impaired, and Michelle, who is emotionally disturbed.

This lesson is the introduction to meter and will begin with the children listening to the piano and hitting the floor whenever they hear first a random and then a regularly spaced accent. The next step in the lesson will be to speak familiar rhymes and pat the first beat and clap softly for the other beat(s).

Four familiar songs will be included in the lesson. The two songs in duple meter are "Who Did?" (Fig. 10-4) and "Ain't Gonna Rain" (Fig. 10-5), and the two in triple meter are "Springfield Mountain" (Fig. 10-6) and "There's a Hole in My Bucket" (Fig. 10-7). Each song will use two different accompaniments. The first uses contrasting rhythm instru-

FIGURE 10-4 Appears in *MUSIC AND YOU*, Grade 3, Barbara Staton and Merrill Staton, Senior Authors (New York: Macmillan, 1988).

Who Did?

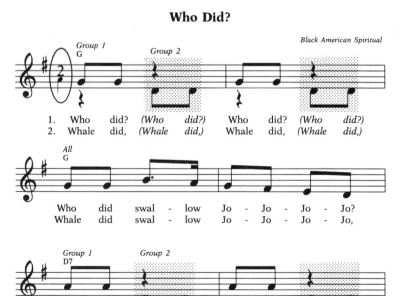

All
D7

Who did swal - low Jo - Jo - Jo - Jo?
Whale did swal - low Jo - Jo - Jo - Jo,

Group 1   Group 2
G

Who did? (Who did?) Who did? (Who did?)
Whale did, (Whale did,) Whale did, (Whale did,)

All
G

Who did swal - low Jo - Jo - Jo - Jo?
Whale did swal - low Jo - Jo - Jo - Jo,

Group 1
D7   Group 2

Who did swal - low Jo - nah? (Who did swal - low
Whale did swal - low Jo - nah, (Whale did swal - low

D7   All   G

Jo - nah?) Who did swal - low Jo - nah down? ____
Jo - nah,) Whale did swal - low Jo - nah up. _____

3. Daniel, *(Daniel,)* Daniel, *(Daniel,)*
Daniel in the li-li-li-li, *(3 times)*
Daniel in the lion's, *(Daniel in the lion's,)*
Daniel in the lion's den.

4. Gabriel, *(Gabriel,)* Gabriel, *(Gabriel,)*
Gabriel blow your trump-trump-trump-trump, *(3 times)*
Gabriel blow your trumpet, *(Gabriel blow your trumpet,)*
Gabriel blow your trumpet loud.

Ain't Gonna Rain

AMERICAN FOLK SONG

1. The wood-chuck, he's a - chop-pin' wood,

The pos - sum, he's a - haul - in'.

My poor old dog fell off a log And killed him - self a - bawl - in'.

REFRAIN
It ain't gon-na rain, it ain't gon-na rain, It ain't gon-na rain no more.

Come on down, ev-'ry-bod-y sing. It ain't gon-na rain no more.

2. Just bake them biscuits good and brown,

It ain't gonna rain no more.

Swing your ladies round and round,

It ain't gonna rain no more. *Refrain*

3. I'll tune the fiddle, you get the bow,

It ain't gonna rain no more.

The weatherman just told me so,

It ain't gonna rain no more. *Refrain*

4. Oh, what did the blackbird say to the crow?

"It ain't gonna rain no more.

It ain't gonna hail, it ain't gonna snow,

It ain't gonna rain no more." *Refrain*

FIGURE 10-5   From *Silver Burdett MUSIC*, Centennial Edition, Grade 3. © 1985 by The Silver Burdett Company.

ments on the first and other beat(s), and the second includes a do-sol ostinato on the Orff metallophones.

The lesson evaluation will also be taped sections of the songs as in first grade, but the third graders will decide on a set of movements for 2s and 3s and change their movements while listening to the tape. His master plan for third grade also includes making an overhead transparency of the familiar songs to use when discussing meter signatures. His planned conclusion is to clap rhythm echoes in both meters and have the class decide which meter they clap.

Springfield Mountain

American Ballad

1. On Spring-field Moun - tain there did dwell
2. One Mon - day morn - ing he did go

a hand - some youth; I knew him well. _____
down in the mea - dow for to mow. _____

Refrain

Too loo - re - ay, too loo - re - oo,

Too loo - re - ay, too loo - re - oo.

3. When he had mowed but half the field,
   a pesky sarpent bit his heel.

4. He took his scythe and with a blow,
   he laid the pesky sarpent low.

5. He took the sarpent in his hand
   and straightway went to Molly Bland.

6. "Oh, Molly, Molly, here you see
   the pesky sarpent what bit me."

7. Now, Molly had a ruby lip
   with which the pizen she did sip.

8. But Molly had a rotten tooth
   and so the pizen kill'd them both.

FIGURE 10-6 Appears in *MUSIC AND YOU*, Grade 3, Barbara Staton and Merrill Staton, Senior Authors (New York: Macmillan, 1988).

The two mainstreamed children in this class certainly have contrasting problems, and Bill remembers that planning for this class always takes a long time. Todd has a moderate binaural conductive hearing impairment and wears a portable FM hearing system. Todd's hearing loss is the result of an accident when he was five. (Bill Cole has learned a great deal about hearing impairments since Chapter 6.)

Michelle has been in Main Street School for over a year, and her parents finally consented to having her tested by the school psycholo-

There's a Hole in My Bucket

Dialogue Song

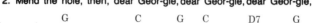

1. There's a hole in my buck-et, dear Li-za, dear Li-za,
2. Mend the hole, then, dear Geor-gie, dear Geor-gie, dear Geor-gie,

There's a hole in my buck-et, dear Li-za, a hole.
Mend the hole, then, dear Geor-gie, dear Geor-gie, mend the hole.

3. With what shall I mend it, dear Liza, dear Liza?
   With what shall I mend it, dear Liza, with what?

4. With a straw, dear Georgie, . . . with a straw.

5. The straw is too long, dear Liza, . . . too long.

6. Cut the straw, then, dear Georgie, . . . cut the straw.

7. With what shall I cut it, dear Liza, . . . with what?

8. With a knife, dear Georgie, . . . with a knife.

9. The knife is too blunt, dear Liza, . . . too blunt.

10. Whet the knife, then, dear Georgie, . . . whet the knife.

11. With what shall I whet it, dear Liza, . . . with what?

12. With a stone, dear Georgie, . . . with a stone.

13. The stone is too dry, dear Liza, . . . too dry.

14. Wet the stone, then, dear Georgie, . . . wet the stone.

15. With what shall I wet it, dear Liza, . . . with what?

16. With the water, dear Georgie, . . . with the water.

17. In what shall I get it, dear Liza, . . . in what?

18. In the bucket, dear Georgie, . . . in the bucket.

19. There's a hole in my bucket, dear Liza, . . . a hole.

FIGURE 10-7   From *Holt Music 1988 Grade 3* by Meske, Andress, Pautz and Willman, copyright © 1988 by Holt, Rinehart and Winston, Inc., reprinted by permission of the publisher.

gist. Following the testing, teachers were told that her unusual behavior and inability to learn at the normal rate were indeed (as all the teachers already knew) the result of an emotional disturbance. However, at Main Street School, these children are labeled behaviorally disordered! Part of Michelle's recently developed IEP includes a behavior modification plan, and Mrs. Adams has described the checklist that Bill must keep during each week's music class. In addition, Bill must have a "time-out" place in his room, and before beginning his music teaching, he must review his classroom rules so that Michelle understands that his expectations are exactly the same as those of Mrs. Adams.

The two children are almost opposites when they come to music class. Todd always nods and smiles at every direction and activity and gives an outward appearance of understanding all that is happening in class. Michelle is usually withdrawn, often quite sullen, and never volunteers to participate. She is chosen for a turn by another child only if Bill tells the class that everyone must have a turn. One week, she did not want to play an instrument and threw the maraca so hard it cracked completely open.

Mrs. Adams always brings the class into the music room and checks to see that everyone is sitting quietly before she leaves and then hands Michelle's checklist to Bill Cole. He makes a note in his plan to be sure that Todd is sitting close to the piano for the lesson introduction and tries to remember where he put the charts with the words for the rhymes. He used them in the first grade in November and now it is April. Finally, he looks between two cabinets, finds all ten clipped together, and pulls out the two for this third-grade lesson. When he puts sequence pictures or song words on the easel, Todd's singing always improves. Reading the charts will mean that Todd doesn't have to remember the words, and therefore he will be able to focus on the feeling of meter.

The music room is carpeted, and the third graders always sit on the floor near the piano. Bill makes a note on his form to put a small chair near the piano so that he can quickly make the transition from the improvised piano playing to the nursery rhyme section of the lesson. At the same time, he remembers that the psychologist told Mrs. Adams that Michelle should not have unnecessary distractions. So he makes another note to take the rhythm instruments he is going to need out of the cabinet and keep them in a black carrying case, which he will put behind the piano.

Then Mr. Cole looks at the next part of the third-grade lesson, which involves experiencing duple and triple meter in familiar songs. The picture sequence charts for "Ain't Gonna Rain" and "There's a Hole in My Bucket" not only will be useful for the learning disabled third graders but also will help Todd. If he writes a short list of words on the board before the class arrives, Todd should have no trouble with the first song ("Who Did?"), either. The charts and the list should help Michelle also, since she is reading only at beginning second-grade level.

Bill thinks to himself, "How can I structure the transitions between passing out instruments and taking turns and four songs?" He knows this is an important part of the lesson to think about because Michelle has had behavior problems during other lessons when the children were exchanging instruments. He makes a note on his lesson-plan form to have this class sit in rows, with six children in each row. The instruments will be played initially by children in the first row and then passed back. This will eliminate the lost time and waiting while children get up and try to give an instrument to their best friend.

This seating arrangement will also help structure the movement section of the lesson. The class can be easily directed to stand by rows and to move with arms spread out so that each child has his or her own space; the movement to 2s or 3s will not result in chaos, either. With this structure, no child will have an opportunity to make a fuss when he or she gets close to Michelle! Bill realizes that this arrangement will also make it much easier to line the class up at the end of the period, since he can direct the quietest row to stand and move in a duple or triple way to the door.

Mr. Cole's mind flips back to Todd. Are there any other ways that the lesson can be made clearer for him? He needs as much visual assistance as possible. Bill Cole remembers that he had some additional visual adaptations for Danny in Miss Tynan's class. The lesson plan for that class includes using colored chalk to draw light and dark rectangles to represent heavy and light beats. It probably would be a good reinforcement for Todd also, but considering the need for structure and control in Mrs. Adams's class, drawing the rectangles on the board is not a good idea. He makes a note to cut them out ahead of time and glue sandpaper to the back so that they will stay on a flannel board.

This lesson plan is now ready to go into his book.

GRADE __3__   TEACHER __Mrs. Adams__

MAINSTREAMED __Todd, Michelle__

ACTIVITIES	MATERIALS	ADAPTATIONS
		Review class rules
		Sit class in rows
Improvising—accents on floor		*Time-out chair*
		Todd near piano
Rhymes—Humpty, Jack Horner, Oliver Twist	*Charts*	*Have a small chair ready*
Songs		
Ain't Gonna Rain	*Rhythm instruments*	*Instruments in box*
		Sequence chart
Who Did?	*2 metallophone and mallets*	*Words on board*
Hole in My Bucket		*Sequence chart*
Springfield Mountain		
Tape of song phrases	.	*Colored rectangles for light/ heavy to show meter*
Transparencies		

Bill files the paper in his looseleaf notebook and picks up his last unfilled lesson-plan sheet. He always leaves this class until last because it is the hardest planning job of the week.

Grade Five

In Mr. Cain's fifth grade, there are twenty-seven students, including four mainstreamed children. Each of the four has a different type of deficit. Robby has a moderate hearing impairment, Chris is visually impaired, Carolyn is physically handicapped, and Carlos is behaviorally disturbed. Planning for (and teaching) this class is the real challenge of Bill Cole's week.

This week's lesson is the third lesson on form for the fifth graders, and the focus is on having the students discover how repeated rhythmic and harmonic structure provide variety and repetition in phrases and sections. He has planned to use two songs, both in AB form—"Going to Boston" (Fig. 10-8) and "Mineira de Minas" (Fig. 10-9)—and a listening piece, a rondo—*Symphonie de Fanfares*, "Rondeau" (see Fig. 10-10). He selected the first song because it is clearly printed, with the repeated rhythms in each line directly under each other. The repeated melody

FIGURE 10-8   Appears in *MUSIC AND YOU*, Grade 5, Barbara Staton and Merrill Staton, Senior Authors (New York: Macmillan, 1988).

rhythm of the second song is more difficult for fifth graders to find, but Bill prepared a chart last year that combined each set of two lines into one. That helped the students understand the rhythmic repetition. And in this song, there are different arrangements of chords in the two sections.

The form of the listening piece is ABACA, and while the text provides both notation and a call chart (Call Chart 2; Fig. 10-10), Bill remembers that he has already made a modified call chart (Chapter 5) for Jeffrey, who is in Mr. Moore's class. Perhaps he will be able to use that chart for one of the four children in Mr. Cain's class.

After Bill Cole writes the names of the four children on the first line of the lesson-plan form, he mentally reviews what he knows about each child. Robby has a severe conductive hearing loss and wears a portable hearing aid unit. Even with the unit, his speech reception threshold is barely at a functional level, and his spoken language is sometimes quite hard to understand. Robby tries to lip-read, and that sometimes helps him in music, but Bill Cole knows he must have as many visual aids for Robby as possible.

The next two children, Chris and Carolyn, are slightly easier to plan for. Chris's visual impairment is described in his file as moderate. He wears very thick glasses and can read print if the text or the paper is within a 3- to 6-inch range. Large musical symbols and ikons have been helpful for Chris in other lessons. Carolyn has cystic fibrosis, and on the surface, she seems like other class members except that she is always coughing. She misses many days of school and has been absent on music days many times this year. Bill knows from reading her file that he must watch her very carefully when including movement activities to be sure she doesn't perspire or get overtired.

The final child, Carlos, is a challenge to the entire school! The label behaviorally disordered doesn't begin to describe him adequately. At times, he seems to be very concerned with following the behavior contract that the school psychologist, Dr. Bowden, has written and has given to all his teachers. On some other days, however, he has temper tantrums and uses a vocabulary that would shock a sailor. Bill has been very fortunate this year because Carlos has only "flipped" once in his class. When Carlos cannot be controlled by any teacher, Dr. Bowden is called, and he takes him to his office until the end of the day.

Some of the adaptations that Bill has already planned (Chapter 5) will be helpful in this class also. He already has prepared an enlarged transparency of the song and has planned to emphasize the similar rhythm in each section with two colored markers. If he makes a photocopy of the transparency for Chris and has an extra set of markers, Chris will be able to circle the sheet and see the rhythms. The use of simple gestures to indicate Autoharp chord changes in the B section of "Mineira de Minas" will be a good way to help both Chris and Robby understand when to change chords. And Carlos really shines at playing the Autoharp. Bill decides that for this class, the lesson order should be changed so that the Autoharp activity is last. This strategy will make it possible to mention at the beginning of class that Autoharps will be used in the last activity, and that knowledge may help Carlos keep "on track" through the entire period.

Bill Cole looks again at "Going to Boston" and thinks about the four mainstreamed fifth graders. Each of these children will really benefit from a more concrete experience with the uneven pattern in the A section and the two sixteenth-note patterns in the B section. So, in addition to a transparency and highlighting the rhythms with different colors, this class will reinforce the rhythmic differences by playing instruments. Passing out and exchanging instruments can cause some class disruption (not needed when Carlos is in the class), but there is already quite a bit of structure in place. Fortunately, the fifth graders sit in chairs, and posted on the side bulletin board is a class checklist,

FIGURE 10-10   From *Silver Burdett MUSIC*, Centennial Edition, Grade 5. © 1985 by The Silver Burdett Company.

RONDO FORM: REPETITION AND CONTRAST OF SECTIONS

The diagram at the top of the page will help you discover how the sections in a piece of music are put together to create a rondo form. Study the diagram and answer the following questions:

• Which section repeats?
• How many contrasting sections does the diagram show?
• Which section do you find at the end of the diagram?

CALL CHART 2: Rondo   **Mouret:** *Symphonic de fanfares,* "Rondeau"

This piece for trumpet, organ, and timpani is in rondo form.
Follow the chart as you listen. It will help you hear what is
going on as the music goes along.

Another time, try following the notation of the music in each
section.

1	SECTION A	TRUMPET SOLO; FOUR PHRASES— PHRASES 1 AND 3 ARE EXACTLY ALIKE, PHRASES 2 AND 4 ARE NEARLY ALIKE.
2	SECTION B	NO TRUMPET; TWO PHRASES, ALIKE IN RHYTHM AND MELODY
3	SECTION A	PHRASES 3 AND 4 ONLY
4	SECTION C	NO TRUMPET; LONG AND SHORT PHRASES
5	SECTION A	SAME AS NUMBER 1

showing who has had a turn playing an instrument. Bill reads the
suggested dance activity in the teacher's book and immediately decides
against it—a class with Carlos should not involve a lot of movement, and
Carolyn should never have any strenuous activity.

The next lesson section for this class, then, will be listening to the rondo and following a chart. Chris will be able to follow the chart in the text (see Fig. 10-10) if Mr. Cole makes a larger copy of the entire page and then cuts off the notation and directions to eliminate any distractions. Robby will need to be seated very near the phonograph for optimum hearing and will probably follow the form best if he uses the graphic chart. Carolyn will not need any special adaptations in this section, and Carlos will only need very clear directions (and continual monitoring by Mr. Cole). The ikon chart (Fig. 10-11) will be a good way to emphasize harmonic change in each section, and having the class discover the visual and aural texture differences will provide a good transition to the second song.

Once again, Bill Cole runs through his mental file on each of the four children and thinks about how each child will be able to play an Autoharp. Finally, he decides that this class should have assigned partners. He quickly writes up the list and makes a note to put the list on a large piece of poster paper next week. Preassigning the pairs of children eliminates social rejection for Carolyn, who is rarely chosen by her classmates, and for Carlos, whom the students treat very warily. It also is a good way to have a caring and patient helper for Robby, who often needs extra time to understand the directions and get ready to participate.

Since there are only five Autoharps, Mr. Cole looks carefully at the song and teacher directions and decides that some sets of partners can emphasize the meter changes in the two sections. The only complicated part will be passing out and collecting the instruments. Because of Carlos, each transition must be carefully structured. He decides that the partner chart will also include the name of the instrument and each partner will be designated either a C or an N (for "Mr. Cain"—A and B are being used for form this week). Class directions will have the C students pick up their harmonic, rhythmic, or melodic instruments in turn.

It is now 3:00, and only this class form needs to be filled in before it is time for bus duty. Bill Cole picks up his pen and begins.

GRADE __5__   TEACHER __Mr. Cain__

MAINSTREAMED __Robby, Chris, Carolyn, Carlos__

ACTIVITIES	MATERIALS	ADAPTATIONS
Going to Boston	Rhythm instruments Colored markers	Transparency and copy for Chris
Mouret "Rondeau" Mineira de Minas	Ikon transparency Rhythm instruments	Fix call chart for Chris Partner list

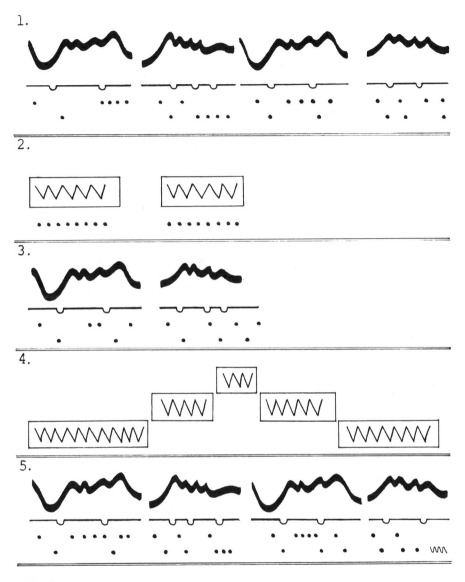

FIGURE 10-11 Graphic Call Chart for *Symphonie de Fanfares,* "Rondeau"

After he fills in the form, he looks at his original plan for fifth grade. He has forgotten to include the evaluation activity. However, after he looks at the page, he sees that the "What Do You Hear?" form uses a large print, so all that will need to be remembered is to reseat the class so that Robby is near the phonograph again. Just then, the bell rings and Mr. Cole closes his planning notebook and heads for bus duty. He thinks, "Well, at least it is not raining this Friday!"

CONCLUSION

Of course this scenario is fiction! Bill Cole is a wonder teacher who plans for an entire week and eight mainstreamed children (just in this chapter) in an hour. He uses material from all three series, and these classes do not include any learning disabled, educable retarded, multiply handicapped, or gifted children (or a partridge in a pear tree, either).

All of Bill Cole's teaching is in general music, and instrumental specialists or secondary teachers may think that it is not possible to generalize the fictional contents of this chapter to their settings. Both summary chapters have described general elementary music classes primarily because of basic mainstreaming realities. A national music education survey (Gilbert and Asmus, 1981) included the finding that it is into these classes that most exceptional children are mainstreamed. However, any teacher at any level can follow the process described in the introduction of this chapter: Read the student's file, talk to other resource or guidance personnel, observe the student in your setting, and then plan for appropriate instructional materials and strategies.

Bill Cole planned to use some materials for the students in this chapter that he had previously planned for the fictional children in Chapter 5. This approach is highly recommended because it implies a consideration of individual learning strengths and weaknesses, not a reliance on definitions or labels. Deciding on the appropriate adaptations of instructions and materials for an exceptional child should not be a process of extracting "the" five (or ten) teaching suggestions in a particular chapter. A more generalized approach is recommended in which teachers consider all the changes that have been illustrated in the text as an enormous menu. The ways that teaching can be adjusted (structure, transitions, rate) or that materials can be adapted (size, graphic, intensification) are the headings on the menu—not the labels that describe singular children.

The labels used in education are useful because they alert teachers to a range of possible handicaps and a range of possible teaching strategies. Almost every label that has been discussed in this text can be modified with another set of words—mild, moderate, severe. Those terms imply the possibility for vast differences between any two children who are defined with the same exceptional label. And the use of this additional descriptive terminology underlines the reality that the most effective planning for mainstreamed children is *individual* planning.

The fictional teacher described in this chapter followed this suggestion in his planning. First he thought about *how* each child approached learning in music, and then he made decisions on how to best teach that single child. To inexperienced (and to some experienced) teachers, it may seem that Bill Cole is a "superhero" and that ordinary mortals cannot plan in this manner. But when you were in fourth or fifth grade and watched and listened to a teacher play all the possible choices of instruments you could learn, you were also awed by the skill needed to play those instruments (even if the teacher was a clarinetist playing a scale on a trombone)! Think of your ability as a musician right now. How did you acquire *that* skill?

Good teachers are not born or produced in methods classes. Good teachers are lifelong learners! Teaching is a process that involves constant decisions and judgments that are the result of observing, diagnosing, and evaluating classroom content and individual responses. Through this process, teachers are continually learning how best to structure instruction for individuals. Music teachers, who have perfected incredible skills and abilities in music performance, must practice teaching in the same manner. In this way, the individual students defined as exceptional or special or mainstreamed will receive an adequate and equal music education in the least restrictive environment as mandated by federal law.

QUESTIONS

1. Why must music teachers include planning for individuals as well as groups?
2. What steps should music teachers follow when they plan for and teach mainstreamed students?
3. Why is the partner movement activity in the grade-one plan a helpful adaptation for both of the mainstreamed children?
4. Why did Bill Cole decide that Todd should sit close to the piano?
5. How could Bill Cole adapt "Hole in My Bucket" for the two mainstreamed children in the third-grade class?
6. Why should a music teacher carefully consider including movement in classes that include mainstreamed emotionally disturbed children?
7. Describe other music teaching adaptations from this text that are useful for more than one exceptionality.

ACTIVITIES

1. Write a lesson plan for another grade level, an instrumental lesson, or a rehearsal. Describe two fictional exceptional children, and then write the possible instructional and material adaptations for those students.
2. Observe a music class that includes mainstreamed students described in Chapters 6–9. Discuss the students' learning strengths and weaknesses with their teacher and with their music teacher. Write a short description of each child and plan a follow-up lesson with appropriate adaptations.
3. Reread the scenarios at the beginning of Chapters 6, 7, 8, and 9. Use the lesson-plan form in this chapter, and write a music lesson plan and suitable mainstreaming adaptations for each of those classes.

Self-Contained Classes for Multiply Handicapped Students

CHAPTER ELEVEN

ONE MAINSTREAMING REALITY

Harmon Street School

It is the first week of school, and it is also the first week of Miss Allen's music teaching career. When she was hired in July, the job was described by the assistant superintendent, Mr. MacDonald, because the building principal was on vacation. He told Miss Allen that she would be teaching the four sections of each grade level in the elementary school and also would be teaching the children in the special center twice a week. At that time, she did not ask what or where the special center was. Mr. MacDonald did not volunteer a description and had immediately asked her about her piano-playing skills, since he was most concerned that she be able to play piano for the PTA meetings.

At lunch today, Miss Allen saw a group of children at one table with a number of adults. The children certainly looked different: Some were in wheelchairs; some had very noticeable and different facial characteristics; some were signing, while others were speaking very loudly; two of them appeared to be preschoolers, and others were taller than the teachers. At the end of the school day, she asked the art teacher about the unusual class she had seen. Then she learned what the words *special center* meant.

She was told that the special center is a separate wing of the school, connected by a covered walkway, which houses two classes of multi-handicapped students. The students are bused from the entire county to this center. All the students in these classes are quite retarded, and each

198

has one or more additional handicaps. The only time they are seen in the school is at lunch—the center even has its own playground. Miss Allen looked at her schedule and realized she was going to teach those two classes the next day!

The next morning, she came to school quite early and headed for the telephone. She planned to ask her music supervisor, the high school choral director, for some advice. His rehearsal would not be over until after her first class began, however, so Miss Allen walked over to the special center and introduced herself to the head teacher. "I was wondering if you could tell me what the music teacher did in your class last year?" The head teacher, Tom Ross, looked at her and groaned very loudly.

"She brought a cart of books every week—third-grade books—and she played the records that came with the books. Our kids held the books and tried to listen to the records. Sometimes she brought a filmstrip about a composer and a record to go with the filmstrip. You can't believe how bad it was last year. Your predecessor couldn't cope with the idea that our kids are different. They can't read, and they don't have a clue to what a composer is."

Miss Allen replied, "Well, how do you suggest I start? Do you sing any songs together or listen to any records? What do you think the class will be able to learn today? May I eat lunch with you so that I can learn the names of the children? Do you have any free time before lunch to talk to me?"

Tom Ross looked at her with amazement and said he had a prep period at 10:40. He said that the other teachers would be delighted to have her eat lunch with their classes.

What Did Miss Allen Learn?

In this special center, the children are divided into two classes roughly by age. The younger class includes children from 4 to 11, and the older class includes students as old as 21. The students who are over 14 spend the latter half of every day at the sheltered workshop on the other side of town, where they learn work skills that will enable them to be employable as adults. The younger class includes children who are autistic, deaf-blind, and nonverbal and children with cerebral palsy, and all the students are also retarded. This class has listened to Ella Jenkins records, and the class teacher has taught songs that emphasize names and songs about body parts. The older class includes students with moderate retardation; some of them also have cerebral palsy, and one is blind. These students listen to the radio a great deal. Many of them have earned enough money at the workshop to buy Walkmans or tape recorders. The teacher of this class sometimes uses listening to music as a reward for excellent work.

The students in these classes call the teachers and the aides by their first names—this is easier for those that have some language ability. The teachers and the aides stay in the class during music and are willing to help in any way. Both of the teachers graduated from a college where they had to take a course in music for special children, and they know how much their children love music. Tom Ross was sure that on the days the class did not have music, the teachers would be glad to practice any song or activity that Miss Allen taught.

After Miss Allen finished talking to Tom Ross, she felt much better. At lunch, she talked to both classroom teachers and decided to begin with songs and activities that they had taught in order to focus on dynamic contrasts. Her first week of teaching was a success!

DEFINITIONS

The definition for the children in this special center is found in the Federal Register description of Public Law 94-142.

> "Multihandicapped" means concomitant impairments (such as mentally retarded-blind, mentally retarded-orthopedically impaired, etc.), the combination of which causes such severe educational problems that they cannot be accommodated in special education programs solely for one of the impairments. The term does not include deaf-blind children.

The final sentence excludes a group of children because those students are defined under a separate paragraph in these regulations.

> "Deaf-blind" means concomitant hearing and visual impairments, the combination of which causes such severe communication and other developmental and educational problems that they cannot be accommodated in special education programs solely for deaf or blind children. (Federal Register)

As readers can imagine, these definitions present a vast variety of possible handicapping conditions. Although the definition does not describe where these children are to be taught, in public schools the "least restrictive environment" for them is usually a special class. Seldom are they mainstreamed into music classes.

Although the focus of this text is on how to provide a positive and successful music education for mainstreamed handicapped learners, not every exceptional student is mainstreamed. Future teachers may well find themselves in a position similar to Miss Allen's when they take a new job, and it is for that reason that the present chapter is included. A familiarity with severe and multiple handicaps is also a much-needed part of a music teacher's preparation. It is hoped that the words *special center*, or whatever terminology is used, will be clearly defined during your interview.

A self-contained class of multihandicapped students appears different from a normal class in a school. The class is smaller and has more aides than a regular class. Many of the students also act in a manner different from other children. They do not have adequate adaptive behaviors or social skills, and those deficits, in addition to cognitive and physical handicaps, contribute to the children's dissimilarity.

Teachers of such classes have a different focus and a different purpose from those of teachers of graded classrooms. There are no daily reading groups with different levels, nor is there a daily list of work assignments on the blackboard. Academic subjects are taught at a very simple level. Students may be learning to count to ten or to recognize these numbers in a simulated store. They may be learning colors and practicing how to respond correctly to the changing colors on a stoplight. Classroom instruction may also include daily emphasis on self-help skills such as dressing, setting the table, and shampooing one's own hair. At other times during the day, the teacher may be teaching simple social skills to one or more of the students, such as learning to say "how are you" or practicing handshakes with the correct tone and eye contact.

Each preceding chapter that has focused on one handicapping condition has included a general description of some of the possible learning styles and behaviors. It is not possible to describe all the possible variations of physical and mental handicaps that are subsumed under the label multihandicapped. However, there are three descriptors that music educators may meet in reading or in professional discussions that have not previously been described in this text. These include *trainable mentally retarded, autism,* and *communication disorders.*

Mental Retardation

One category or descriptor of most students in self-contained classes is *moderate retardation* or *trainable mentally retarded* (or *handicapped*). This term indicates that students have been tested by psychologists and have demonstrated an intelligence score between 35/40 and 50/55. (The precise numbers used depend upon state or local definitions.) A second facet used to define this population is deficits in adaptive behavior. Adaptive behavior includes language, self-help skills, socialization abilities, and sensorimotor skills (see Chapter 2 for an elaboration of those terms).

The learning ability of these retarded individuals may eventually be the same as that of children who are aged 4 to 8, but cognition develops very slowly—at one-fourth to one-half the rate in a normal child (Gearheart, 1972). Many of these students may learn basic number concepts of how to read and write their own names, but they are unable to master the more complex academic tasks of reading and computation. Some of the emphasis in instruction is on the self-care skills that are part of daily human functioning and may, even in a public school, include toileting. There also is instruction in skills such as using money and the social abilities that enable individuals to shop in a mall or at a neighborhood store.

In addition to a more severe degree of retardation, multihandicapped students may have any of the physical handicaps that have been described in previous chapters. Indeed, Chapter 8 pointed out that 50 percent of the students with cerebral palsy are also retarded. Music teachers may be teaching classes that include blind or deaf or physically handicapped individuals who are also trainable mentally handicapped. This reality means that students in self-contained classes also cannot be easily categorized into a homogeneous group. Each child's abilities and disabilities must be considered when planning music instruction.

Autism

Autistic students exhibit a variety of peculiar social behaviors and unusual language development. The types of abnormal behaviors that are characteristic of these children have been described by the National Society for Children and Adults with Autism as follows (Hinerman, p. 5):

Abnormal ways of relating to people, objects, and events
Abnormal responses to sensations (sight, hearing, touch, pain, balance, smell, taste)
Immature rhythms of speech, limited understanding of ideas, and use of words without the usual meaning to them
Slow development or lack of physical, social, and learning skills

It was once theorized that autistic children's behavior was the result of faulty parental upbringing or lack of parental affection, but researchers in the medical community are now investigating autism as a brain disorder. An announcement in May 1988 described a finding by researchers in San Diego that autistic patients had a deficiency of Purkinje cells. These cells convey messages from the cerebellum to the cerebral cortex within the brain. In addition, the same announcement described a finding of a brain abnormality in the autistic patients. Portions of the patients' cerebellums appeared underdeveloped when tested with magnetic resonance imaging (*Portland Press Herald*, June 8, 1988).

In a classroom, autistic children may behave in a very withdrawn, aloof manner or may appear to be living in their own world. Some of the behaviors that these children may demonstrate include avoiding eye contact, lack of facial emotion, an insistence on repetition in routines, an absence of responsiveness to people, and deficits in both receptive (understanding) and expressive (speaking) language. Approximately 50 percent of all autistic children are mute (Rutter, 1978).

Future music educators may, at this point, become dismayed. Teaching autistic children sounds too difficult! One important fact to remember is that autism is an uncommon condition. Indeed, in the previously cited newspaper article, it was estimated that the occurrence is between 2 and 5 out of every 10,000 live births. Most readers may never teach an autistic child or an autistic class. Those who do should be aware that in addition to all the aforementioned (and more) problems of autism, some autistic children have special abilities in math, art, and music—subjects that do not depend on the use of language. The author once observed an autistic child in a special school cling to the wall and refuse to look at the music teacher while simultaneously naming the triads she played on a piano by both the letter name of the root and the quality (major, diminished, and so on).

Once again, the degree and types of behavior included under this label cannot be generalized, but vary from child to child. Music educators who teach one or more autistic children must employ the same set of strategies repeatedly suggested throughout the text for teaching exceptional children who are mainstreamed. During the first step— reading files and talking to other teachers—you may discover that extensive behavior modification techniques are being used with autistic individuals or classes. A 1983 text (Hinerman) describes the use of this approach in teaching autistic children to communicate. If this technique is used with autistic children, music class must provide continuity and consistency in behavioral expectations, rewards, and punishments (see Chapter 9). On the other hand, you may discover that the autistic student you teach exhibits exceptional musical abilities. In that case, you will want to adapt your instruction so that you can provide musical experiences that will challenge and engage the child.

Classes of autistic students will be an enormous challenge, but there is a methodology in music education that has been used in therapeutic settings with autistic individuals. The use of Orff-*Schulwerk* with autistic children (Hollander and Juhrs, 1974) resulted in improvements in a variety of nonmusical areas, including positive reactions, an increase in gestural and sign communications, and language development. These are not the focus of music education, certainly, but the appeal of Orff instruments and the many levels of involvement possible in this teaching method make it worthy of special consideration for autistic students in the public school.

Communication Disorders

Many multihandicapped children also have deficits in the use or the understanding of language. Students who are autistic, trainable mentally retarded, deaf-blind, and others may also have severe communication deficits. You may also meet the term *aphasia*. This word literally means "lack of speech" and includes such deficits as lack of comprehension, inability to speak, and an incapacity to think using language as a result of brain damage (Myklebust, 1954).

However, teachers must be aware that although some children lack expressive capacity, they may well understand what they hear. This understanding may be communicated very simply, as in a movement of the hand or a shifting of the eyes. Other students may use more formal gestures or may have learned some sign language (described in Chapter 6). It is suggested that when instructing classes or individuals with severe language deficits, you use short and simple sentences, speak slowly, wait between sentences for a response, and assume that the child understands what you have said (Fraser and Hensinger, 1983).

Some language disabled students communicate through a device called a communication board (see Chapter 8). For very young children, these boards contain squares with pictures of objects. Older children may use boards that contain words. The user points to the symbol or the word as a means of initiating conversation or as a way of responding to questions.

Other multihandicapped students may be learning to use sign language in their special class as a means of communication. Music teachers who teach these children will want to consider taking a course in signing. These courses are offered by a number of agencies and colleges, usually at little or no cost.

This description of communication disorders is included to inform music educators of some of the possibilities they may encounter if they teach classes of multihandicapped students. Most of this section describes what students with communication disorders *cannot* do. In order to plan successful musical experiences, however, teachers must try to determine what these students *can* do, how they communicate, and how they respond.

It is entirely possible that a multihandicapped student who is unable to speak may be very gifted. In fact, the winner of the 1987 Whitbread Book of the Year prize in Britain is an author named Christopher Nolan who is profoundly handicapped and mute. At age 11, he learned to type using a stick that is attached to his head. At times, it may take him over fifteen minutes just to type one word, but he has written not one but two prize-winning books (Joffee, 1988). With the constant invention of ways to adapt computers for handicapped students and the availability of software programs for music composition, it is possible that someday a similar article will describe a multihandicapped prize-winning composer. It is hoped that that student's talents will have been first discovered in a music class.

MUSIC TEACHING

Once a music teacher has completed the initial steps of investigation and discussion and has discovered that in a single class no two children have the same handicap, the next step involves careful thought. Planning musical instruction for these classes involves selecting appropriate activities to illustrate and provide experiences with each of the elements of music while simultaneously providing ways for each child to participate at some time at his or her own level of ability. Some of the factors that need to be considered during the planning phase include language, the regular class curriculum, the overall rate of learning, and lesson structure.

Language

There are two aspects of language that need to be carefully planned in music instruction: the words of songs and the teacher's spoken directions and questions. Songs should contain simple and highly repetitious vocabulary that is within the children's experience. The illustration of song vocabulary with pictures and objects should always be included in lesson planning, and the pictures should be used every time the song is sung. Some examples of songs that can be illustrated in this manner include "John the Rabbit," "Who Has the Penny," "Jack-in-the-Box," and "Five Angels." All of these can be found in *Reaching the Special Learner through Music* (Nocera, 1979). The publishers of this text also sell an accompanying set of charts and sequence pictures, which are very helpful in illustrating song vocabulary.

Music teachers must also consider the age level and the social skills of students when selecting songs. A 16-year-old who listens to rock music stations should not be asked to participate in singing what is clearly a "baby" song. However, songs that have adequate repetition and that are socially appropriate can be found in a variety of sources, including the series texts and the books listed in the bibliography in this chapter. Some examples are "Head Shoulders Baby, One, Two, Three" (*Silver Burdett MUSIC*, Kindergarten, p. 113), "Rocky Mountain" (*Holt MUSIC*, Grade 2, p. 43), and "Long Legged Sailor" (*Macmillan MUSIC AND YOU*, Grade 2, p. 203). Readers who plan for older classes of multihandicapped students will also want to investigate the *Music*

Curriculum for Moderately Retarded Adolescents by Beal and Gilbert (1982).

The language used in teacher directions and questions should be very simple, and sentences or questions need to be very short. A statement such as "Listen to this new song and tell me how many angels there are" may be much too complicated. The direction probably should simply be "Listen and watch."

Functional Music

Some of the songs and musical experiences that music teachers include in their planning for multihandicapped classes may serve two functions. The primary focus should always be musical education. However, musical education can be accomplished with material that reinforces the skills or the knowledge that the students are learning daily in their classroom. Songs or activities that describe body parts, reinforce body image, or assist in color discrimination can be found in all primary series texts as well as in the sources at the end of this chapter.

The selection of such songs or activities should certainly be coordinated with what the classroom teacher feels is most important and is teaching each day. Music teachers should, however, always remember that their primary purpose is to present musical experiences. If the classroom teacher is working on colors and a song such as "Who Has a Green Dress?" (Graham and Beer, p. 109; see Fig. 11-1) is selected to reinforce what the class is learning, the song must also fit into the music

FIGURE 11-1 "Who Has a Green Dress" adapted from "Who Has a Penny" by Angela Diller & Kate Stearns Page, from *A Pre-School Music Book.* Copyright © 1936, 1963 by G. Schirmer, Inc. All Rights Reserved. Used by Permission.

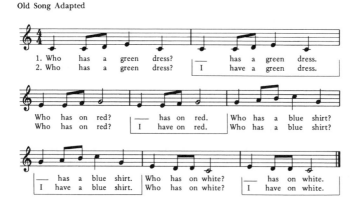

lesson and illustrate a musical element that you have been teaching or are going to teach.

It is when music educators begin to teach multihandicapped classes that the distinction between therapy and education can become blurred. Music therapy uses music to achieve nonmusical goals and is a very valid, useful profession. Readers of this text who teach handicapped students will certainly benefit from reading any of the music therapy texts listed in the chapter bibliography.

But music educators are not trained as therapists and must always try to provide all students, no matter how severe the handicap, with a *music* education. The color song referred to earlier can be taught to help the teacher reinforce colors, and it can be easily adapted for any child by changing the color and the word *dress* to *shirt* or *pants*, and so on. The song can also be sung with varying tempos, dynamics, accompaniments, and so on, depending upon the focus of the lesson. It is in this way that the two functions, musical and extramusical, can be served simultaneously.

Rate

Probably the most difficult aspect of teaching multihandicapped classes is the adjustment of teacher expectations. In regular general music classes, the teacher includes a new song or activity (sometimes two) during each lesson and reviews the material the following week. After two or three weeks (assuming there have been adequate material selection and competent teaching), the entire class demonstrates their ability to sing, listen, play, or move at an acceptable level. It is not possible to follow this procedure with a multihandicapped class.

Students who are trainable mentally retarded learn extremely slowly, which, translated into lesson-planning reality, means that it may take two or three or four times as long for a class to learn songs, movement sequences, or accompaniments. Although the teacher may feel that repeating the same material for four lessons (or more) is incredibly boring, the students do not. And because of the variety of handicaps that students may have in one class, repetition provides the opportunities for different levels of participation. One or two students may learn all the words after two or three lessons, whereas another student or two may learn only the beginning or the end phrase. In the same class, one student may only be able to indicate his or her awareness that the music is beginning.

An important musical factor that affects students' rate of learning is tempo. The initial presentations of new songs or activities should be at a very slow speed, with very clear teacher diction and enunciation. Recorded versions of the song should rarely be used—certainly never as an introduction—since the accompaniment and the tempo make it very difficult for children with language deficits to comprehend what words are being sung. A fine song and activity is "Play Your Instrument and Make a Pretty Sound" (Ella Jenkins, Folkways # 7665). At the recorded tempo, the song is beyond the comprehension of many students in multihandicapped classes. When taught slowly and repeatedly, the song can be used to teach tone colors—"Play your maraca [triangle, drum, etc.] and make a pretty sound"—or dynamics—"Play your bells and make a soft sound." Even after participating in this activity for many months, some students may still need prompting or assistance when it is their turn, whereas others may demonstrate an ability to take turns and recognize the different musical instruments and contrasts.

Structure

One aspect of planning for these classes is easier: The beginning and ending activities should be the same in each lesson. Beginning every lesson with "Hello, Everybody" or "If You're Happy and You Know It" or another greeting song provides a signal to every class member—whether or not he or she is able to sing any or all of the words or participate in the movements—that now music class is beginning. Ending each class with "Goodbye, Everybody" or a similar song also provides a musical signal. Teachers may wish to conclude each lesson with a song such as "All Night, All Day," which is found in many texts, or "My Father's House," which is illustrated with hand signs in Nocera's text. The soothing quality of these songs may help some students come to adequate closure and more easily transfer their attention to the next activity in their school day.

The classroom physical structure should also be consistent from lesson to lesson. Since many multihandicapped classes include children in wheelchairs, one suitable seating arrangement is a semicircle or a circle. This type of seating enables aides and classroom teachers to sit next to a child who needs help holding an instrument, waiting his or her turn, or simply attending. Music teachers will find that they are able to maintain constant eye contact with the entire class, easily distribute and collect classroom instruments, and demonstrate movements in the center space.

SUMMARY OF TEACHING SUGGESTIONS

Illustrate song vocabulary.
Select socially appropriate musical material.
Use simple directions.
Coordinate music selection with academic instruction.
Plan to repeat musical activities.

Provide for different levels of individual participation.
Present new songs at a slow tempo.
Include a consistent lesson introduction and conclusion.
Provide a consistent seating arrangement.

Instrumental Music

Instrumental teachers may have decided by this point in the chapter that certainly these are students that they will never have to deal with! However, trainable retarded individuals have been taught to play instruments, and there are places in our country where these students make up a complete band. Reports by music educators have described two of these successful instrumental ventures.

A program at the Rocky Mountain Rehabilitation Center in Colorado Springs (Mills, 1975) had an enrollment of fifty-eight students, who learned recorder, piano, chord organ, guitar, trumpet, accordion, clarinet, and drums. The students initially learned by rote, but the author describes devising written materials so that the students' parents could assist in practice periods. The first book for all instruments emphasized the difference between right and left, using games, songs, and pictures, followed by a section on finger numbers. The author wrote books for each of the aforementioned instruments and introduced manageable amounts of material and simple rhythms for each instrument. For example, the book for clarinet used only three notes played by the left hand and included simple tunes using these notes.

The Great Expectations Band (Fig. 11-2) in Great Falls, Montana (Williams, 1985), was begun in 1975 and includes students who play brass and percussion instruments (plus two who play saxophones). The teachers used the *Tap Master* program, taped examples, systematic listening, and breathing exercises to increase the students' tone quality and rhythmic ability. The members of this band are taught to use standard music notation, and this facet of the program is especially noteworthy, since several students have been subsequently mainstreamed into public school music instrumental groups. Students who graduate are also allowed to continue to play in this band, which made a guest appearance at the Music Educators National Conference in Chicago in 1984.

Summary

Readers should understand that planning for classes of multihandicapped students will require quite different approaches. Certainly, the process of finding material that incorporates age-appropriate language and provides for different levels of participation ability is a challenge. An important aspect of instruction in these classes is being aware of the

FIGURE 11-2   The Great Expectations Band. Photograph courtesy of Dr. Larry Williams, Bozeman Public Schools, Bozeman, Montana.

balance of functional music and the necessity of providing a music education. Music educators must adapt their expectations, since a class of multihandicapped students may include students who each learn at a different rate.

But you should be aware that teaching these students is incredibly rewarding and joyful. You will receive immediate satisfaction and continual positive reinforcement because many of the students in these classes who have inadequate adaptive or social behavior speak their thoughts immediately. You will be told you are loved and truly appreciated, even hugged and kissed before and after each class, and told repeatedly that you and music are wonderful. Teaching this type of class is a healthy antidote to teaching students who are determined to not appear to enjoy anything lest their peers consider them not "cool."

It is obvious that students in self-contained special classes are not going to be the concertgoers of the future. That does not mean that the value of music is any less for these individuals. Everyone who receives a public education also deserves exposure to the expressiveness and feelings of music. The selection of appropriate lesson content and the adjustment of teaching techniques to fit these classes will ensure that multihandicapped students also receive their musical education.

INTEGRATION OF MULTIHANDICAPPED STUDENTS

Some readers of this text may eventually teach multihandicapped students who are mainstreamed into music classes. It is the belief of some special educators that the "least restrictive environment" should refer not only to the physical classroom setting but also to a total school environment that prepares multihandicapped students to function and interact with nonhandicapped peers (Certo, Haring, and York, 1984). In some communities, this setting is achieved by moving special classes out of separate buildings and into neighborhood elementary and secondary schools.

In communities where these classes are already housed in a public school, some students may be individually mainstreamed, or structured experiences with nonhandicapped students may be provided in peer-tutoring sessions. A program pairing peer-tutors with autistic children in Oregon (Almond, Rodgers, and Krug, 1979) benefited both the handicapped students, by providing additional preacademic instruction, and the nonhandicapped students, who learned interpersonal skills necessary to relate to nonverbal individuals. This volunteer work especially contributed to a sense of self-worth in the slower students from regular classes. In addition, cooperative playground contacts between the two groups increased significantly, and classroom teachers indicated school-wide understanding and acceptance of the autistic children.

A description of peer-helpers in music class was published in *Music Educators Journal* in 1979 (Dykman). One school in Madison, Wisconsin, was chosen as the target school for several classes of multihandicapped students, some of whom had formerly been institutionalized. The music-teacher author and the school's art and physical education instructors proposed a plan whereby students signed up to help in the special education classes. Examples of musical activities that were made possible through these helpers included wheelchair dances, correct rhythmic responses, and guitar and recorder accompaniments. The account also describes how children from emotionally disturbed classes participated as helpers for the multihandicapped students.

A different approach is that of the "Special Friends" project (Voeltz, 1984), which has been used for four years in twelve public schools in Hawaii. This project provides opportunities for the multihandicapped child to acquire social skills and for the nonhandicapped child to learn positive attitudes and ways of interacting with handicapped peers. Attractive leisure activities (video games, pinball, and so on) are used to provide positive social peer interactions.

Successful mainstreaming of multihandicapped students into music depends upon a careful consideration of the individual's abilities in conjunction with a detailed matching of the demands and expectations of class instruction. Teachers should certainly be open to providing an opportunity for a mainstreamed musical experience for a multihandicapped child. However, music educators must be alert to the implication that music is a nondemanding and nonacademic period, into which any exceptional child can be placed at any time. For example, the following quote is from a chapter describing the program and curriculum innovations involved in integrating severely handicapped students in public schools: "Nearly all severely handicapped children can be included within regular classrooms for various selected activities and programs, e.g., story time, art, and music in elementary grades, etc." (Voeltz, 1984 p. 159). Unfortunately, that is not an unusual statement or attitude and can be countered only by music educators who have developed a coherent curriculum and are able to clearly articulate what and how they are teaching.

Teachers who do participate in integrating severely handicapped students into music classes must provide an accepting and positive model for the nonhandicapped students. Instruction must be adapted so that there are opportunities for cooperation and successful interactions between the students. Many nonhandicapped students may have negative attitudes toward multihandicapped students that have gradually developed from inferences in the media or from significant adults. Because of the prevalence of such feelings among students, it may be necessary to carefully structure interactions and provide positive reinforcement for both the nonhandicapped and the handicapped in mainstreamed and cooperative learning settings.

This strategy was employed in a music education research study reported by Jellison, Brooks, and Huck (1984). The experimental period was four weeks, during which severely retarded and multihandicapped students ($n = 26$) aged 8–15 were mainstreamed into four music classes ($n = 100$) with students aged 9–12. The music classes met twice a week. Nonhandicapped students were pretested and posttested with an "Acceptance within Music Scale," and classes were observed for helping and reciprocal social interactions during both large-group and small-group activities. The small groups were instructed to work together, and cooperation was clearly defined by the music teacher. In addition, the small groups were promised that the most cooperative group would receive a reward (listening to rock music).

The researchers report that positive social interactions were highest during the small-group activities. Reciprocal interactions were observed, but few helping interactions were observed in three of the four classes. Significant differences in acceptance were reported for all but one class. Specific instructional strategies that facilitate the mainstreaming of multihandicapped students into music classes are suggested in the conclusion of this report: "a) students know specifically what is expected of them; b) opportunities are provided for students to do what is expected; c) contingencies of reinforcement are arranged so that students want to do what is expected" (p. 259).

Future researchers should note this study as one that could be duplicated with children of other ages. The experimental classes in this study were one third- and fourth-grade combination, one fourth grade, one fifth- and sixth-grade combination, and one sixth grade. It would be of interest to read a duplication of this study with younger students.

In these particular music classes, students were given five minutes of free time at the end of the second class period of each week. Some readers may question the need for this "free time" in music instruction and also the inclusion of rock music listening as a reward. Another future researcher may wish to structure a similar experiment and either omit the reinforcer or use only praise as a reinforcer.

A nonmusic research study (Rynders et al., 1980) investigated integrated groups who were learning to bowl. While the subject may seem far afield for this text, the groupings and the results do complement the foregoing music education study. In this project, junior high students and students from a school for trainable students were integrated and divided into three groups to learn bowling. One group was instructed to use cooperative behaviors to improve their group scores (verbal praise, reinforcement, assistance). The second group focused on individual competitive behaviors: Scores were rank-ordered, and individuals were instructed to monitor the scores of other group members to determine if they were ahead or behind. The members of the third group were instructed to try to improve their own individual scores over the previous session.

The groups' interactions and language were noted by trained observers. Each handicapped student had an average of twenty-nine positive interactions per hour with nonhandicapped peers in the cooperative group, in contrast to two per hour in the competitive and four per hour in the individual groups. At the conclusion of the eight sessions, each subject was individually interviewed: He or she was asked to rank-order photographs of the other group members from most to least favorite person to bowl with, and to explain why. The ranking of handicapped students was significantly higher by members of the cooperative group than in either of the other two groups.

These findings are especially noteworthy, since the cooperative group was instructed to try to improve their previous group score by 50 points each week. The handicapped students bowled much more poorly than their peers, but their poor performance did not alter or affect the students' cooperative behaviors and language or their later feelings about each other. The results of this study are similar to those of Jellison et al. and support the efficacy of prestructuring small groups and indicating acceptable cooperative behaviors to provide social acceptance of multihandicapped learners.

ADDITIONAL RESEARCH

The first three studies described in this section were conducted with students who were not educated in public schools. Two of the projects were conducted prior to the passage of Public Law 94-142, and students with similar disabilities may now possibly be educated in a noninstitutional setting. The authors all describe clearly structured and appropriate instruction that was effective for their subjects. These studies are summarized to provide readers with additional information on teaching multihandicapped students. The final report in this section concerns the use of musical vocabulary by therapists and trainable retarded students, and the conclusions are also applicable to music education.

Instrumental Instruction

A description of teaching trainable retarded students to play piano and other instruments is found in a dissertation by Weber (1966). The researcher began by stimulating student response to such familiar melodies as "Pop Goes the Weasel" and "When the Saints Go Marching In"; he then played those melodies on instruments. He devised a simplified symbolic code for each instrument to stand for the six notes C through A. For example, the clarinet code was 3-2-1-t-0-A, which is related to the fingerings for the tones that can be played with only the left hand. The piano code was the six alphabet letters. The students were then taught to discriminate the code and finally to associate the symbols and sounds.

The report is not a statistical study but is a narrative description of each of the five students who were taught by the researcher over the course of a year. He reports that one 10-year-old, after the year's instruction, could play one hundred melodies on the piano using his simplified chord and note symbol system. The students had several common difficulties, which included initial problems differentiating similarly shaped letters, tracking from left to right, keeping their place in a series of repeated letters, and moving down the page. The last two problems were solved by having the children point to the symbol with their nonplaying hand.

Classroom Music for Neurologically Impaired Students

A very different population, neurologically handicapped children with no verbal abilities, was the subject of an instructional experiment by Pirtle and Seaton (1973). The researchers taught the students ($n = 15$) twice a week for six months. This experimental group was matched (mental age and intelligence) with a control group from the same residential setting, and all subjects were administered pretests and posttests of musical concepts and language. Test responses were nonverbal and included movements, pointing to pictures, and playing an instrument.

The instruction used by the researchers was carefully structured to assist the students in the development of auditory discrimination and memory and did result in improvement. The experimental group made significant improvement in the tests of both musical concepts and language. The researchers conclude that music experiences have transfer effects for this population and provide "one nonthreatening experience in which he can function on a nonverbal level" (p. 300).

Music Curriculum for the Deaf-Blind

A report by Weidenbach (1981) describes the development of a music curriculum for six young multihandicapped deaf-blind children who had been classified as ineducable. Although the subjects were institutionalized, the report is of interest because of the emphasis on finding a way to educate these children similarly to their nonhandicapped peers, using singing, listening, playing, moving, and creating. Each of these music education approaches is also described as serving functional and therapeutic ends, such as increasing auditory attention and discrimination, improving fine and gross motor skills, and learning skills needed for group cooperation. The report is a narrative description and includes this statement in the conclusion: "There were occasions when their spontaneous expressions of pleasure closely resembled those encountered in a regular classroom" (p. 497).

Music Vocabulary in Adults and Students

A report by Hair and Graham (1983) summarizes a study that compared the vocabulary used by music therapists ($n = 19$) to describe musical characteristics and that used by trainable retarded students ($n = 32$). The subjects were tested individually with a taped test containing ten variations (loud, soft, fast, slow, and so on) of known melodies. The expected finding of statistical differences between the two groups is reported. What is of interest is the children's ability to hear changes but their inability to express the correct term.

The report includes the percentages of correct responses by both groups for each of the ten musical alterations. The initial loud dynamic change was described accurately by 72 percent of the students and 89 percent of the therapists. The final change, rhythmic alteration, was described correctly by 53 percent of the therapists, while the students used terms such as *dancing, different, gentle,* and *sounds better.* The researchers conclude that their findings indicate a need for more effective strategies to teach musically specific vocabulary to trainable retarded students.

The conclusion of this study corresponds to similar findings by Hair (1981) with nonhandicapped children who used any musical term to describe a perceived musical change when the correct term was not known. While the preceding study was conducted with therapists, the conclusion is certainly generalizable to music educators. Trainable retarded children can discriminate and perform musical contrasts, and included in this aspect of their musical education should be the usage of correct and descriptive terminology.

Research tells us that some

Multiply handicapped students can be successfully mainstreamed in music if small-group instruction is carefully structured.

Trainable retarded students can learn to play instruments.

Neurologically handicapped children with no verbal ability can learn musical concepts.

Deaf-blind children labeled ineducable responded to music similarly to nonhandicapped children.

CONCLUSION

It has taken much longer for multihandicapped students to become accepted in public school settings than for students with single disabilities. Some compassionate and fine educators (and schoolboard and community members) would still prefer to keep these children "out of sight." These often unarticulated sentiments are quite similar to those expressed by many individuals when a sheltered home for retarded adults is proposed for their community. "Not in my neighborhood" is, unfortunately, a standard response.

Although we would prefer to concentrate on teaching subject matter only, it is not possible for educators to ignore social issues. Indeed, teachers already attempt to deal with many social ills that were once the province of the entire community, including hunger, drug addiction, smoking, drinking, and now AIDS. The inclusion of multi-handicapped children in public schools should not be allowed to become a similar negative social issue; rather, it should be an opportunity for an entire faculty to model and teach accepting and cooperative social skills to all the students in a school.

One music professor in Winston-Salem, North Carolina, has found a way to provide trainable retarded adolescents who attend a special school with positive musical and social interactions. Lee Beall (1985) has described the performance of *Oliver* given by students from a special school and students from nonhandicapped classes. A different musical is presented each year. Dr. Beall prepares the musical aspects, and the other teachers help with teaching the script and the choreography. Every trainable mentally handicapped student (58) participated in the production of *Oliver* along with a chorus of nonhandicapped fifth graders. Teachers of these students were in the cast and always on stage to help out, and nonhandicapped fifth and sixth graders were leaders in the dances. What is especially noteworthy about this project is that Dr. Beall is neither a music educator nor a music therapist. He is a compassionate and caring musician who found a way to provide cooperative learning experiences for severely handicapped students and share his musical talents with others.

The love of music and the sharing of that love with young people is what we are all about. The students may not look similar or react in the same way, nor is there a standard set of materials or procedures that will work with all classes. We share our love of music by planning for and teaching individuals and groups in a manner that is consistent with *their* abilities.

No textbook can teach the most important quality needed for music teachers who will instruct the students described in this chapter—an acceptance of human differences. All a textbook can provide is generalizations about labels and learning differences, suggestions for materials and instructional strategies, and summaries of relevant research. Attitudes come from within each of us, but even the slowest and most different of children can sense acceptance and caring in a teacher. Multihandicapped children need music teachers who have both a knowledge of the contents of this chapter and a nonjudgmental approach. Teaching a single multihandicapped child or an entire class is truly the challenge for your future!

QUESTIONS

1. Why is the "least restrictive environment" often different for multihandicapped students?
2. Discuss the implications for instrumental music teachers who teach a trainable retarded student.
3. What are the similarities and differences between students labeled autistic and those labeled trainable mentally retarded?
4. What communication techniques can be used when teaching music to students who do not speak?
5. What is functional music?

6. Why must music teachers adjust their expectations when teaching multihandicapped classes?
7. Why is a consistent structure recommended for a multihandicapped class?
8. What are some instructional strategies to use if multihandicapped students are mainstreamed into general music classes?

ACTIVITIES

1. Plan a music lesson for a primary class of multihandicapped children who have severe communication disorders. Include materials, activities, and teacher directions.
2. Observe a multihandicapped class and describe each student's language and learning ability. Describe the classroom setting and lesson content.
3. Prepare a proposal for an administrator that details how you will set up a peer-tutoring experiment for a class of multihandicapped students who have just been moved to your building.

BIBLIOGRAPHY

BOXILL, E. H. 1985. *Music Therapy for the Developmentally Disabled.* Rockville, Md.: Aspen Systems Corporation.
CORMIER, L. J. 1980. A Guide in the Use of Music in the Training and Development of Rubella Deaf-Blind Children. Master's thesis, Michigan State University.
HARDESTY, K. W. 1979. *Music for Special Education.* Morristown, N.J.: Silver Burdett Company.
MICHEL, D. E. 1976. *Music Therapy.* Springfield, Ill.: Chas. C Thomas.
NORDOFF, P., and C. ROBBINS. 1971. *Music Therapy in Special Education.* New York: Harper & Row, Pub.
PRATT, R. R., and M. PETERSON. 1981. *Elementary Music for All Learners.* Sherman Oaks, Calif.: Alfred Publishing Co.
PURVIS, J., and S. SAMET, eds. 1976. *Music in Developmental Therapy.* Baltimore: University Park Press.
SLYOFF, M. R. 1979. *Music for Special Education.* Fort Worth: Harris Music Publications.
VERNAZZA, M. 1978. *Music Plus for the Young Child in Special Education.* Boulder, Colo.: Pruett Publishing Co.

Success
for Mainstreamed
Learners
CHAPTER TWELVE

INTRODUCTION

The overriding premise of this book is that music educators must adapt instruction in ways that will enable all exceptional students to participate in successful musical experiences. While some of these students may be taught in small self-contained classes, most will be mainstreamed into various music settings. Those students who are integrated into general music, lessons, band, or chorus have been described in previous chapters by singular terms such as learning disabled, educable mentally retarded, physically handicapped, and emotionally disturbed.

Do these labels contribute to success? For the purpose of organization, the chapters of this text have been arranged under the distinct names given to disabilities by educators. Music teachers should be aware, however, that ever since the earliest attempts to provide a differentiated education for exceptional children, there has been an awareness of the dangers that labels pose. Alfred Binet, who devised the first intelligence test in 1904, wrote that "it will never be to one's credit to have attended a special school" (Bryan, p. 81). Sixty-four years later, in the seminal article that proposed that exceptional children be educated in the mainstream and that the proliferation of special classes be halted, Lloyd Dunn wrote, ". . . we must examine the effects of these disability labels on the pupils themselves. Certainly none of these labels are badges of distinction" (p. 9).

Subsequently, Public Law 94-142 was passed, which, while not including the specific term *mainstreaming*, mandated the integration of many exceptional students who were formerly taught in the self-contained classes that Dunn opposed. The paradox is that while the proliferation of special classes has been halted, the law has actually promoted the labeling process. Students must be categorized in order for school districts to receive state and federal funding.

Music teachers should be acutely aware of how labels are used in their own setting. One approach is to consider any label as only a signal that alerts you to a possible range of learning behaviors. A label, then, is just a generalization. The various designations provide a background with which to better understand individual children, and they also provide a foundation for more focused planning, competent instruction strategies, and adaptation of materials for mainstreamed students.

A major disadvantage of any exceptionality label is that teachers will not perceive the student as a unique individual but, rather, will perceive the student as being representative of the generalization. Every label that has been used in this text includes degrees of severity from mild to severe. That fact alone should serve to discourage present readers from ever believing that a single term can describe an individual exceptional child.

Do teachers already have preconceptions based on the specificity of single labels? Several researchers have found that teachers have low expectations of and negative feelings toward exceptional students. One report in the music education literature (Jellison and Wolfe, 1987) contains a description of how teachers rated music objectives for two groups of students. For each set of teachers, one group of students was defined as unlabeled and a second group of students was labeled either severely handicapped or gifted. The researchers report significant differences in the comparisons between the labeled and unlabeled students. Objectives were more important for nonhandicapped than for severely retarded and were also more important for gifted than for nonlabeled.

Another research project that has particular relevance to this text (Stone, 1980) addressed the labeling question and also queried teacher attitudes toward mainstreaming. This report is described in some detail because the findings have important implications for music educators who will be involved in teaching mainstreamed students.

The researcher's questionnaire focused on several broad areas: preparation, sympathy, communication, awareness of potential restrictions, and ability to help exceptional children learn. Important effects were reported for age, years of experience, special education courses, and subject area specialization. Older teachers (41–50) indicated the most overall positive attitudes, while teachers who were 30 and younger had the most negative attitudes. This finding alone should be a gigantic flashing danger signal in undergraduate preparation of music teachers. Methods courses must include experiences that will prepare future teachers to be accepting and understanding of exceptional children.

Future teachers should have adequate exposure to, information about, and structured positive experiences with mainstreamed students so that they will not develop negative attitudes.

Findings about the teachers' perceptions of individual labels were correlated with the amount of teacher preparation and subject matter specialization. Negative or positive attitudes about individual labels were not affected by the number of special education courses (1–4) taken by the teachers. Of particular note to readers is the fact that *all* labels were perceived negatively by teachers of art and music. The researcher's conclusion regarding this finding is that "their attitudes might arise from being accustomed to the 'perfection' of their art forms, and obvious imperfections in students might create discomfort. If these teachers could be helped to strive for improvement in individual students, rather than 'perfection,' their attitudes might become more positive" (p. 111). This conclusion reinforces the previous statement that music educators should consider labels as guides, not as definitive descriptions.

As reported in Chapter 1, researchers in our own field have indicated that music teachers at the secondary level have the least amount of interaction with exceptional students. That may have been the case with the respondents of this survey. However, even with this caveat, it is still quite startling to read that any music educators (whose motto for so long was "Music for every child, every child for music") would indicate completely negative attitudes toward exceptional students.

Negative attitudes toward exceptional students can be caused by many factors, of course. Both beginning and experienced teachers often feel insecure when faced with the inclusion of labeled students in music classes, lessons, or rehearsals. One reason for this lack of assurance may be lack of preparation in methods classes or inadequate experiences during student teaching. A second reason is that some students do present unique patterns of behavior or learning that deviate from the group norm; most music teachers are prepared to teach groups (trumpets, second graders, concert choir), not individuals within groups. Teachers also realize that exceptional students demand extra teacher time, and for most music teachers, time is a precious commodity.

It is certainly difficult to eliminate a negative attitude about any label (or stereotype) without positive experiences with individuals to whom the label is applied. It is hoped that readers of this text will simultaneously experience some successful, fulfilling, and rewarding musical experiences with a variety of exceptional students. Music educators must always remember the positive uses and the dangers of the labels used in exceptional education. Categories of exceptional students are truly vague indicators of the ways that one individual may learn and are never a definitive description of any student.

Identification

An important question is, "How do music teachers know that students in their classes are exceptional learners?" Some readers may think that this is a silly question. It is not. The reality is that some teachers do *not* know! The author conducted a research study of achievement in learning disabled students in grades two and five in 1987 and was informed by the music supervisor of a quite large city that there were no learning disabled children in any music classes! The music teachers all agreed with the supervisor in an introductory meeting. This statement was subsequently negated by the director of special education. Each class contained several learning disabled students, but the music teachers did not know who they were.

Such ignorance does not result in the equal treatment of all children. All music educators have an understandable desire to produce pleasing and musical results in each lesson. Certainly, a child who cannot coordinate the mallet and actually hit the Orff instrument won't be chosen by the teacher very often (if ever, after the one time). Without any explanation or understanding of why the child has gross motor difficulties, the teacher will most certainly select students who will succeed at this musical task. Lacking any explanation or understanding of the child's deficits, the teacher has no incentive to find ways to adapt the activity or ensure success in future musical experiences for that one student.

Some directors of special education clearly identify the exceptional students in their district at the beginning of the school year to all the teachers who will be interacting with them. If you teach in a school where this is not the practice, it would be worthwhile to request such information every year. Similarly, some classroom teachers will ensure that you know immediately which of their students require careful consideration. If neither of these types of communication exists, then it is your responsibility to read and ask questions and discover which are the exceptional learners.

The reasons for early identification of mainstreamed learners are related to the title of this chapter. Quite simply, teachers cannot provide success for mainstreamed individuals during group instruction without a knowledge of who the individuals are in each class. In addition, each group of students comes to music instruction with a class social structure that is established during the first few days of the year and that subsequently does not change (Engstrom, 1982). Teachers who are prepared to immediately provide opportunities for musical success for exceptional students can help influence the perceptions of the nonhandicapped class members during this critical time.

MUSICAL SUCCESS

As with many educational mandates that are politically motivated, the practice of mainstreaming by itself does not automatically ensure success for any student in music. Mainstreaming or providing education in "the least restrictive environment" was in great measure a reaction and a response to the often indiscriminate placement of children from both lower economic levels and racial minorities in classes for retarded students. Many people in and out of education believe that music is a nondemanding, nonacademic period, in which any child can easily be accommodated; music teachers know that that perception is erroneous.

In general music for primary children, what appears to be fun and games is actually a clearly defined curriculum that focuses on concrete experiences. These activities are the means of providing a foundation for teaching subsequent musical abstractions. Students who cannot participate in these readiness experiences because of physical handicaps will have greater difficulty in their later musical education. Students whose motor and cognitive abilities are unequal to those of their peers are also at risk in music when abstractions and higher-order thinking skills become the important focus in music instruction.

Music educators must face some basic truths about mainstreaming. Some (perhaps even many) exceptional students will be unable to participate in many aspects of music instruction at the same level or rate as their classmates, and many music classrooms will still often be considered one of the few "least restrictive environments"! The law is not going to change or disappear, and neither are the mainstreamed exceptional students.

After accepting those realities, teachers can proceed to a determination of how to provide as much musical success as possible for mainstreamed students. Each chapter in this text has included numerous suggestions for general and specific curriculum accommodations at all levels. By incorporating one or more of these suggestions, a teacher may enable a single child to more clearly understand or participate in music learning. In addition to incorporating the suggestions that have been included in individual chapters, teachers should consider the following general ways of approaching music planning and teaching, which will assist in making successful music experiences for mainstreamed students a reality.

Intensification

Many of the ways that visual and aural material can be clarified for mainstreamed students are subsumed under the descriptor of *intensification*. Throughout the preceding chapters, numerous suggestions have been included that were based on several common principles: increasing size, adding color, changing rate, and using different combinations of auditory, visual, and motor activities. Each of these generic terms describes a variety of mainstreaming approaches that may be helpful for students with very different disabilities.

Musical success, therefore, may be possible for some mainstreamed students solely through the inclusion of intensified materials. Increasing the size of a visual example, whether it be words, notation, or graphics, may assist not just a visually impaired child but also, perhaps, a learning disabled or an emotionally disturbed learner. Intensifying the same visual example with color may help students who are identified by the same labels or who are educable mentally retarded. Using a slower rate or tempo in giving directions, singing songs, or teaching movements is also a means of intensifying and making more meaningful some musical activities. Each of these types of intensification can be adapted by teachers of general music classes, instrumental lessons, or performance organizations.

The ways that materials or instruction can be adapted are based on a belief that multisensory learning is more effective for many students. Music educators, whose subject is sound, often rely extensively on students' aural abilities and often neglect to consider the use of other senses in reinforcing and illustrating sound; yet, a present-day reality is that most students are much more visually oriented. It has been estimated that most children begin school with an accumulated *average* television viewing time of 5,000 hours. These kindergartners have developed a high degree of visual dependence, and that fact must not be ignored when planning music instruction.

Grouping

Musical success for many mainstreamed learners does not necessarily have to be continual individual success. There are instructional approaches other than one teacher and one learner or one teacher and a large group that can be incorporated into classroom and performance music teaching. Two of those approaches, peer tutoring and small cooperative groups, were described in Chapter 11 as ways of facilitating the inclusion of multihandicapped students in music classes. Both approaches are also worthy of consideration for all other mainstreamed students.

There are many possibilities for incorporating peer tutoring in music. In general music classrooms, students can help handicapped children learn special accompaniments on Orff instruments, recorders, or resonator bells. Peers can teach a saxophone part or a soprano part in a piece of music to mainstreamed peers in a performance group at any level. Teachers should also note that peer-tutors may also be exceptional children who can teach other students a skill they have acquired. This approach was described by Osguthorpe and Custer (1983), who conducted an experiment in which educable mentally retarded students acted as peer-tutors for sixth graders in sign language. The researchers reported dramatic increases in social contact between the two groups of students in nonstructured social settings and increases in self-confidence in the retarded students.

The "Special Friends" concept (Voeltz, 1984), in contrast to peer tutoring, is not a situation where teaching and learning take place but, rather, an opportunity for social interaction. Special friends can be a way of providing contact beyond mere physical proximity of handicapped and nonhandicapped students. Promoting such friendships through assigning pairs of children to projects is also a suggested approach (Pappanikou and Paul, 1977). Many activities in music provide opportunities for such social and musical cooperation to occur. Music rooms can provide a place for students to "hang out" with their special friends or their partners and use electronic keyboards, Autoharps, or listening stations together.

It may be difficult for many performance-oriented music educators to accept that musical success for some students may not necessarily involve accurate musical reproduction of notation. Many exceptional learners will never read music, but that does not mean that they enjoy music any less than their peers. Musical success for some mainstreamed students may be opportunities to improvise according to their own ability, listen as perceptively as they are able, and experience feelingful reactions to music—valid musical experiences, indeed. This success may be more possible if it is the result of musical experiences with a peer or a "special friend."

Dividing classes into smaller groups and defining a cooperative learning structure is another type of instructional grouping that could be incorporated into many music teaching situations. General music groups could work out a composition, an accompaniment, or a rhythm ostinato. Three trumpet players could work on a trio in their beginning book, or a quartet might work on their vocal parts in one piece of music. Mere grouping, however, is not sufficient. Teacher directions must clearly indicate that the group outcome is most important, not how each individual performs: This is the premise of cooperative learning.

Three different approaches to learning—cooperative, competitive, and individualistic—have been researched extensively in groups that include mainstreamed children (Johnson and Johnson, 1986). In Chapter 11, an experiment in teaching bowling was described. That study is just one of twenty-five projects that have been conducted over a ten-year period in a continuing research program. The studies have been conducted at varying levels (grade one to grade eleven) and have included exceptional children who are mentally retarded, learning disabled, emotionally disturbed, gifted, and hearing impaired. The results of all these studies indicate that cooperative learning facilitates greater interpersonal attraction between handicapped and nonhandicapped students.

Musical success for some exceptional learners may not be an individual musical performance, no matter what the grade or setting; rather, it may consist of being a member of a group that cooperates to reach a common musical goal. The variables described by Johnson and Johnson that contribute to greater social acceptance for exceptional students include greater peer approval, positive interactions, unconditional self-acceptance, academic success, and expectations for future positive interactions. For some students, greater social acceptance and working toward a common musical outcome may provide success in musical learning.

Another type of grouping is called the "Teams-Games-Tournaments" model (Slavin, 1978). Again, cooperative learning is stressed, but in this approach, students of different ability levels train and work together to prepare for tournaments or quizzes, which are administered individually. This model could be adapted in music instruction, both in preparing for individual sectional auditions in performing groups and in general music classes where a review of prior learnings is planned.

The structure and the directions for any of these groupings are of great importance, and teachers must be able to clearly define cooperative learning, goals, outcomes, and acceptable processes for their own musical setting. Forming groups without a clear structure will result in close physical proximity but not necessarily any cooperation, acceptance, or liking. In fact, small groups who are not working cooperatively can provide very negative experiences for mainstreamed learners.

Small-group activities certainly approximate more closely the types of sharing that adults are expected to be able to do. One researcher (Resnick, 1987) describes the difference between learning in school, where students are judged on an individual basis, and participation in activities out of school, where adults are evaluated on their ability to contribute to a shared enterprise. Alternative grouping in music instruction might better prepare all students for adult musical cooperation and participation by including more experiences that require students to work toward a common musical goal. Such grouping already exists for many advanced adult musicians under the title of chamber music. Of course, for many adolescents, small groups already exist in every community under the label of rock band.

Organization

The final area that music teachers should consider when deciding how to provide successful musical experiences for mainstreamed students is how each period will be structured. The type of structure may refer to different instructional groupings described in the preceding section or to the actual lesson content and types of questions that will be asked of students. As was described in Chapters 5 and 10, lesson planning for classes that include mainstreamed students should involve a prior determination of what is necessary to provide opportunities for musical success.

All students learn best when there is a clear focus in a lesson and when objectives are clearly articulated to the learners. Assuming that the kids will "get it" because each song, dance, chant, and movement activity is in triple meter is fallacious. And assuming that a performance group understands why they are to "begin again at letter A" is similarly false. What is true for nonhandicapped learners is similarly or even more true for mainstreamed students: Instruction of any kind at any level must not be a guessing game.

Effective lesson structure for classes with mainstreamed learners should include a variety of musical experiences with opportunities for involvement at many levels. In an article in *Music Educators Journal* in 1982, Alice S. Beer and her coauthors described a series of thirteen steps that could be used in teaching "Five Angels" (Fig. 12-1). The steps are arranged in increasing order of difficulty and are suggested as a way to teach ascending melodic direction to groups that include mainstreamed learners. The song and the steps are included as an illustration of one way to provide success in music for many different children.

1. Listen to the song and observe a picture of five angels.
2. Count the angels.
3. Describe the angels' actions.
4. Listen to the song and point to each angel at the appropriate time.
5. Sing only the repeated phrase.
6. Sing the song, dramatizing the words.
7. Play a triangle on the words, "first, second," and so on.
8. Indicate with some motion the upward direction of the repeated melodic phrase.
9. Sing the song as five children take turns indicating the direction of the melody at the appropriate time, using a large visual representation of the scale passage.
10. Sing and play the repeated phrase on step bells, resonator bells, xylophone, metallophone, or piano.
11. Determine whether the patterns are alike.

FIGURE 12-1 From *Reaching the Special Learner through Music* by Sona Nocera. © 1979 by The Silver Burdett Company.

12. Make a visual representation of the part played on the bells.
13. Use the term *repeated pattern*.

These steps provide a variety of levels of possible involvement for mainstreamed children. One student may only be able to attain level 5, while another may be able to participate through level 8. Classroom and instrumental instruction for mainstreamed learners should be predicated on a similar type of construction. Planning for different levels of musical experience is necessary within each musical activity as well as within the entire lesson.

Another factor in preparing adequate lesson structure involves asking appropriate questions of mainstreamed students. Suitable individual questions require a clear understanding of single students' cognitive levels. Mainstreamed gifted students should be prodded and challenged with questions that will focus them in creative and productive musical thought. Such questions might involve interpretation, analysis, application, or synthesis. A source that describes how to structure such questions is Bloom's cognitive taxonomy (1956). In contrast, mainstreamed educable mentally retarded students might be asked lower-order questions that focus on specific facts or knowledge.

The types of questions used during instruction is one of several effective teacher behaviors described by Larrivee (1982), who investigated the skills needed by teachers who teach mainstreamed classes. The researcher identified successful teachers of classes that included exceptional children. Then through observation, daily records, self-report, and interviews, she assessed the common characteristics that contributed to their effectiveness.

One salient skill was effective questioning techniques. The questions asked by these teachers were related specifically to the content being covered, and "teachers received correct answers to their questions from the first student to respond an average of 80% of the time, indicating their ability to gear their questions to their target group or individual" (p. 4). These successful teachers demonstrated a skillful inclusion of suitable questions based on an understanding of each child's abilities.

Certainly, it is easier to gear questions toward individuals when you teach those students all day. Music teachers cannot be faulted for not knowing seven hundred students as well as a teacher of a self-contained class knows twenty-four students. But most music teachers do teach students for more than one year. A music teacher who teaches each class once a week for 40 minutes will teach students for a total of 145 hours during their elementary schooling. A secondary teacher who meets a performance group three times a week for 50 minutes will teach students for a total of 262 hours. Music teachers can provide effective instruction for mainstreamed students during this time when they understand how each individual learns. Such knowledge will then enable music teachers to construct questions appropriate to the student's ability.

Summary

Successful learning for mainstreamed students involves many factors and may, at times, seem overwhelming to the teacher. All good teaching involves continually reassessing past learning and integrating past and present experiences for students while understanding a future goal. Music teachers always have such goals. The goal may be an individual one, such as preparing a student to perform a solo for a district or state solo festival so that eventually the student may be an All-State participant. Or it may be a long-term goal for a group: to teach every child to sing on pitch by the end of grade two.

Teaching exceptional students should also include establishing immediate and long-term musical goals. Such goals can be defined only when teachers understand the specific learning deficits and strengths of each mainstreamed student. This understanding occurs through a generalized knowledge of different exceptionalities, observation of the individual, reading files, and discussing the student with resource and classroom teachers.

Such a foundation then becomes the reference that is used to decide how to adapt instruction to provide musical success. The adaptations may involve any of the techniques that have been suggested as viable for providing successful musical learning: clarifying materials and activities through the use of differing intensifications, changing grouping within instruction, incorporating different participatory levels within single activities and lessons, and varying the types of questions asked of different learners.

ADVOCACY

In Chapter 1, the IEP document and process were described as an opportunity for music educators to become involved in the placement of and planning for individual exceptional students. If that option is not available to you, then an alternative stance—that of an advocate—is strongly recommended. A dictionary definition of an advocate is "one who pleads the cause of another" (Webster, p. 18). Music educators must find alternative ways to become actively involved in determining which child is placed in which class for which good reason.

One way to begin to establish a climate for effective advocacy is to inform your professional peers (including administrators) that your music instruction is based on a valid curriculum and involves more than fun activities and entertainment. One does not accomplish such a goal by "preaching in the teachers' room." Bulletin boards that illustrate musical learning are one nonverbal way. Mentioning to each teacher at the end of each period what the class has learned is also an important step in the process. This simple step can have a far-reaching and positive cumulative effect if consistently followed.

Another part of the process involves establishing curriculum credibility with your administrator. You certainly don't want to be blowing your own horn every time you talk to your principal. An effective suggestion is to use your plan book to educate the reader (the administrator). Don't list page numbers and song titles in those little squares—use musical terminology! Not many administrators understand what metrical organization or melodic register is. When they ask (and some will), you will have the opportunity not only to explain the terminology but also to describe how different learners cope with the demands of music instruction. If they don't ask, you are indicating that you teach content and you are establishing yourself as a professional. This stance will precede you when you decide it is time to advocate for changes in how students are mainstreamed into music class.

One of the most difficult perceptions to overcome is that music is purely a nonacademic period and is therefore the class that will provide a social experience for all exceptional students. Many administrators are vaguely familiar with the wording of P. L. 94-142. They truly believe that the law dictates that every exceptional child be mainstreamed at some time during the school day.

An important aspect of being an advocate for exceptional children includes being knowledgeable about this law. Under the section defining "least restrictive environment," the wording includes the following:

> That to the maximum extent appropriate, handicapped children . . . are educated with children who are not handicapped.
> That special classes . . . occur only when the nature or severity of the handicap is such that education in regular classes with the use of supplementary aids and services cannot be achieved satisfactorily. (Federal Register, p. 42497)

Music educators will note that the law does not state that every child must be mainstreamed into music! The law does state that students are to be "educated," and if necessary, "supplementary aids and services" are to be provided.

An additional paragraph in the rules and regulations regarding placement of exceptional children reads as follows:

> With respect to determining proper placements, the analysis states ". . . it should be stressed that, where a handicapped child is so disruptive in a regular classroom that the education of other students is significantly impaired, the needs of the handicapped child cannot be met in that environment. Therefore regular placement would not be appropriate to his or her needs." (p. 42497)

This specific statement should be remembered and used by teachers to advocate for the education of nonhandicapped students if an exceptional child is inappropriately placed in a music class. Suggesting a change in placement is most likely to succeed when the request is accompanied by documentation. Noting after each music class the specific behaviors or learning deficits and how they contrast with class expectations will enable you to compile a comprehensive supporting statement for such a request.

In most educational settings, including music, mainstreamed students require more teacher time, and the inclusion of several mainstreamed children can require so much extra teacher attention that the academic level of the entire class is affected (Bradfield et al., 1973). When one child is mainstreamed into a class and requires some additional teacher time, the remainder of the class will not be overly affected. "However, the mainstreaming of seven children into that class may very well increase the likelihood of compromising the education of non-handicapped class members" (Bender, 1985). Certainly, the musical education of an entire class will be at risk when large numbers of handicapped children are mainstreamed into one class, especially if the music teacher does not receive adequate assistance or preparation time.

Music educators should, therefore, be assertive in advocating that entire self-contained classes of exceptional students *not* be mainstreamed into music. And this is a very common way by which administrators attempt to meet what they understand as the "mainstreaming" requirement of the federal law. An illustration of this type of mainstreaming was the basis for the opening scenario in Chapter 1. A music teacher wrote the following on a survey questionnaire:

> Nine of the Special Education students are mainstreamed into my top reading group of fifth graders. They usually arrive late to class and my fifth graders often roll their eyes. I have been told that Special Education students need to be mainstreamed to help them be accepted by their peers. (Atterbury, 1986)

Clearly, those students were never going to be "accepted by their peers" in that setting. Numerous researchers have concluded that physical proximity of handicapped and nonhandicapped students does not result in positive social experiences. A review of research (Gresham, 1982) includes sixteen citations of research that indicate that mainstreamed exceptional children interact less and more negatively with nonhandicapped peers. In addition, mainstreaming does not automatically result in social acceptance for exceptional children. Gresham cites numerous other studies that indicate that placement without instructional adaptations results in poor acceptance of handicapped children by their peers.

Part of being an advocate for exceptional children must include efforts by the teacher to eliminate inappropriate placements of exceptional children—whether it be one student or an entire class. This statement does not imply that music educators should be against mainstreaming. It does mean that children can receive an adequate education—of any kind—only when they are included in a classroom where the teacher has time to use all the ways to provide musical success (intensification, grouping, and so on) that have been described in this text.

Another important part of advocacy is the insistence that you receive similar help from aides—the most important asset that classroom teachers of exceptional children have. Many schools have aides hired solely to assist in the education of one child. Music class should not be their break time. Advocating for their participation and help is also a way to provide musical success for some mainstreamed learners.

Classroom teachers also have aides who help them prepare materials, collect money, mark papers, and work with small groups. Music educators who have identified the exceptional children they will be teaching and who understand the implications of learning differences should advocate for similar types of assistance. It may mean that you have to present to your administrator a list that identifies all the exceptional children that you meet in a week, along with a description of the necessary instructional adaptations for their participation and success in music. Then do it—every week if necessary! When you are advocating for adequate educational opportunities for all students, you have a powerful argument.

Some readers may feel that becoming an advocate for exceptional students is not part of being a music teacher. In a way it is not. Such advocacy has nothing to do with melody, rhythm, or harmony—the musical content of any lesson. But it has everything to do with your own feelings as a professional. When teachers feel that they are not in control—of classroom discipline, of lesson content, of the number of required musical performances, or of determining which students are mainstreamed into which music class—they are certainly at risk for "burnout." They may, however, just become bitter and unhappy. None of these conditions enables a teacher to enthusiastically share the joy and excitement that music teaching demands.

And the joy of music is the most important reason to become an advocate for exceptional children. Music must be a part of *every* child's education. Each exceptional student should be properly placed in a class setting where he or she will be able to participate in successful musical creation and recreation and experience the aesthetic pleasure that music contains. Your advocacy on their behalf can make that a reality.

QUESTIONS

1. Discuss the positive and negative implications of labels.
2. Why should music teachers know which students are mainstreamed into a class?
3. Describe some alternative groupings for classroom and performance settings.
4. Discuss the ways teachers should organize individual lessons to provide musical success for exceptional students.
5. How can music educators advocate for musical success for exceptional children?

ACTIVITIES

1. Interview an experienced music teacher to determine how exceptional learners are identified in their school.
2. Prepare a list of instructional adaptations for one cognitive disability and one physical disability that illustrate the principle of intensification.
3. Write a lesson plan that includes different levels of participation both within the entire lesson and within each activity. Briefly describe the exceptional students for whom these levels would be suitable.

References

ALMOND, P., S. RODGERS, and D. KRUG. 1979. Mainstreaming: A Model for Including Elementary Students in the Severely Handicapped Classroom. *Teaching Exceptional Children* 11:135–39.

ALOIA, G., and D. MACMILLAN. 1983. Influence of the EMR Label on Initial Expectations of Regular Classroom Teachers. *American Journal of Mental Deficiency* 88:255–62.

ANSUINI, A. M. 1979. Identifying Competencies for Elementary School Music Teachers in Planning Learning Experiences for Children with Learning Disabilities. Ed.D. diss., State University of New York at Buffalo.

APGAR, V., and J. BECK. 1972. *Is My Baby All Right?* New York: Pocket Books.

APTER, S. J. 1982. *Troubled Children Troubled Systems.* Elmsford, N.Y.: Pergamon Press.

ATKINS, W., and M. DONOVAN. 1984. A Workable Music Education Program for the Hearing Impaired. *Volta Review* 86:41–44.

ATTERBURY, B. W. 1982. A Comparison of Rhythm Pattern Perception and Performance in Normal and Learning Disabled Readers, Age Seven and Eight. Ph.D. diss. Northwestern University.

———. 1988. Music Achievement in Learning Disabled and Normal-Achieving Readers, Grades Two and Five. Research presentation given at MENC Convention, Indianapolis, 1988.

———. 1986. Musical Differences in Learning-Disabled and Normal-Achieving Readers, Aged Seven, Eight and Nine. *Psychology of Music* 13:114–23.

———. 1987. The Perplexing Issues of Mainstreaming. *Council for Research in Music Education* 94:17–28.

———. 1986. Success in the Mainstream of General Music. *Music Educators Journal* 72:34–36.

BARRAGA, N. C. 1976. *Visual Handicaps and Learning, A Developmental Approach.* Belmont, Calif.: Wadsworth.

BARRON, F. X. 1963. *Creativity and Psychological Health.* New York: D. Van Nostrand.

BEAL, M. R., and J. GILBERT. 1982. *Music Curriculum Guidelines for Moderately Retarded Adolescents.* Springfield, Ill. Chas. C Thomas.

BEALL, L. 1985. The Making of a Special "Oliver." *Music Educators Journal* 71:30–32.

BEER, A. S., N. L. BELLOWS, and A.M.D. FREDERICK. 1982. Providing for Different Rates of Music Learning. *Music Educators Journal* 68 (April): 40–43.

BELL, W. 1981. An Investigation of the Validity of the *Primary Measures of Music Audiation* for Use with Learning Disabled Children. D.M.A. diss., Temple University.

BENDER, W. N. 1985. The Case against Mainstreaming: Empirical Support for the Political Backlash. *Education* 105:279–85.

BENIGNO, J. 1984. Opening Doors for Gifted Young Musicians. *American Education* 20:24.

BENTLEY, A. 1959. *Measures of Musical Abilities*. London: Harrap.

BESS, F. H., B. A. FREEMAN, and J. S. SINCLAIR, eds. 1981. *Amplification in Education*. Washington, D.C.: Alexander Graham Bell Association for the Deaf.

BICKEL, F. 1985. A Comparison of Gifted and Randomly Selected Children's Perceptions of Music Duration. *Council of Research in Music Education* 84:14–19.

BISHOP, V. E. 1986. Identifying the Components of Success in Mainstreaming. *Journal of Visual Impairment and Blindness* 80:939–46.

BLECK, E. E., ed. 1982. *Physically Handicapped Children: A Medical Atlas for Teachers*. New York: Grune & Stratton.

BLOOM, B., ed. 1985. *Developing Talent in Young People*. New York: Ballantine.

BLOOM, B. S., ed. 1956. *Taxonomy of Educational Objectives Handbook I: Cognitive Domain*. New York: D. McKay.

BOARDMAN, E., and B. LANDIS. 1966. *Exploring Music*. New York: Holt, Rinehart & Winston.

BOWLEY, A. H., and L. GARDNER. 1972. *The Handicapped Child*. Edinburgh: Churchill Livingston.

BOXILL, E. H. 1985. *Music Therapy for the Developmentally Disabled*. Rockville, Md.: Aspen Systems Corporation.

BRADFIELD, R. H., J. BROWN, P. KAPLAN, et al. 1973. The Special Child in the Regular Classroom. *Exceptional Children* 39:384–92.

BROWNE, N. J. 1984. A Music-Based Cognitive Assessment Procedure for Nonhandicapped, Nonverbal, and Blind Young Children. Ph.D. diss., University of Kansas.

BROWNING, E. R. 1983. *Teaching Students with Severe Emotional and Learning Impairments*. Boston: Allyn & Bacon.

BRUNER, J. S. 1966. *Toward a Theory of Instruction*. Cambridge: Harvard University Press.

BRUSCIA, K. E., and S. LEVINSON. 1982. Predictive Factors in Optacon Music-Reading. *Visual Impairment and Blindness* 76:309–12.

BRYAN, T. H., and J. H. BRYAN. 1978. *Understanding Learning Disabilities*. Sherman Oaks, Calif.. Alfred Publishing Co.

BUKER, G. N. 1966. A Study of the Ability of the Educable Mentally Retarded to Learn Basic Music Rhythm Reading through the Use of a Specific, Structured Classroom Procedure. Ed.D. diss., University of Oregon.

CASSIDY, J., and N. JOHNSON. 1986. Federal and State Definitions of Giftedness: Then and Now. *Gifted Child Today* 9:15–21.

CATTELL, R. B., and R. W. COAN. 1976. The Cattell Early School Personality Questionnaire. Champaign, Ill.: Institute for Personality and Ability Testing.

CENTER, Y., and J. WARD. 1984. Integration of Mildly Handicapped Cerebral Palsied Children into Regular Schools. *The Exceptional Child* 31 (July): 104–13.

CERTO, N., N. HARING, and R. YORK, eds. 1984. *Public School Integration of Severely Handicapped Students*. Baltimore: Paul H. Brooks Publishing Co.

CHANDLER, H. N. 1986. Mainstreaming: A Formative Consideration. *Journal of Learning Disabilities* 19:125–26.

CHRISTIANSEN, R. O., and R. L. HINTZ. 1982. Juvenile Diabetes Mellitus. In *Physically Handicapped Children: A Medical Atlas for Teachers*, ed. E. E. Bleck. New York: Grune & Stratton.

CLARIZLO, H. F., and W. A. MEHRENS. 1985. Psychometric Limitations of Guilford's Structure-of-Intellect for Identification and Programming of the Gifted. *Gifted Child Quarterly* 29:113–20.

CLEALL, C. 1983. Notes on a Young Deaf Musician. *Psychology of Music* 11:101–2.

COATES, P. 1986. Piano Sessions for the Handicapped. *The American Music Teacher* 36 (September): 27.

COLES, G. S. 1978. The Learning-Disabilities Test Battery: Empirical and Social Issues. *Harvard Educational Review* 48:313–40.

COLWELL, R. 1970. *Music Achievement Test.* Chicago: Follett Educational Corporation.

CORMIER, L. J. 1980. A Guide in the Use of Music in the Training and Development of Rubella Deaf-Blind Children. Master's thesis, Michigan State University.

CRONBACH, L. J. 1970. *Essentials of Psychological Testing.* New York: Harper & Row, Pub.

CROOK, E., et al. 1985. *Silver Burdett MUSIC,* Centennial Edition. Morristown, N.J.: Silver Burdett Company.

CULLINAN, D., M. H. EPSTEIN, and J. M. KAUFFMAN. 1984. Teachers' Ratings of Students' Behaviors: What Constitutes Behavior Disorder in School? *Behavioral Disorders* 10:9–19.

CULLINAN, D., M. H. EPSTEIN, and J. W. LLOYD. 1983. *Behavior Disorders of Children and Adolescents.* Englewood Cliffs, N.J.: Prentice-Hall.

CURTIS, C. R. 1981. A Comparative Analysis of the Musical Aptitude of Normal Children and Mildly Handicapped Children Mainstreamed into Regular Classrooms. Ph.D. diss., Vanderbilt University.

CYPRET, D. 1963. A Musical Test for the Discrimination of Rhythm, Melody, and Timbre in Hard-of-Hearing and Normal Hearing Children. Masters thesis, University of Wichita.

DALLMAN, R. M. 1970. A Survey of Creativity in Music through Composition in the Elementary Schools of Colorado. Ed.D. diss., University of Northern Colorado.

DAMER, L. K. 1979. A Study of Attitudes of Selected Public School Music Teachers toward the Integration of Handicapped Students into Music Classes. Ed.D. diss., The University of North Carolina at Greensboro.

DARROW, A. 1979. The Beat Reproduction Response of Subjects with Normal and Impaired Hearing: An Empirical Comparison. *Journal of Music Therapy* 16:91–98.

———. 1983. A Comparison of Rhythmic Responsiveness in Normal and Hearing Impaired Children and an Investigation of the Relationship of Rhythmic Responsiveness to the Suprasegmental Aspects of Speech Perception. Ph.D. diss., The Florida State University.

———. 1987. Exploring the Arts of Sign and Song. *Music Educators Journal* 74 (September): 33–35.

———. 1987. An Investigative Study: The Effect of Hearing Impairment on Musical Aptitude. *Journal of Music Therapy* 24:88–96.

———. 1985. Music for the Deaf. *Music Educators Journal* 71:33–35.

DAVIS, G. A., and S. B. RIMM. 1985. *Education of the Gifted and Talented.* Englewood Cliffs, N.J.: Prentice-Hall.

DAVISON, E. L. 1972. Music for Emotionally Disturbed Children in the Public Schools. Masters thesis, The American University, Washington, D.C.

DECUIR, A. A., and C. E. BRASWELL. 1978. A Musical Profile for a Sample of Learning-Disabled Children and Adolescents: A Pilot Study. *Perceptual and Motor Skills* 46:1080–82.

DICKINSON, P. I. 1976. *Music with ESN Children.* Windsor, England: NFER Publishing Company.

DOLL, E. A. 1965. *Vineland Social Maturity Scale.* Circle Pines, Minn.: American Guidance Service.

DUNN, L. 1968. Special Education for the Mildly Retarded, Is Much of It Justifiable? *Exceptional Children* 34:5–22.

DYKMAN, R. A. 1979. In Step with 94-142, Two by Two. *Music Educators Journal* 65 (January): 58–63.

EDDY, C. 1972. No Fingers to Play a Horn. *Music Educators Journal* 58 (April): 61–62.

EDGINGTON, D. 1976. *The Physically Handicapped Child in Your Classroom*. Springfield, Ill.: Chas. C Thomas.

EDWARDS, E. M. 1974. *Music Education for the Deaf*. South Waterford, Maine: Merriam-Eddy Company.

ELLIOTT, B., et al. 1982. *Guide to the Selection of Musical Instruments with Respect to Physical Ability and Disability*. St. Louis: Magnamusic-Baton.

ELLIS, D. L. 1982. Differences in Music Achievement among Gifted and Talented, Average, and Educable Mentally Handicapped Fifth and Sixth Grade Students. Ed.D. diss., University of North Carolina at Greensboro.

ENGSTROM, MARY. 1982. The Social Behaviors and Attitudes of Sixth Grade Students and Their Mainstreamed Peers in Two Different Environments: A Case Study. Ph.D. diss., University of Boulder.

EPSTEIN, M. H., and D. CULLINAN. 1983. Academic Performance of Behaviorally Disordered and Learning Disabled Pupils. *Journal of Special Education* 17:303–7.

ERICKSON, L. B. 1973. Keyboard Fun for Children with Osteogenesis Imperfecta and Other Physical Limitations. *Inter-clinic Information Bulletin* 12 (January): 9–17.

Federal Register, vol. 42, no. 163, August 23, 1977, 42497.

FISCHER, S. D. 1982. An Orientation to Language. In *Deafness and Communication*, ed. D. G. Sims, G. C. Walter, and R. L. Whitehead. Baltimore: Williams and Williams.

FOLTS, M. L. 1977. Deaf Children Cannot Play a Musical Instrument . . . Can They? *Volta Review* 79:453–56.

FORD, T. 1985. The Effect of Musical Experiences and Age on the Ability of Deaf Children to Discriminate Complex Tones. Ed.D. diss., The University of North Carolina at Greensboro.

FRASER, B. A., and R. N. HENSINGER. 1983. *Managing Physical Handicaps*. Baltimore: Paul H. Brookes Publishing Company.

GALLAGHER, J. J. 1975. *Teaching the Gifted Child* (2nd ed.). Boston: Allyn & Bacon.

GARDNER, H. 1983. *Frames of Mind, The Theory of Multiple Intelligences*. New York: Basic Books.

GAVIN, A.R.J. 1983. Music Educator Practices and Attitudes toward Mainstreaming. Ed.D. diss., Washington University, St. Louis, Mo.

GEARHEART, B. F. 1972. The Trainable Mentally Retarded. In *Education of the Exceptional Child*, ed. B. F. Gearheart. Scranton, Pa.: Intext Educational Publishers.

GENGEL, R. W. 1969. Practice Effects in Frequency Discrimination by Hearing Impaired Children. *Journal of Speech and Hearing Research* 12:847–55.

GERBER, S. E., and G. T. MENCHER. 1980. *Auditory Dysfunction*. San Diego, Calif.: College-Hill Press.

GETZELS, J. W., and P. W. JACKSON. 1962. *Creativity and Intelligence*. London: John Wiley.

GFELLER, K., and S. K. HEDDEN. 1987. Mainstreaming in Music Education: The State of the State. *Iowa Music Educator* 40:24–27.

GIACOBBE, G. A. 1973. The Responses of Aggressive Emotionally Disturbed and Normal Boys to Selected Music Stimuli. Ph.D. diss., University of Georgia.

GIBBONS, A. C. 1983. Rhythm Responses in Emotionally Disturbed Children with Differing Needs for External Structure. *Music Therapy* 3:94–102.

GILBERT, J. P. 1983. A Comparison of the Motor Music Skills of Nonhandicapped and Learning Disabled Children. *Journal of Research in Music Education* 31:147–55.

GILBERT, J. P., and E. P. ASMUS, JR. 1981. Mainstreaming: Music Educators' Participation and Professional Needs. *Journal of Research in Music Education* 29:31–38.

GORDER, W. D. 1980. Divergent Production Abilities as Constructs of Musical Creativity. *Journal of Research in Music Education* 28:34–42.

GORDON, E. 1965. *Music Aptitude Profile.* Boston: Houghton Mifflin Co.

———. 1979. *Primary Measures of Music Audiation.* Chicago: G.I.A. Publications.

GOTTLIEB, J. 1981. Mainstreaming: Fulfilling the Promise? *American Journal of Mental Deficiency* 86:118.

GOTTLIEB, J., M. ALTER, and B. W. GOTTLIEB. 1983. Mainstreaming Mentally Retarded Children. In *Handbook of Mental Retardation,* ed. J. L. Matson and J. A. Mulick. Elmsford: N.Y.: Pergamon Press.

GRAHAM, R. M., ed. 1975. *Music for the Exceptional Child.* Reston, Va.: Music Educators National Conference.

GRAHAM, R. M., and A. S. BEER. 1980. *Teaching Music to the Exceptional Child.* Englewood Cliffs, N.J.: Prentice-Hall.

GRESHAM, F. 1982. Misguided Mainstreaming: The Case for Social Skills Training with Handicapped Children. *Exceptional Children* 48:422–33.

GRESHAM, F. M., and D. J. RESCHLY. 1986. Social Skill Deficits and Low Peer Acceptance of Mainstreamed Learning Disabled Children.*Learning Disability Quarterly* 9:23–32.

GROSSMAN, H. J., ed. 1983. *Classification in Mental Retardation.* Washington, D.C.: American Association on Mental Deficiency.

GUILFORD, J. P. 1967. *The Nature of Human Intelligence.* New York: McGraw-Hill.

HAIR, H. I., and R. M. GRAHAM. 1983. A Comparison of Verbal Descriptors Used by TMR Students and Music Therapists. *Journal of Music Therapy* 20:59–68.

HARDESTY, K. W. 1979. *Music for Special Education.* Morristown, N.J.: Silver Burdett Company.

HARLEY, R. K., and G. A. LAWRENCE. 1984. *Visual Impairment in the Schools* (2nd ed.). Springfield, Ill.: Chas. C Thomas.

HARRIS, M. 1976. Auditory Training of Learning Disabled Using Orff Music. Ed.D. diss., Memphis State University, Memphis, Tenn.

HARVEY, D.H.P., and A. P. GREENWAY. 1984. The Self-Concept of Physically Handicapped Children and Their Non-Handicapped Siblings: An Empirical Investigation. *Journal of Child Psychology and Psychiatry and Allied Disciplines* (Great Britain) 25:273–84.

HERLEIN, D. G. 1975. Music Reading for the Sightless: Braille Notation. *Music Educators Journal* 62 (September): 42–45.

HEWETT, F. M. 1977. The Orchestration of Success. In *Mainstreaming Emotionally Disturbed Children,* ed. A. J. Pappanikou and J. L. Paul. Syracuse: Syracuse University Press.

HINERMAN, P. S. 1983. *Teaching Autistic Children to Communicate.* Rockville, Md.: Aspen Systems Corporation.

HOLLANDER, F. M., and P. D. JUHRS. 1974. Orff-Schulwerk, an Effective Treatment Tool with Autistic Children. *Journal of Music Therapy* 11:1–12.

IANACONE, R. N. 1976. The Measurement of Music Aptitude for the Mentally Retarded. Ed.D. diss., University of Florida.

ITARD, J. M. 1962. *The Wild Boy of Aveyron.* New York: Appleton-Century-Crofts.

JAQUES-DALCROZE, E. 1931. *Eurhythmics, Art and Education.* New York: A. S. Barnes and Company.

JAN, J. E., R. D. FREEMAN, and E. P. SCOTT. 1977. *Visual Impairment in Children and Adolescents.* New York: Grune & Stratton.

JELLISON, J. A., B. H. BROOKS, and A. M. HUCK. 1984. Structuring Small Groups and Music Reinforcement to Facilitate Positive Interactions and Acceptance of Severely Handicapped Students in the Regular Music Classroom. *Journal of Research in Music Education* 32:243–64.

JELLISON, J. A., and D. E. WOLFE. 1987. Educators' Ratings of Selected Objectives for Severely Handicapped or Gifted Students in the Regular Classroom. *Contributions to Music Education* 14:36–41.

JENSEMA, C. J., and R. J. TRYBUS. 1978. *Communication Patterns and Educational Achievement of Hearing Impaired Students.* Washington, D.C.: Gallaudet College.

JOFFEE, L. A Voice from a Mute World Sings. *Christian Science Monitor.* January 27, 1988, pp. 1, 6.

JOHNSON, D. J. 1971. Educational Principles for Children with Learning Disabilities. In *Educational Perspectives in Learning Disabilities,* ed. D. D. Hammill and N. R. Bartel. New York: John Wiley, pp. 133–43.

JOHNSON, D. J., and H. R. MYKLEBUST. 1967. *Learning Disabilities, Educational Principles and Practices.* New York: Grune & Stratton.

JOHNSON, D. W., and R. T. JOHNSON. 1986. Impact of Classroom Organization and Instructional Methods on the Effectiveness of Mainstreaming. In *Mainstreaming Handicapped Children: Outcomes, Controversies and New Directions,* ed. C. J. Meisel. Hillsdale, N.J.: Lawrence Erlbaum Associates, Publishers.

KANNER, L. 1964. *A History of the Care and Study of the Mentally Retarded.* Springfield, Ill.: Chas. C Thomas, p. 115.

KAPLAN, P. R. 1977. A Criterion-Referenced Comparison of Rhythmic Responsiveness in Normal and Educable Mentally Retarded Children. Ph.D. diss., University of Michigan.

KAVALE, K., and P. D. MATTSON. 1983. One Jumped Off the Balance Beam: Meta-Analysis of Perceptual-Motor Training. *Journal of Learning Disabilities* 16:165–73.

KEPHART, N. C. 1971. *The Slow Learner in the Classroom.* Columbus, Ohio: Chas. E. Merrill.

KERSTEN, F. 1979. An Analysis of Music Education Methods and Materials for the Visually Impaired Synthesized from Documents Written between 1891 and 1978. D.Ed. diss., Pennsylvania State University.

———. 1981. Music as Therapy for the Visually Impaired. *Music Educators Journal* 67:63–65.

KINSEY, T. 1988. Excuse Me, We're Gifted, Too. *The Instrumentalist* 42(9):99–100.

KIRK, S. A., J. J. McCARTHY, and W. D. KIRK. 1968. *Illinois Test of Psycholinguistic Ability.* Urbana: University of Illinois Press.

KLAJMAN, S., E. KOLDEJ, and A. KOWALSKA. 1982. Investigation of Musical Abilities in Hearing-Impaired and Normal-Hearing Children. *Folia Phoniatrica* 35:229–33.

KNAPP, R. A. 1980. A Choir for Total Communication. *Music Educators Journal* 66 (February): 54–55.

KORDUBA, O. M. 1975. Duplicated Rhythm Patterns between Deaf and Normal Hearing Children. *Journal of Music Therapy* 12:136–46.

KRACKE, I. 1975. Perception of Rhythmic Sequences by Receptive Aphasic and Deaf Children. *British Journal of Disorders of Communication* 10:43–51.

KRAUT, J. The Meaning of "Legally Blind." *Boston Sunday Globe.* March 6, 1988, p. 91.

KROLICK, B. 1979. Dictionary of Braille Music Signs. Washington, D.C.: Library of Congress, Division for the Blind and Physically Handicapped, ED190141 (ERIC).

LAM, R. C., and C. CECILIA WANG. 1982. Integrating Blind and Sighted through Music. *Music Educators Journal* 68 (April): 44–45.

LANDECKER, A. W. 1980. Lifting and Carrying. In *Educating the Severely Physically Handicapped, Basic Principles and Techniques,* Volume 1, ed. J. Umbreit and P. J. Cardullias. Reston, Va.: The Council for Exceptional Children.

LARRIVEE, B. 1982. Identifying Effective Teaching Behaviors for Mainstreaming. *Teacher Education and Special Education* 5:2–6.

LARSON, B. A. 1977. A Comparison of Singing Ranges of Mentally Retarded and Normal Children with Published Songbooks Used in Singing Activities. *Journal of Music Therapy* 14:139–43.

LEVINE, E. L., and E. M. WEXLER. 1981. *PL 94-142 An Act of Congress.* New York: Macmillan.

LEVINE, J. S. 1968. The Recorded Aid for Braille Music. *Journal of Music Therapy* 5:1–2.

LEWIS, M. F. 1974. A Handbell Choir for Blind Students. *Journal of Visual Impairment and Blindness* 68:297–99.

LIEBMAN, J., and A. LIEBMAN. 1973. On Stage *Every*body, Music Theatre for Physically Handicapped Children. *Music Educators Journal* 60 (October): 45–46.

LING, D., ed. 1984. *Early Intervention for Hearing-Impaired Children: Oral Options.* San Diego, Calif.: College-Hill Press.

LOWENFELD, B., ed. 1973. *The Visually Handicapped Child in School.* New York: Harper & Row, Pub.

MAAG, J. W., and R. B. RUTHERFORD, JR. 1986. Perceived Social Competence of Behaviorally Disordered, Learning Disabled, and Nonlabeled Students. *Journal of Instructional Psychology* 13:10–18.

McCANN, B. J. 1985. Assume Every Child Will Succeed. *Music Educators Journal* 71 (February): 18–21.

McKINNEY, J. D., and L. FEAGANS. 1983. Adaptive Classroom Behavior of Learning Disabled Students. *Journal of Learning Disabilities* 16:360–67.

MacKINNON, D. 1962. The Nature and Nurture of Creative Talent. *American Psychologist* 17:484–95.

McLEISH, J., and G. HIGGS. 1982. Musical Ability and Mental Subnormality: An Experimental Investigation. *British Journal of Educational Psychology* 52:370–73.

McREYNOLDS, J. C. 1988. Helping Visually Impaired Students Succeed in Band. *Music Educators Journal* 75:36–38.

MADDEN, N. A., and R. E. SLAVIN. 1983. Mainstreaming Students with Mild Handicaps: Academic and Social Outcomes. *Review of Educational Research* 53:519–69.

MANION, S. 1986. On Teaching Piano to Blind Students. *The American Music Teacher* 36:46, 57.

MATSON, J. L., and J. A. MULICK, eds. 1983. *Handbook of Mental Retardation.* Elmsford, N.Y.: Pergamon Press.

MECKLEY, W. A. 1984. The Development of Individualized Music Learning Sequences for Non-Handicapped, Handicapped and Gifted Learners Using the Logo Music Version Computer Language. Ph.D. diss., Eastman School of Music, The University of Rochester.

MELILLO, S. 1985. Reaching Gifted Students through Music. *Early Years* 15:51–52.

MERLE-FISHMAN, C. R., and M. L. MARCUS. 1982. Musical Behaviors and Preferences in Emotionally Disturbed and Normal Children: An Exploratory Study. *Music Therapy* 2:1–11.

MESKE, E. B., et al. 1988. *Holt MUSIC.* New York: Holt, Rinehart & Winston.

MICHAL, E. T. 1987. Teaching Piano Skills to Handicapped Persons through Use of Systematic Instruction: A Proposal. Doctoral dissertation, Ohio State University, D.A.I. 48/05A, 1051.

MICHEL, D. E. 1976. *Music Therapy.* Springfield, Ill.: Chas. C Thomas.

MILLER, J. J. 1982. Juvenile Rheumatoid Arthritis. In *Physically Handicapped Children: A Medical Atlas for Teachers,* ed. E. E. Bleck. New York: Grune & Stratton, pp. 423–30.

MILLS, S. R. 1975. Band for the Trainable Child. *Education and Training of the Mentally Retarded* 10:268–70.

MOOG, H. 1979. On the Perception of Rhythmic Forms by Physically Handicapped Children and Those of Low Intelligence in Comparison with Non-Handicapped Children. *Council for Research in Music Education* 59:73–78.

MOONEY, M. K. 1972. Blind Children Need Training, Not Sympathy. *Music Educators Journal* 58 (April): 56–59.

MOORES, D. F. 1982. *Educating the Deaf, Psychology, Principles, and Practices* (2nd ed.). Boston: Houghton Mifflin Co.

MORSE, W. C. 1976. The Crisis or Helping Teacher. In *Conflict in the Classroom: The Education of Emotionally Disturbed Children*, ed. N. J. Long, W. C. Morse, and R. G. Newman. Belmont, Calif.: Wadsworth.

MURRAY, F. B. 1986. Micro-Mainstreaming. In *Mainstreaming Handicapped Children: Outcomes, Controversies, and New Directions*, ed. C. J. Meisel. Hillsdale, N.J.: Lawrence Erlbaum Associates, Publishers.

MUSIC EDUCATORS NATIONAL CONFERENCE. 1983. *Documentary Report of the Ann Arbor Symposium on the Application of Psychology to the Teaching and Learning of Music: Session III, Motivation and Creativity*. Reston, Va.: Music Educators National Conference.

MYERS, P., and D. HAMMILL. 1976. *Learning Disabilities: Basic Concepts, Assessment Practices, and Instructional Strategies*. Austin, Tex.: Pro-Ed.

MYKLEBUST, H. R. 1954. *Auditory Disorders in Children*. New York: Grune & Stratton.

NAPIER, G. D. 1972. The Visually Disabled. In *Education of the Exceptional Child*, ed. B. R. Gearheart. Scranton, Pa.: Intext Educational Publishers.

NEWCOMER, P. L. 1980. *Understanding and Teaching Emotionally Disturbed Children*. Boston: Allyn & Bacon.

NIHIRA, K., et al. 1974. *AAMD Adaptive Scale*. Washington, D.C.: American Association on Mental Deficiency.

NIX, G. W. 1976. *Mainstream Education for Hearing Impaired Children and Youth*. New York: Grune & Stratton.

NOCERA, S. 1979. *Reaching the Special Learner through Music*. Morristown, N.J.: Silver Burdett Company.

NOCERA, S. D. 1981. A Descriptive Analysis of the Attainment of Selected Musical Learnings by Normal Children and Educable Mentally Retarded Children Mainstreamed in Music Classes at the Second and Fifth Grade Level. Ph.D. diss., University of Wisconsin at Madison.

NORDOFF, P., and C. ROBBINS. 1971. *Music Therapy in Special Education*. New York: Harper & Row, Pub.

OSBORN, A. F. 1957. *Applied Imagination* (3rd rev.). New York: Scribner's.

OSGUTHORPE, R. T., and J. D. CUSTER. 1983. Music as a Tool for Social Acceptance: Training Handicapped Students to Tutor Their Nonhandicapped Peers. In *Second International Symposium of Music Education for the Handicapped*, ed. R. R. Pratt. Bloomington, Ind.: Frangipani Press.

PAPPANIKOU, A. J., and J. L. PAUL, eds. 1977. *Mainstreaming Emotionally Disturbed Children*. Syracuse: Syracuse University Press.

PERKINS, C. E. 1979. Music to Their Ears. *Instructor* 89:134–36.

Pillsbury Foundation Series. 1978. *Music of Young Children*. Santa Barbara, Calif.: Pillsbury Foundation for Advancement of Music Education.

PIRTLE, M., and K. P. SEATON. 1973. Use of Music Training to Actuate Conceptual Growth in Neurologically Handicapped Children. *Journal of Research in Music Education* 21:292–301.

PITMAN, D. J. 1965. The Musical Ability of Blind Children. *American Federation for the Blind Research Bulletin* 11:63–79.

POND, D. 1981. A Composer's Study of Young Children's Innate Musicality. *Council for Research in Music Education* 68 (Fall): 1–12.

PRATT, R. R., and M. PETERSON. 1981. *Elementary Music for All Learners*. Sherman Oaks, Calif.: Alfred Publishing Co.

PRESTI, G. M. 1984. A Levels System Approach to Music Therapy with Severely Behaviorally Handicapped Children in the Public School System. *Journal of Music Therapy* 21:117–25.

PROBST, W. 1985. Instrumental Lessons with Handicapped Children and Youth. *Bulletin of the Council for Research in Music Education* 85:166–74.

Purvis, J., and S. Samet, eds. 1976. *Music in Developmental Therapy*. Baltimore: University Park Press.

Quigley, S. P., and P. V. Paul. 1984. *Language and Deafness*. San Diego, Calif.: College-Hill Press.

Ravitch, D. 1983. *The Troubled Crusade, American Education 1945–1980*. New York: Basic Books.

Redl, R. 1966. *When We Deal with Children*. New York: Free Press.

Reimer, B. 1970. *A Philosophy of Music Education*. Englewood Cliffs, N.J.: Prentice-Hall.

Renzulli, J. S., S. M. Reis, and L. H. Smith. 1981. *The Revolving Door Identification Model*. Mansfield Center, Conn.: Creative Learning Press, Inc.

Resnick, L. 1987. Learning in School and Out. *Educational Researcher* 16:13–20.

Ricca, J. 1984. Learning Styles and Preferred Instructional Strategies of Gifted Students. *Gifted Child Quarterly* 28:121–26.

Richards, M. H. 1964. *Thresholds to Music*. Belmont, Calif.: Fearon.

Rider, R. 1981. The Assessment of Cognitive Functioning Level through Musical Perception. *Journal of Music Therapy* 18:110–19.

Rileigh, K.A.K. 1971. Perception of Rhythm by Subjects with Normal and Deficient Hearing. Ph.D. diss., Vanderbilt University.

Robbins, C., and C. Robbins. 1980. *Music for the Hearing Impaired, A Resource Manual and Curriculum Guide*. St. Louis: Magnamusic-Baton.

Rose, M. C., B. P. Cundick, and K. L. Higbee. 1983. Verbal Rehearsal and Visual Imagery: Mnemonic Aids for Learning-Disabled Children. *Journal of Learning Disabilities* 16:352–54.

Rosene, P. E. 1976. A Field Study of Wind Instrument Training for Educable Mentally Handicapped Children. Ed.D. diss., University of Illinois.

———. 1982. Instrumental Music . . . A Success Opportunity. *Music Educators Journal* 68:37–39.

Rosenstein, J. 1957. Tactile Perception of Rhythmic Patterns by Normal, Blind, Deaf, and Aphasic Children. *American Annals of the Deaf* 103:399–403.

Ross, D. M., S. A. Ross, and S. L. Kuchenbecker. 1973. Rhythm Training for Educable Mentally Retarded Children. *Mental Retardation* 11:20–23.

Ross, M. 1982. *Hard of Hearing Children in Regular Schools*. Englewood Cliffs, N.J.: Prentice-Hall.

Rutter, M. 1978. Language Disorder and Infantile Autism. In *Autism: A Reappraisal of Concepts and Treatment*, ed. M. Rutter and E. Schoper. New York: Plenum.

Rutter, M., and E. Schoper, eds. 1978. *Autism: A Reappraisal of Concepts and Treatments*. New York: Plenum.

Rynders, J. E., R. T. Johnson, and D. W. Johnson. 1980. Producing Positive Interaction among Down Syndrome and Nonhandicapped Teenagers through Cooperative Goal Structure. *American Journal of Mental Deficiency* 85:268–73.

Safran, S. P., J. S. Safran, and R. Barcikowski. 1985. Differences in Teacher Tolerance: An Illusory Phenomena? *Behavioral Disorders* 11:11–15.

Schleuter, S. L., and L. J. Schleuter. 1985. The Relationship of Grade Level and Sex Differences to Certain Rhythmic Responses of Primary Grade Children. *Journal of Research in Music Education* 33:23–30.

Scholl, G. T., ed. 1986. *Foundations of Education for Blind and Visually Handicapped Children and Youth: Theory and Practice*. New York: American Foundation for the Blind.

Scruggs, T. E., and M. A. Mastropieri. 1986. Academic Characteristics of Behaviorally Disordered and Learning Disabled Students. *Behavioral Disorders* 11:184–90.

Sears, C. J. 1985. Recognition of Learning Problems Accompanying Primary Handicapped Conditions and Their Impact on Instructional Programs for Multihandicapped Students. ED257276 (ERIC).

SEASHORE, C. 1960. *Seashore Measures of Musical Talent*. New York: Psychological Corp.

SEBREE, S. M. 1987. A Survey of Gifted and Talented Academic and Fine Arts (Music) Programs in the Urban School Districts of Ten North Central States. Ed.D. diss., The University of Toledo.

SHELLEM, G. W. 1982. The Integration of Profoundly Hearing Impaired Children in the Public School Setting: A Descriptive Profile. Ph.D. diss., Gallaudet College, Washington, D.C.

SHINN, M. R., G. A. TINDAL, D. SPIRA, and D. MARSTON. 1987. The Practice of Learning Disabilities as a Social Policy. *Learning Disability Quarterly* 10:17–28.

SIMPSON, D. J. 1969. The Effect of Selected Musical Studies on Growth in General Creative Potential. Ed.D. diss., University of Southern California.

SISK, D. 1987. *Creative Teaching of the Gifted*. New York: McGraw-Hill.

SKAUGHT, B. J. 1987. Songwriting Should Be Taught in Your Gifted Program. *Gifted Child Today* 10:40–41.

SLAVIN, R. E. 1978. Student Teams and Achievement Divisions. *Journal of Research and Development in Education* 12:39–49.

SLEETER, C. E. 1986. Learning Disabilities: The Social Construction of a Special Education Category. *Exceptional Children* 53:48–54.

SLYOFF, M. R. 1979. *Music for Special Education*. Fort Worth: Harris Music Publications.

Soundpost. 1987. The Conquest of Silence with Sign and Song. 3 (Summer): 1, 15.

SPOSATO, M. A. 1982. Implications of Maximal Exploitation of Residual Hearing on Curriculum Planning in Music Education for Hearing-Impaired Children. Ed.D. diss., State University of New York at Buffalo.

SQUIRES, V. L. 1982. The Beat Maintenance/Beat Reproduction Responses of Hearing Impaired and Normal Hearing Children on Sustained and Percussive Temporal Intervals. Master's thesis, University of Kansas.

STATON, B., et al. 1988. *Music and You*. New York: Macmillan.

STEELE, A. L. 1977. Directive Teaching and the Music Therapist as Consultant. *Journal of Music Therapy* 14:17–26.

STERN, V. 1975. They Shall Have Music. *Volta Review* 75 (November): 495–500.

STERRITT, G. M., B. W. CAMP, and B. S. LIPMAN. 1966. Effects of Early Auditory Deprivation upon Auditory and Visual Information Processing. *Perceptual and Motor Skills* 23:123–30.

STONE, S. J. 1980. A Study of Teacher Attitudes that Affect the Quality of Education for Exceptional Students. Ed.D. diss., The University of Tennesse, Knoxville.

STRATFORD, B., and E. Y. CHING. 1983. Rhythm and Time in the Perception of Down's Syndrome Children. *Journal of Mental Deficiency Research* 27:23–38.

SWAIKO, N. 1974. The Role and Value of an Eurhythmics Program in a Curriculum for Deaf Children. *American Annals of the Deaf* 119:321–24.

SWANNER, D. L. 1985. Relationships between Musical Creativity and Selected Factors Including Personality, Motivation, Musical Aptitude, and Cognitive Intelligence as Measured in Third Grade Children. Ph.D. diss., Case Western Reserve University, Cleveland, Ohio.

TATARUNIS, A. M. 1981. Exceptional Programs for Talented Students. *Music Educators Journal* 68 (November): 55–60.

TEPLITZ, M. 1985. An Exciting Day in My Life. *The Exceptional Parent* 15 (April): 7–9.

TERMAN, L. M. 1947. *Genetic Studies of Genius*, vol. IV. Stanford, Calif.: Stanford University Press.

THOMAS, R. n.d. *Manhattanville Music Curriculum Program Synthesis*. Elnora, N.Y.: Media, Inc.

THOMPSON, K. 1985. Review of "A Comparative Analysis of the Musical Aptitude of Normal Children and Mildly Handicapped Children Mainstreamed into Regular

Classrooms" and "A Descriptive Analysis of the Attainment of Selected Musical Learnings by Normal Children and by Educable Mentally Retarded Children Mainstreamed in Music Classes at the Second and Fifth Grade Levels." *Council for Research in Music Education* 82:80–89.

Todd, J. H. 1986. Resources, Media and Technology. In *Foundations of Education for Blind and Visually Handicapped Children and Youth: Theory and Practice*, ed. G. T. Scholl. New York: American Foundation for the Blind.

Torrance, E. P. 1963. *Education and the Creative Potential*. Minneapolis: The University of Minnesota Press.

———. 1974. *Tests of Creative Thinking*. Lexington, Mass.: Ginn.

U. S. Congress. Educational Amendment of 1978, Public Law 95-561, IX, A.

United States Code and Administrative News, 93rd Congress, First Session, PL 93-112, September 26, 1973, 454.

Urwin, C. 1984. Language for Absent Things: Learning from Visually Handicapped Children. *Topics in Language Disorders* 4:24–37.

Vaughan, M., and R. E. Myers. 1971. An Examination of Musical Process as Related to Creative Thinking. *Journal of Research in Music Education* 19:337–41.

Vaughan, M. M. 1971. Music as Model and Metaphor in the Cultivation and Measurement of Creative Behavior in Children. Ph.D. diss., University of Georgia.

Vernazza, M. 1978. *Music Plus for the Young Child in Special Education*. Boulder, Colo.: Pruett Publishing Co.

Voeltz, L. M. 1984. Program and Curriculum Innovation to Prepare Children for Integration. In *Public School Integration of Severely Handicapped Students*, ed. N. Certo, N. Haring, and R. York. Baltimore: Paul H. Brookes Publishing Co.

Walker, A. R. 1985. Mental Imagery and Musical Concepts: Some Evidence from the Congenitally Blind. *Bulletin of the Council for Research in Music Education* 85:229–37.

Wallas, G. 1926. *The Art of Thought*. London: Watts.

Weber, R. D. 1966. An Approach to the Use of Musical Instruments in the Education of the "Trainable" Mentally Retarded. Ed.D. diss., Columbia University.

Webster, P., C. Yale, and M. Haefner. 1988. Test-Retest Reliability of *Measures of Creative Thinking in Music* for Children with Formal Music Training. Paper presented at MENC Conference, Indianapolis.

Webster, P. R. 1977. A Factor of Intellect Approach to Creative Thinking in Music. Ph.D. diss., Eastman School of Music, The University of Rochester.

———. 1983. An Assessment of Musical Creative Thinking in Young Children: Technical Report. In *Contributions to Symposium/83 the Bowling Green State University Symposium on Music Teaching & Research*, ed. P. Thomas Tallarico. Bowling Green State University, Bowling Green, Ohio.

———. 1987. Refinement of a Measure of Creative Thinking in Music. In *Applications of Research in Music Behavior*, ed. C. K. Madsen and C. A. Prickett. Tuscaloosa, Ala.: The University of Alabama Press.

Webster's New Collegiate Dictionary. 1977. Springfield, Mass.: Merriam.

Weidenbach, V. 1981. Music in the Education of the Young Multiply Handicapped Deaf-Blind Child. *Prospects* 11:490–98.

Westervelt, V. D., and A. P. Turnbull. 1980. Children's Attitudes toward Physically Handicapped Peers and Intervention Approaches for Attitude Change. *Physical Therapy* 60 (July): 896–901.

Westling, D. L. 1986. *Introduction to Mental Retardation*. Englewood Cliffs, N.J.: Prentice-Hall.

White, L. D. 1984. A Follow-up Study of the Attitudes of Selected North Carolina Public School Music Teachers toward the Mainstreaming of Handicapped Students into Music Class. Paper presented at XVI ISME International Conference, Eugene, Ore.

WHORTON, J. E., and D. N. DANIEL. 1987. A Psychometric Comparison of Learning Disabled and Educable Mentally Retarded Children. *Reading Improvement* 63: 63–67.

WIIG, E. H., and E. M. SEMEL. 1976. *Language Disabilities in Children and Adolescents.* Columbus, Ohio: Chas. E. Merrill.

WILLIAMS, L. 1985. A Band That Exceeds All Expectations. *Music Educators Journal* 71:27–29.

WILSON, B. 1981. Implications of the Pillsbury Foundation School of Santa Barbara in Perspective. *Council for Research in Music Education* 68:13–15.

WOODELL, G. 1984. Gifted Children in General Music. *Music Educators Journal* 70 (January): 43–46.

ZENATTI, A. 1975. Melodic Memory Tests: A Comparison of Normal Children and Mental Defectives. *Journal of Research in Music Education* 23:41;–52.

Index

Abbé de l'Épée, 4
Academic achievement, of educable
     mentally retarded, 28–29
Acceleration, 66–67
"Acceptance within Music Scale," 212
Achievement scores, 70
Adaptive behavior, 19, 20
Advanced Placement courses, 67
Advocacy for mainstreamed students,
     230–33
Almond, P., 211
Aloia, G., 79
Alter, M., 29
Amblyopia, 126
American Association on Mental
     Deficiency, 20
American Printing House for the Blind,
     139
American Sign Language, 109–11
Amplification device, 103
Ansuini, A. M., 47
Apgar, V., 20, 36, 145–46, 156
Aphasia, 204
Applied Music–Individual Study
     Course, 68
Apter, S. J., 166, 173
Asmus, E. P., Jr., 10, 11, 196
Asthma, 147

Astigmatism, 125
Atkins, W., 120
Attention, 21–22, 25–27, 45
Atterbury, B. W., 11, 12, 53–54
Audiogram, 106–7
Auditory input, 41
Autism, 202–3
Autoharp, 38, 98, 101, 115, 225

Barcikowski, R., 168
Barraga, N. C., 135
Barron, F. X., 63
Beal, M. R., 206
Beall, Lee, 217
Beck, J., 20, 36, 145–46, 156
Beer, A. S., 12, 206, 227
Behaviorally impaired, 162. *See also*
     Emotionally disturbed
Behavior modification, 160, 164–66, 170,
     203
Bell, William, 53
Bender, W. N., 232
Benigno, J., 66
Bentley, *Measures of Musical Abilities*,
     32, 34, 73
Bess, F. H., 121
Bickel, F., 70–71
Binet, Alfred, 5, 219

Bishop, V. E., 138
Bleck, E. E., 156
Blind, legally. *See* Legally blind
Blindness, 124
Bloom, B., 65, 69
Bowley, A. H., 145
Boxill, E. H., 218
Bradfield, R. H., 232
Braille, Louis, 4
Braille materials, 125, 128, 130–32,
    135–36, 138, 178
Brainstorming, 68
Braswell, C. E., 53
Broca, P., 40
Brooks, B. H., 9, 212
Browne, N. J., 136
Browning, E. R., 164, 173
Bruner, Jerome, 25
Bruscia, K. E., 132
Bryan, J. H., 57
Bryan, Tanis, 48, 57, 81
Buker, G. N., 33, 35
Bulletin boards, 24
Burdett, Teri, 114
Bureau of Education for the
    Handicapped, 5

Calhoun, G., 28
Camp, B. W., 118
Cassidy, J., 60
Cattell, R. B., 74
Center, Y., 155
Cerebral palsy, 119, 144–45, 148, 155–56,
    178–79, 202
    classifications, 145
    concomitant problems, 145
Certo, N., 211
Chadwick, D., 151
Chandler, H. N., 9
Ching, E. Y., 31
Chomsky, Noam, 109
Christiansen, R. O., 147
Chromosome 21, 21
Chunking, as aid to memory, 25
Clarizlo, H. F., 62
Clark, C., 151
Cleall, C., 119

*Clinically Adapted Instruments for the
    Multiply Handicapped*, 151
Coates, P., 156
Coles, G. S., 55
Color blindness, 126
Colwell, R., 33
Communication board, 152, 204
Communication disorders, 175, 204
Communication modes, 110
Computers, 68, 71–72, 133, 151, 155,
    204–5
Conductive hearing loss, 105–6, 119
Consistency, in teaching, 163–64, 203
Convergent thinking, 62, 76
Cooperative learning, 212–14, 217,
    225–26
Cormier, L. J., 137, 218
Council for Exceptional Children, 9
Creativity, 62–63, 67–68
    growth after music instruction, 75
    instruction, 72
    measurement, 73
    taught in schools, 74
Cronbach, L. J., 62
Cullinan, D., 166
Curtis, C. R., 28, 32
Custer, J. D., 225
Cypret, D., 117
Cystic fibrosis, 146–47

Dallman, R. M., 74
Damer, L. K., 11
Daniel, D. N., 40
Darrow, A., 110, 116, 118, 120
Davis, G. A., 77
Davison, E. L., 169
Deaf, 104
Deaf-blind, 200, 215
Decibels, 106
Decuir, A. A., 53
Developmental period, 18, 20
Diabetes, juvenile, 147
Diagnostic teaching, 43
Dickinson, P. I., 34–35
Differentiated curriculum, 66
Discrepancy clause, 39

Disinhibition, 45
Distractibility, 45, 168
Divergent thinking, 62, 76
Doll, E. A., 20
Donovan, M., 120
Down's syndrome, 20–21, 31, 85
Duchenne dystrophy, 146
Dunn, Lloyd, 219
Dykman, R. A., 211
Dyslexia, 42

Ear, anatomy, 104–5
Early Education for the Handicapped, 4–5
Early School Personality Questionnaire, 74
Eddy, Clark, 143–44
Edgington, D., 146, 157
Educable mentally retarded
  academic achievement, 28–29
  adaptive behaviors, 20
  definition, 19, 36
  developmental period, 20–21
  intellectual functioning, 19–20
  learning
    attention, 21–22, 25–27, 36
    memory, 22–24, 26–27, 36
    organization, 24–27, 36
  musical achievement, 33
  music performance, 26, 33
  research in music education
    achievement, 33
    aptitude, 32–33
    pitch, 30
    rhythm, 30–31
    singing range, 31–32
    training, 33–34
  social acceptance, 28–30
  teacher expectations for, 35
Education for All Handicapped Children
  Act, 4, 6, 12. *See also* Public Law
  94–142
Edwards, E. M., 120
Elaboration, in creative thinking, 72–73
Elementary and Secondary Education Act
  of 1965, 5
Elliott, B., 157
Ellis, D. L., 33

Emotionally disturbed
  academic achievement, 166
  behaviors, range and variety, 162
  definitions, 160
  environment for success, 172
  learning in music, 166–69
  models of diagnosis and treatment
    behaviorist, 162
    medical, 161
    psychodynamic, 161
  research in music, 169–71
  teacher attention as a reinforcer, 168
  teacher competencies needed, 163–66,
    170
Engstrom, M., 222
Enrichment, 67–69, 86, 100
Environment, least restrictive. *See* Least
  restrictive environment
Epstein, M. H., 166
Equal protection, 4
Erickson, L. B., 157
Evaluation, 84, 90, 95
Exclusion clause, 39
Exploring Music, 82–83, 178–79
Extinction, in behavior modification, 165
Eye, anatomy, 124

Feagans, L., 45
Federal legislation, 5–6
Federal Register, 9, 200
Fernald, G., 40
Finger spelling, 110
Fischer, S. D., 109
Flexibility, 63, 72–73
Fluency, 63, 72–73
FM systems, 107–8
Folts, M. L., 114
Ford, T., 117
Fraser, B. A., 145, 152, 157
Freeman, B. A., 121
Freeman, R. D., 124, 132, 139
Functional music, 206–7

Gallagher, J. E., 65, 67, 77
Gallaudet, Thomas Hopkins, 4
Gardner, H., 61, 63–64, 70, 76
Gardner, L., 145

Gavin, A. R. J., 12
Gearheart, B. F., 4, 202
Gengel, R. W., 117
Gerber, S. E., 106–7
Getzels, J. W., 62
Gfeller, K., 11, 51
Giacobbe, G. A., 171
Gibbons, A. C., 171
Gifted and talented
    characteristics and concomitant
        problems, 65
    creativity instruction for, 72–73
    creativity measurement, 73–74
    definition, 60
    differences between groups, 71
    hostility toward, 60
    instructional adaptations
        acceleration, 66–67, 76
        differentiated curriculum, 69–70
        enrichment, 67–69
    learning, 64–66
    learning preferences, 69
    neglect of, 60
    performance opportunities for, 68–69
    research, 70–75
    state definition cutoffs, 60
Gifted hypocrisy, 60–61
Gilbert, Janet Perkins, 10, 11, 46, 196, 206
Goldstein, K., 40
Gorder, W. D., 73
Gordon, E., 32, 34, 53, 73–74, 116–17
Gottlieb, J., 9, 29, 36
Graham, R., 12, 137, 139, 206, 215
Great Expectations Band, 209, 210
Greenway, A. P., 153
Gresham, F., 9, 48, 232
Grouping, alternatives for mainstreaming,
    224–26
Guilford, J. P., 61, 73, 75

Hair, H. I., 215–16
Hall, R. Vance, 165
Hammill, D., 47
Haptic input, 42
Hardesty, K. W., 218
Hard of hearing, 104
Haring, N., 211
Harley, R. K., 139

Harris, M., 53
Harvey, D. H. P., 153
Hearing, 104
Hearing impaired
    academic achievement, 111, 113
    age of onset, 109
    amplification range of aid, 108
    assessment, 106
    communication modes, 110–12
    conductive hearing loss, 105–6, 119
    definition, 104
    degrees of loss, 106, 109
    ear anatomy, 104–5
    effect of music instruction, 117
    hearing aids, 106–9
    instrumental instruction, 113–14
    lag in language development, 111
    level of noise in room, 108
    in music, 112–15
    musical training, 118
    note taking, 113
    profoundly hearing impaired
        in music, 113
        research subjects, 116
    research in music education
        aptitude, 116–17
        musical training, 117–18
        pitch, 117
        rhythm, 115–16
    reverberation in music room, effect of,
        108
    sensorineural hearing loss, 106, 119
    spatial memory, 110
    strategies used in rhythmic
        reproduction, 115
    training of pitch discrimination, 118
    visual memory, 110
Hearing loss, mixed, 106
Hedden, S. K., 11
Hemophilia, 147
Hensinger, R. N., 145, 152, 157
Herlein, D. G., 137
Hertz, 106
Hewett, Frank, 172
Higgs, G., 32
Hinerman, P. S., 202–3
Hintz, R. L., 147
Hollander, F. M., 203

Holt Music, 89, 91–92, 186, 205
Huay, Victor, 4
Huck, A. M., 9, 212
Hyperactivity, 45
Hyperopia, 124

Ianacone, R. N., 32
Ikons, 25–26, 49–50, 134
Improvisation, 68, 72–73
Incidental learning, 27
Independent study, 66
Individualized Education Program, 12–13, 230
Instructional acceleration, 66–67
Instructional adaptations
  educable mentally retarded, 21–27
  emotionally disturbed, 166–69
  gifted and talented, 66–70
  hearing impaired, 112–14, 118
  learning disabled, 41–44
  in lesson planning, 86, 92, 96, 98–100
  physically handicapped, 149–53
  visually impaired, 127–35
Instrumental music
  adaptations, 101, 143, 151–52
  for educable mentally retarded, 25–27
  for emotionally disturbed, 166–67
  for hearing impaired, 113–14
  for learning disabled, 47
  for multiply handicapped, 205–8
  performance for gifted and talented, 66
  for physically handicapped, 143–44, 151–53
  with preschoolers, 71
  for trainable retarded, 209, 214
  for visually impaired, 128, 139
Integration of inputs, 42–43
Intelligence quotient, 19–20, 60, 62
Intelligence tests
  Stanford-Binet, 5, 19, 61
  Wechsler (Revised), 19, 61
Intensification of materials, 51, 223–24
Involvement, levels of in activities and lessons, 203
Itard, Jean Marc Gaspard, 4

Jackson, P. W., 62
Jan, J. E., 124, 132, 139
Jaques-Dalcroze, E., 74, 129

Jellison, J. A., 9, 212–13, 220
Jenkins, Ella, 199, 208
Jensema, C. J., 110
Joffee, L., 204
Johanna Bureau for the Blind and Visually Handicapped, Inc., 139
Johnson, D. J., 40–41, 56–57
Johnson, D. W., 225
Johnson, N., 60
Johnson, R. T., 225
Juhrs, P. D., 203

Kanner, L., 5
Kaplan, P., *Test of Rhythmic Responsiveness*, 30–31, 116
Kauffman, J. M., 166
Kavale, K., 47
Kephart, Newell, 47
Kersten, F., 137, 139
Kirk, W. D., 40, 53
Klajman, S., 118
Knapp, R. A., 110
Koldej, E., 118
Korduba, O. M., 115, 118
Kowalska, A., 118
Kracke, I., 116, 118
Kraut, J., 123
Krolick, B., 132
Krug, D., 211
Kuchenbecker, S. L., 34

Labeling, of exceptional learners, 220–21
Lam, R. C., 137
Landecker, A. W., 149
Lane, H., 111
Language
  acquisition of
    by hearing impaired, 111
    by visually impaired, 127
  consideration with multiply handicapped, 205–6
  definition, 109
  development, 20, 111
Larson, B. A., 31
Laterality, 47
Lawrence, G. A., 139
Learning
  educable mentally retarded, 21–27

Learning (*cont.*)
  emotionally disturbed, 166–69
  gifted and talented, 64–66
  hearing impaired, 111
  learning disabled students, 49–52
    providing verbal rehearsal and visual
      imagery, 49
    providing visual and verbal
      continuity, 49
  physically handicapped, 148–53
  visually impaired, 127–32
Learning disabilities
  behavior, 44–48
  definition, 39
  intensification of input, 51–52
  label misused, 40, 44
  model, 40–44, 56
  motor ability, 46–47
  perceptual motor ability, 47
  placements, 29
  research in music education, 52–55
  social ability, 47–48
  social construct, 55
Least restrictive environment, 4, 7, 9, 16,
    200, 211, 223, 231
Legally blind, 123, 125–26, 132, 138, 178
Levine, J. S., 128
Levinson, 132
Lewis, M. F., 137
Liebman, A., 157
Liebman, J., 157
Ling, D., 106, 110
Lipman, B. J., 118
Listening, 104, 133
Lloyd, J. W., 166
LOGO computer language, 71–72
Lowenfield, B., 127

Maag, J. W., 168
McCann, B. J., 47
McCarthy, J. J., 53
McKinney, J. D., 45
MacKinnon, D., 63
McLeish, J., 32
MacMillan, D., 79
McReynolds, J. C., 128
Madden, N. A., 28

Mainstreaming
  academic improvement, 9, 28–29
  administrative support, 11
  contrasts, 3
  effect on exceptional children, 11
  entire classes in music, 232
  examples, 1–3, 17–18, 37–38, 58–59,
    103–4, 122–23, 140–42, 158–60
  identification of exceptional learners in,
    222
  impact, 10–12
  individualized instruction in, 28
  instructional adaptations made by music
    teachers, 11
  levels of involvement, 227–28
  models, 7–8
  multiply handicapped students, 211–12
  musical success during, 23–24, 48,
    223–29
  music teacher
    attitudes toward, 11
    familiarity with, 12
    preparation, 11
  placements, 39, 56, 142
  planning for, 78–79, 85–86, 91–93,
    95–100, 166–69, 176–77, 180–81,
    185–88, 191–94
  pro and con, 8–9
  questioning techniques, 229
  social acceptance, 28, 48
  social integration, 9, 10
Manhattanville Curriculum, 67, 76
Manion, S., 137
Marcus, M. L., 170–71
Mastropieri, M. A., 166
Matson, J. L., 36
Mattson, P. D., 47
*Measures of Creative Thinking in
    Music*, 74
Meckley, W. A., 71
Mehrens, W. A., 62
Melillo, S., 70
Memory
  educable mentally retarded, 21–27
  for language, 111
  visual, 110
Mental age, 19, 21, 30–32, 34

Mentors, 69
Merle-Fishman, C. R., 170–71
Michal, E. T., 157
Michel, D. E., 218
Miller, J. J., 147
Mills, S. R., 209
Modeling of acceptance, 212
Moderate retardation, 201
Moog, H., 153
Mooney, M. K., 137
Moores, D. F., 104, 110, 121
Morse, W. C., 162
Motor ability, of learning disabled
    children, 46–47
Motor alternatives, 150
Motor coordination, 39, 46–47
Motor development, 20
Movement, 17–18, 23, 43, 46, 86, 129,
    150
Mulick, J. A., 36
Multiply handicapped, 175
    age-appropriate materials, 205
    autism, 202–3
    class description, 199–201
    communication disorders, 204–5
    definition, 200
    functional music, 206–7
    instructional focus, 201
    instrumental music for, 209
    language use with, 205
    least restrictive environment, 211
    mainstreamed in music, 211–12
    music teaching, 205–10
    research in music education, 212
    structure of lessons, 208
    teacher expectations, 207
    trainable mentally retarded, 201–2
    use of records with, 207–8
Multisensory approach, 51–52, 224
Murray, F. B., 9
Muscular dystrophy, 146
Music Achievement Test, 33–34, 73
Musical intelligence, 64
Musically talented, 65, 72
Musical prodigies, 66
Music and You, 84, 87, 90, 94, 180, 182,
    185, 189, 205

Music Aptitude Profile, 32, 34, 73
Music Educators Journal, 68, 110, 128,
    137, 143, 211, 227
Music Educators National Conference
    *Documentary Report of the Ann Arbor
    Symposium III*, 77
    historical center, 71
    *The School Music Program: Description
    and Standards*, 13
Music notation, teaching
    educable mentally retarded, 22
    hearing impaired, 112
    learning disabled, 44
    visually impaired, 128, 131–32
Myers, P., 47
Myers, R., 72–73
Myklebust, H., 40–41, 56–57, 204
Myopia, 124

Napier, G. D., 5
National Library Service for the Blind and
    Physically Handicapped, 128, 139
National Society for Children and Adults
    with Autism, 202
Newcomer, P. L., 160, 162, 173
Nihira, K., 20
Nix, G. W., 121
Nocera, S., 28, 32–33, 36, 57, 173, 228
Nolan, Christopher, 204
Nonverbal input, 41–42
Nordoff, P., 218
Normal curve of distribution, 19

Omnichord, 100
Operant conditioning, 164–66
Optacon, 132
Orff-*Schulwerk*, 23, 52–53, 203
Organization, educable mentally retarded,
    21, 25–27
Originality in creativity, 72–73
Orton, S., 40
Osborn, A., 68, 76
Osguthorpe, R. T., 225
Ostinato, 41

Pappanikou, A. J., 174, 225
Partially sighted, 124

Paul, J. L., 174, 225
Paul, P. V., 111–12
Pavlov, I., 162
Peer-tutors, 211, 224–25
Perkins, C. E., 120
Perkins School for the Blind, 4
Peterson, M., 218
Physically handicapped
    adapting communication with, 152
    adapting materials for, 151
    characteristics, 144–47
    definitions, 142
    emergency procedures, 149
    instrumental instruction, 152
    lifting, 150
    need for extra time, 148
    research in music education, 153–54
    rhythmic ability, 153
    self-image, 154
    temporary accommodations, 143
Piaget, Jean, 109
    model, 136
    theory, 71
*Piers-Harris Self-Concept Scale for
    Children*, 154
Pillsbury Foundation School, 71
Pirtle, M., 215
Pitman, D. J., 135
Placek, Robert W., 68
Pond, D., 71
Pratt, R. R., 218
Presti, G. M., 170–71
Primary Measures of Music Audiation,
    53–54, 74, 116, 118
Probst, W., 152
Public education, free appropriate, 6
Public Law 94–142, 4, 6–10, 12, 14, 16,
    19, 39–40, 56, 175, 214, 219, 231
    funding of, 10
    impact of in music, 10–11
Public Law 95–561, 60
Purvis, J., 218

Quigley, S. P., 111–12

Ravitch, D., 5
*Reaching the Special Learner through
    Music*, 228

Reading ability
    educable mentally retarded, 29
    learning disabled, 38, 42
Reading frame, 50, 132
Recording for the Blind, 139
Redl, R., 162, 174
Rehabilitation Act of 1973, 142
Reinforcement, 27, 165
    schedules, 165
Reis, Sally M., 63
Renzulli, J. S., 60, 63, 76
Reschly, D. J., 48
Residual sight, 125
Resnick, L., 226
Retardation. *See* Educable mentally
    retarded; Moderate retardation;
    Trainable mentally retarded
Rheumatoid arthritis, juvenile, 147
Rhythmic ability
    of educable mentally retarded, 30–31
    of emotionally disturbed, 170–71
    of hearing impaired, 115–16
    of physically handicapped, 153
Rhythmic accompaniment, 89
Rhythmic discrimination of learning
    disabled, 53–54
Rhythmic training of educable mentally
    retarded, 33–34
Ricca, J., 69
Richards, M. H., 112
Rider, R., 136
Rileigh, K. I. K., 118
Rimm, S. B., 77
Robbins, C., 218
Robbins, C., 114, 120
Rodgers, S., 211
Rosene, Paul, 25–26, 29, 34–35
Rosenstein, J., 135
Ross, D. M., 34–35
Ross, M., 107, 121
Ross, S. A., 34–35
Rubella, 106
Rutherford, R. B., 168
Rutter, M., 203
Rynders, J. E., 213

Safran, J. S., 168
Safran, S. P., 168

Samet, S., 218
Schleuter, L. J., 46
Schleuter, S. L., 46
Scholl, G. T., 139
Scott, E. P., 124, 132, 139
Scruggs, T. E., 166
Seashore Measures of Musical Talent,
   32–33, 53, 135
Seaton, K. P., 215
Sebree, S. M., 72
Seguin, Edouard, 4
Semel, E. M., 57
Sensorineural hearing loss, 106, 119
Shaping, in behavior modification, 165
Shellem, G. W., 111, 113, 115
Sheltered workshop, 199
Shinn, M. R., 55
Sickle-cell disease, 147
Signed English, 110
Signing Exact English, 110
Sign language, 204
Silver Burdett Competency Test, 33, 54
Silver Burdett Music, 83, 87, 89, 93,
   95–96, 98, 137, 184, 190, 192, 205
Sinclair, J. S., 121
Singing
   lack of pitch levels by hearing impaired
      students, 103
   range of educable mentally retarded,
      31, 85
Sisk, D., 77
Skaught, B. J., 70
Skinner, B. F., 162
Slavin, R. E., 28, 226
Sleeter, C. E., 55
Slow learners, 32, 40
Slyoff, M. R., 218
Smith, Linda H., 63
Snellen eye chart, 126
Social acceptance of retarded students, 28
Social behavior
   gifted students, 64–65
   learning disabled children, 47–48
Song texts, 22
Special center, 198–99, 201, 216
Special friends project, 211, 225
Speech impaired, 175
Spina bifida, 145–46

Spira, D., 55
Sposato, M. A., 120–21
Squires, V. L., 118
Stanford-Binet Intelligence Scale, 19, 61
Steele, A. L., 170–71
Stern, V., 121
Sterritt, G. M., 118
Stokowski, Leopold, 71
Stone, S. J., 220
Stratford, B., 31
Strauss, A., 40, 45
Strauss Syndrome, 45, 56
Structure of Intellect model, 61–62
Suzuki, S., 74, 100, 128
Swaiko, N., 121
Swanner, D. L., 74

Tactual experiences, 127
Talking books, 132
Task commitment, 63
Tatarunis, A. M., 77
Teacher modeling, 113
Teachers, perceptions of, 79
Teaching, as process, 197
"Teams-Games-Tournaments" model of
   grouping, 226
Telemann flute concerto, 83
Teplitz, Mike, 144
Terman, L. M., 63
Textbook use
   educable mentally retarded, 22
   with learning disabled, 48–50
Therapist
   music, 172, 207, 215–17
   speech, 103, 120
Thermoform Brailon Duplicator, 132
Thinking
   convergent, 62, 76
   divergent, 62, 76
Thomas, R., 67
Thompson, K., 32
Thorndike, E., 162
Thresholds to Music, 112
Time-out in behavior modification,
   158–59, 165
Tindal, G. A., 55
Todd, J. H., 132

Tonal discrimination
  educable mentally retarded, 30
  learning disabled, 53–54
Torrance, E. Paul, 62–63, 73
Torrance Tests of Creative Thinking, 73
Total Communication, 110
Trainable mentally retarded, 20, 201–2,
  213, 215
Trybus, R. J., 110
Turnbull, A. P., 154

Vaughan, M., 72–73
Verbal input, 41
Vernazza, M., 218
Vineland Social Maturity Scale, 20
Visual aids, 112
Visual input, 41
Visually impaired
  age of onset, 127
  anatomy of the eye, 124
  audition as compensatory sense, 127,
    130
  color blindness, 126
  definition, 123–24
  environmental adaptations, 130–31
  environmental interaction, 130–33
  instrumental teaching of, 128, 139
  language development, 127
  limited experiences, 127
  mobility, 129–30
  print enlargement, 131
  research in music education, 135–37

Vocabulary, music, 215
Voeltz, L. M., 211–12, 225

Walker, A. R., 136
Wallas, G., 67
Wang, C. C., 137
Ward, J., 155
Watson, J., 162
Weber, R. D., 214
Webster, P., 62, 73–74
Wechsler test (Revised), 19, 61
Weidenbach, V., 215
Wernicke, K., 40
Westervelt, V. D., 154
Westling, David L., 27, 36
Wheelchair, 140, 149–50
White, L. D., 11
Whorton, J. E., 40
Wiig, E. H., 57
Wild Boy of Aveyron, The, 4
Williams, L., 25, 209
Wilson, B., 71
Wing Tests of Musical Ability, 135
Wolfe, D. E., 220
Woodell, G., 77
Writing, 43–44

York, R., 211

Zenatti, A., 30